The Gordon Highlanders
in the
First World War

D1547339

THE LIFE OF A REGIMENT
VOLUME IV

The Gordon Highlanders

in the

First World War

1914-1919

CYRIL FALLS

ABERDEEN

THE UNIVERSITY PRESS

First published 1958

PRINTED IN GREAT BRITAIN AT
THE UNIVERSITY PRESS
ABERDEEN

FOREWORD

WRITING in 1938 my penultimate predecessor said of this volume—"How many dead corpses of so-called Regimental Histories still fill the groaning bookshelves—Regulars, Territorials, K. Troops, there they lie by dozens . . . . But with Guedalla to write for us, we shall prove an exception."

Guedalla's death, added to previous misfortunes, was indeed a disaster. But now, forty years after the end of the First World War, we go to print under the name of one of the foremost military historians of the day.

After Greenhill Gardyne, father and son, we welcome to the ranks of Regimental Historian Captain Cyril Falls and who else, after all these years, could have recaptured the spirit of 1914-18?

We welcome also for the first time to the pages of our History the unsurpassed achievements of our Territorial and New Army Battalions. These pages tell a story of endurance and sacrifice met with courage and equanimity.

Whatever the future may hold, in peace or war, I am confident that met in the spirit of 1914-18 all difficulties will be overcome—

" And be Health and Victory for ever
With the Lads of the Marquis of Huntly."

WILLIAM J. GRAHAM

December 1957   Colonel, The Gordon Highlanders

CONTENTS

LIST OF ILLUSTRATIONS

AUTHOR'S PREFACE

MANY regimental and divisional histories of the First World War were published not long after its close. Some of the authors, assuming that they were addressing in the main readers who had taken part in the war or at least knew a good deal about it as kinsfolk of fighting men, thought it unnecessary to provide much in the way of background. Others, hoping, over-optimistically or not, that their works would be consulted years later, tried to provide pictures of the military setting.

The latter class seems to me to have been the wiser and to have shown the greater historical sense. When, as in the case of the Gordon Highlanders, the publication of a regimental history of the First World War has been delayed until some forty years after it came to an end there cannot be the smallest doubt on the matter. To all but a small minority, rapidly diminishing in numbers, the story must be very hard to follow unless considerable detail is put into its background. I have kept this consideration in mind throughout. It has not been possible to make room for all I wanted to say, but I have done my best. I have kept up a commentary on the nature of the war and its developments.

The developments are highly important. They were particularly striking in the artillery arm and its equipment, but the infantry also acquired greatly increased fire-power. A long series of inventions, technical and tactical, were exploited all through the war. Among these were rolling or creeping artillery barrages; smoke shell for cover; sound-ranging and flash-spotting; toxic, vesicant, and lachrymatory gas; light machine guns; tracer ammunition; camouflage on scientific principles; tanks; air reconnaissance and photography—without which mapping of the enemy's trench system would have been impossible—a little later air bombing, and towards the end low-flying operations in direct support of the infantry; hand and rifle grenades; flame-throwers and " thermit " shell from mortars.

Meanwhile the primitive trenches dug by companies or battalions when deadlock followed open fighting had expanded into vast defensive systems by 1918, 5,000 yards or so deep for a division, not counting further lines in rear constructed as a precaution against a break-through. These fortifications were provided with dug-outs—often with bunks—machine-gun emplacements, snipers' posts, telephone systems, occasionally even water-supply. They came to be regarded as assets, valuable properties, because they took long to replace. The private soldier realized their worth. Good battalions took pride in them, as I have mentioned in describing the work of those of the Gordon Highlanders. Before 1918 they were rarely captured on a big scale. In one notable instance, on the Somme in 1916, when they were captured, though very slowly, the Germans had time to replace them by a well-planned and constructed new system on a shorter front, to which they withdrew in early 1917.

The reader of every book on the First World War needs to keep in mind, especially as regards the Western Front, that the constant overriding problem was the conversion of a " break-in " into a " break-through ". Time after time attempts to do so fell short of success. One factor in these failures was the construction of special entrenchments : the " switch "—the German used the more expressive name *Riegel*, meaning cross-beam or cross-bolt— by means of which an intact system or length of trench could be linked to another in rear when a breach had occurred. The main obstacle, however, was the lack of mobility and speed in driving the attack through. Before it could reach open ground on a wide front reinforcements would appear on the scene and the defences would congeal round the breach. Various devices were tried to get over this difficulty. One of the earliest, and worst, was that of small diversionary attacks. They were made in the hope of tying down the enemy's reserves, but generally with such small resources that he was not compelled to use reinforcements or even alarmed. The introduction of the tank in 1916 made it feasible to obtain surprise by doing without a preliminary bombardment. This method was not tried, however, until the end of 1917, at Cambrai. After that battle the downfall of Russia gave the Germans the initiative and an ascendancy which brought them near to winning the war. In that period, though they had virtually no tanks, they made deeper and swifter advances than had been seen since trench warfare set in. Yet when the allies passed to the offensive they won the war in the period of the " hundred days ". The seeds of the German defeat had been sown in the bloody soil of terrible battles, notably the Somme and Ypres. Criticism of the " useless butchery " of the war overlooks this undoubted fact, though there is plenty of room for criticism with knowledge behind it.

Histories of British regiments are commonly hard to write, perhaps to read. This is particularly the case in the First World War with regiments from great industrial centres, because the expansion was enormous in their case. Many of them had battalions serving in France and Belgium, Egypt and Palestine, Gallipoli, Macedonia, and perhaps Italy. The change of scene is not really an advantage when it is so frequent that the story becomes scrappy. I cannot guarantee that the history of the Gordon Highlanders will be easy to read, but it has been relatively easy to write. Every battalion on active service served in France and Belgium. One battalion only, the 2nd, ever left that theatre, and it served in Italy only for the last year of the war. On many occasions battalions in different divisions were engaged close to each other, in one or two instances shoulder to shoulder. They met often enough when out of the line, and, as I have shown, the city of Arras was for a time almost a Gordon Highlanders' club. This regimental record is practically a Western Front story, and as such compact and manageable.

There would never be a great deal that was interesting to say about battalions which did not go abroad in that war, even if they kept full records, which they rarely did. (There is rather more in the Second World War because in it the threat of invasion was so much sharper.) These battalions had a dual role, that of defence and that of receiving, training, and draft-finding units. The 3rd Battalion takes the foremost place. It was the permanent Special Reserve battalion, the successor under the Haldane scheme to the old Militia. It remained at Aberdeen throughout and for a considerable time provided the garrison of the Torry Batteries. In addition to recruits it took in officers and men who had been wounded, when they came out of hospital or convalescent camp. The 3rd Gordon Highlanders sent to France over 800 officers and 20,000 men. Three 2nd-line Territorial battalions were raised, but never went abroad, and a Garrison battalion served in India. The " Young Soldiers " battalions which served in Germany after the armistice had come into force have a short space allotted to them in the last chapter.

Four regiments affiliated to the Gordon Highlanders took part in the First World War. These affiliations did not take place until after the war, but they had been preceded by unofficial associations. They linked the Gordon Highlanders to one regiment of the British Territorial Army and to Canadian, Australian, and South African regiments. These are : The London Scottish, the Gordon Highlanders (T.A.) ; The 48th Highlanders of Canada (Toronto, Canadian Militia) ; The 5th Australian Battalion (The Victorian Scottish Regiment), and the Queen's Own Cape Town Highlanders.

The title of the London Scottish as given above dates only from 1936 and had predecessors in great variety. The first men of the regiment to go on active service did so in the ranks of the Gordon Highlanders in the South African War. The London Scottish was, like the 4th and 6th Gordon Highlanders, one of the battalions selected to go to France before their divisions were ready. It was highly honoured by its priority and crossed to France about two months earlier than even the 6th Gordons. It was also the first Territorial battalion to go into action, at Messines on October 31st, 1914, where it won the highest praise by its extraordinary gallantry. It missed hardly a great battle in France and Belgium, being engaged in those of Ypres in 1915, 1917, and 1918 ; Loos ; the Somme, 1916 and 1918 ; Arras, 1917 and 1918 ; and Cambrai, 1917 and 1918. The 2nd Battalion had a remarkable war career. After a brief period of service in France it was transferred to Macedonia, and in July 1917 to Egypt, where it was engaged in Allenby's victorious battles in Palestine and the less successful operations beyond Jordan. In 1918 it returned to France and took part in the final victories there. The first draft which it received after its arrival, a large one, was made up of Gordon Highlanders. The commanding officer informed the newcomers that they were not strangers and would continue to wear their own kilts amid the hodden grey. This graceful and charming courtesy was worthy of a fine regiment and an exceptionally good commanding officer, Lieut.-Colonel R. J. L. Ogilby, whose memory will last in a sphere far wider than that of his regiment by reason of his legacy to military museums.

Writing in 1916, the then Colonel of the Gordon Highlanders, General Sir Ian Hamilton, mentioned the number of battalions of the regiment in the *Army List*, and added : " But the true scope of the expansion covers a wider field by far. . . . . Overseas I have had the honour to inspect the superb 48th of Toronto." These words show that the Colonel considered the regiments as good as wedded then, though the ceremony had not yet been performed. This regiment served as the 15th Battalion Canadian Infantry. It formed part of the 1st Canadian Division, the earliest to cross the Atlantic. It won immortal honour in the famous gas attack in the Ypres Salient on April 22nd, 1915, when the French Colonial troops reeled away on the left, baring the Canadian flank. It was to distinguish itself again in this region at Passchendaele in 1917. Other outstanding feats of the 15th Battalion were performed on the Somme in 1916, on Vimy Ridge in 1917, and in the Battle of Amiens, the first blow in the final victorious offensive, in August 1918.

The 5th Australian Battalion began its fighting career on the Gallipoli Peninsula. Famous names ring out from this period of its service : Helles, Krithia, Anzac, Suvla, Sari Bair. It fought on the Somme in 1916—where it won a great grenade tussle at Pozières on July 25th—at Bullecourt in 1917, and later that year at Ypres. Some of its finest work was done in the Battle of the Menin Road and afterwards in that of Broodseinde Ridge. In the German Lys offensive the battalion was heavily engaged. In the advance to victory it took part in the Battle of Amiens and the breaching of the Hindenburg Line.

The Queen's Own Cape Town Highlanders wore the kilt and plaid of Gordon tartan as early as 1885. Its present title dates only from 1947 and was adopted in consequence of the fact that Queen Elizabeth (now the Queen Mother) had become Colonel-in-Chief in 1947. It took part in the campaign in South-west Africa in 1915. It did not, however, form part either of the South African Brigade which fought against the Senussi in North Africa and was later embodied in the 9th (Scottish) Division on the Western Front, or of the larger South African contingent which served in East Africa, but it was drawn upon for drafts.

These links with the forces of the Commonwealth are highly prized by the Gordon Highlanders.

I have used contemporary terms rather than those which have replaced them. In the First World War the smallest units of field artillery and field engineers were " batteries " and " field companies ", not " troops ". All guns and howitzers from 60-pdr. upwards ranked at " heavy ". A " bomber " in those years was a man who threw hand-grenades, and his hand-grenades were called " bombs ". The Grenadier Guards are said to have objected when it was proposed to use officially the word " grenadier " in this sense. I have, however, tried not to be too pedantically consistent where it does not matter. " Aircraft " and " airfield " appear, though " aeroplane "—or even " machine "—and " aerodrome " were the terms generally used. " Truck " has slipped in occasionally, but in principle I have stuck to " lorry ". The numbers of armies are written in full, those of corps are in Roman numerals, and those of divisions and brigades in Arabic numerals—a system which I think it was a pity to abandon.

I have striven to be frank. It is easy enough to say that a battalion or a company was " forced back " or " compelled to retire ", but every soldier knows, in the first place, that the force or compulsion applied has to be greater in the case of some defenders than in that of others ; in the second place, that the same troops show varying powers of resistance when they are at their best and when they have, through exhaustion or depletion, fallen below it. It seems desirable to be honest here, and to seek reasons for such fluctuations.

I hope it is not presumptuous to say in conclusion how much the fine spirit and good record of the Gordon Highlanders have appealed to me in writing this history. Such material is encouraging to the historian, even if at some stages he has to record a series of disappointments, including bloody repulses. War diaries are cold and bleak by nature, with only rare flashes of sentiment or vivacity shedding light on the human side. Yet it is impossible to work through those of the Gordon Highlanders in the First World War without being left with the impression that they were always triers.

C. F.

CHAPTER I

WHEN Britain went to war in 1914, it was to engage in her first " great " war for a century. As usual, her chief strength lay in the Royal Navy. The Army was of high quality, but to begin with trifling in strength by comparison with the forces of the continental nations which conscribed their male citizens capable of bearing arms. Yet the Army entered this war better prepared than it had been for some of its secondary wars, though they required less preparation. The improvement was due to the reorganization carried out by Mr. R. B. (later Lord) Haldane, the Secretary of State for War. His scheme made it possible to form the Expeditionary Force of six infantry divisions and one cavalry division, which could be shipped to the Continent at very short notice.

In addition, there were considerable regular forces on foreign stations which were later organized into divisions. There was the Yeomanry, which formed the cavalry reserve, and the Territorial Force, which was organized in fourteen divisions; but in both cases unfit for war without formation training. The Militia had become the Special Reserve, a title indicating its real task, that of draft-finding.

Haldane, however, was a member of a Liberal Government committed to peace and with a left wing opposed to military expenditure. He had not a free hand financially. If he increased expenditure in one direction he had to cut it in another. Thus, though the Expeditionary Force was well equipped, except in the heavier types of artillery, this was not the case with the reserve forces. In the Territorial Force divisions the artillery was equipped with obsolete guns. Supplies of ammunition, scarcely adequate for the needs of the Expeditionary Force, were inadequate for expansion, and production itself could not be rapidly expanded. As was soon to be revealed, even uniforms, even cloth of which to make them, could not be obtained for a growing Army. Nowhere was there more than a narrow margin and everywhere a certainty of shortages if Britain decided to raise her Army to the continental scale.

Britain's one definite commitment under treaty obligations was the protection of Belgian integrity, to which in fact Germany and France were equally pledged. It was uncertain up to the last moment whether this country would go to war if France were attacked, provided that the neutrality of Belgium was respected. Indeed, it is impossible to be sure even now what would have happened had this neutrality not been violated. The German ultimatum to Belgium brought almost all the peace party in the Cabinet, headed by Mr. Lloyd George, into line with its right wing. The despatch of the Expeditionary Force to France could not be undertaken until this problem had been solved. All the plans had, however, been worked out. After preliminary conversations starting as early as 1906, the Government had from 1911 permitted the General Staffs of Britain and France to draw up in detail a scheme for the landing of the Expeditionary Force in France and its concentration between Maubeuge and Le Cateau. Thus, although no pledge had been given to send it, it was ready to go and the French were ready to receive it.

The order for mobilization was issued at 4 p.m. on Tuesday, August 4th, by which time Germany had violated Belgian neutrality and declared war on France. The 1st Battalion the Gordon Highlanders received the order at 5.20 p.m. at Crownhill, Plymouth. Next day the mobilization equipment and small arms ammunition were drawn. On August 6th 236 reservists arrived from the depot at Aberdeen, and on the 7th 296 more. The system whereby a battalion stationed at home had to rely on reservists for half its war establishment was a handicap, if an inevitable one. The reservists, though trained men, were in some cases far from physically fit. When this was so they proved a weak element in an infantry unit hurried into a war which began with swift movement and long marches, at an early stage in the depressing surroundings of a retreat, on several days in great heat. The technical disadvantages of the system were, however, not so great as in later times. The battalion of 1914 was a simple organization ; apart from a machine-gun section of two guns, the rank and file, just under a thousand strong, were all riflemen. In one particular respect, however, they were highly skilled troops. Musketry had never been better and has never been as good since. The blast of rapid fire from a single line of British troops was shattering. None of the transport forward of the third line, the Divisional Supply Column, was motorized. Even brigade headquarters had to rely on horses, though a brigade commander might in emergency be lent a car from the very small establishment at divisional headquarters. As the war went on mechanical transport increased and troops were more and more frequently moved by it ; but until the end no infantry headquarters below that of the division had a single motor vehicle at its own disposal.

The 1st Battalion the Gordon Highlanders, under the command of Lieut.-Colonel F. H. Neish, formed part of the 8th Brigade (Brig.-General B. J. C. Doran), 3rd Division, and II Corps. It was to serve throughout the war in this sound and hard-fighting division, which kept a high standard from first to last, despite very heavy losses. The battalion began its move to France on August 13th, reached Boulogne from Southampton on the 14th, and travelled by train to Aulnoye, in the zone of concentration, billeting for the night of the 16th at Taisnières, four miles north-west of Avesnes.

On August 20th it moved to Saint-Aubin and on the 21st marched north through Maubeuge to Goegnies-Chaussée, on the Belgian frontier. The day was hot and sultry and the troops, particularly the reservists, found the march on a cobbled road very trying. Next night's halt was at Hyon, less than a mile south of Mons.

August 20th was the day on which the German First Army on the right flank of the offensive wheel entered Brussels and the main Belgian Army fell back into the fortress of Antwerp. The probability, to be confirmed by air and ground reconnaissance and information from civilians, was that General von Kluck, the First Army Commander, would continue his wheel until his direction became only just west of south. If he did, it appeared likely that his right flank would be directed on Mons, or at all events very little further west. In this event, it was hoped that the left wing of the British Expeditionary Force would be able to outflank and turn the enemy's right while the British right, in conjunction with the French Fifth Army, now south of Charleroi between the Meuse and the Sambre, attacked him frontally.

If, however, the prospects looked reasonably good on paper, they were very much less rosy in reality. In the first place, Kluck's right flank was directed nearly twelve miles west of Mons. This, however, was a matter of secondary importance. Much more serious was the fact that all the French armies, with the exception of the Fifth on the British right, had already suffered a series of sharp defeats from German armies at numerical odds of five to four in the French favour, and that this left the whole German right wing of three armies and thirty-four divisions with a free hand to deal with the French Fifth Army and the B.E.F., ten and four divisions respectively, while containing the Belgian Army of six divisions which had been driven into Antwerp.

There can have been few men from coal-mining districts in the 1st Gordon Highlanders at this time, but for any miners in the ranks no scene could have been more familiar. For those who appreciated unspoiled country it could scarcely have been grimmer or drearier. The mining villages, in some cases so close to each other as to form sprawling, straggling, townships, were overlooked by a jumble of engine-house chimneys, pit head-gears, and dark, steep, and lofty shale heaps. It was not good ground for the defensive battle about to develop because the field of fire was nearly everywhere short, but neither was it inviting to an attacker.

On the morning of Sunday, August 23rd, the battalion took up a position following the Mons-Beaumont road, facing east-north-east. Fighting began before 9 a.m., but it was not concerned while outpost troops north of Mons held the enemy, as they did most gallantly, until after 11 a.m. About noon German troops began advancing by rushes, not directly against the battalion front but obliquely across it and that of the 2nd Royal Scots on the right, in the direction of Hill 93. The Germans were in fact

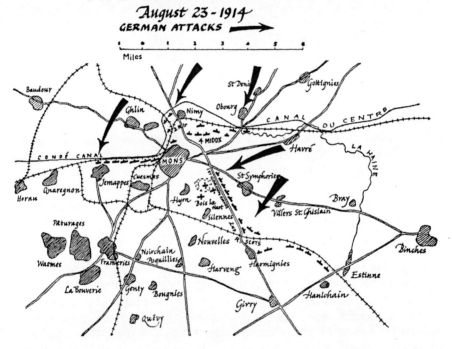

THE BATTLE OF MONS
August 23 - 1914
GERMAN ATTACKS ➡

unaware of the presence of these two battalions until they opened fire. Here was a wonderful piece of luck of which no good regular battalion could fail to take advantage. Both poured in a deadly fire, almost in enfilade. A battery firing shrapnel over the Gordons' heads from the high ridge of Bois la Haut increased the effect. The enemy suffered serious loss and was brought to a dead stop 300 yards from the 8th Brigade's trenches. Shortly before 4 p.m. the left-centre of the Gordons scored another success. When the leading company of a German battalion appeared advancing on Bois la Haut, the Highlanders lay low until it had approached within 500 yards and then turned on such a blast of rapid fire as pinned the survivors to the ground.

North and West of Mons, however, the pressure had been heavier, on the left flank of the 3rd Division and the 5th to its left. Weight of numbers and artillery superiority had compelled a considerable withdrawal, though this was carried out generally in good order and without undue loss. Mons had been abandoned, though the Germans had been unable to debouch south of the city. To the south-west the line ran at nightfall north of Frameries. The right of the 5th Division was still on the Condé Canal, but with orders to retire under cover of darkness to the second position at Wasmes. Further west the 14th Brigade was in the act of withdrawing to this position.

The left of the 8th Brigade had been badly knocked about in the salient north of Mons. In fact, the 2nd Royal Irish and the 4th Middlesex had suffered nearly half the casualties inflicted on the B.E.F. that day. The losses of the 2nd Royal Scots and the 1st Gordon Highlanders had been light. These two battalions were, however, in an awkward situation, with German troops in unknown numbers in rear of the Gordons on the southern outskirts of Mons. At 9 p.m. Brig.-General Doran ordered the two battalions back to the second position at Nouvelles. They withdrew unscathed. The Gordons' casualties were Lieutenant Richmond and two other ranks killed, Majors Simpson and Allan and about a dozen other ranks wounded.

Late in the afternoon No. 12 platoon of the Gordons, commanded by Second Lieutenant I. B. N. Hamilton, had been detached to act as escort to the 23rd Battery R.F.A., which had to be extricated from a precarious position on the summit of Bois la Haut, where its good service has been mentioned. The little column tried to reach the north-south road through Hyon—the village where the battalion had billeted the previous night—by a narrow sunken lane. One section passed through. Then fire was opened by a party of Germans who had entered Hyon from Mons and barricaded themselves at right angles to the end of the lane. The horses of the leading gun were shot and their carcasses blocked the road until they were, by immense exertions, dragged up on to the banks. Next a small attack was beaten off and five prisoners were captured. After a smashed watercart had been laboriously carried away, the gun was man-handled on to the road ; the surviving horses were redistributed ; and the battery withdrew to safety. Nothing was lost but the shot horses and the watercart. Hamilton and his platoon had behaved coolly and intelligently.

The British had reason to be satisfied with their achievement. Only one corps of two divisions, the II, had been seriously engaged ; it had been faced by six German divisions ; and at the end of the day it had retired to a position at some points less than two miles in rear. German losses had certainly been twice or thrice as heavy as British. Yet, apart from the fact that the B.E.F. unexpectedly found itself facing odds of between two and three to one, the news received that night by its commander, Field Marshal Sir John French, showed that it stood in grave danger by reason of the retreat of the Fifth French Army on the right. In face of this news there could be no question of standing on the second position on August 24th, as had at first been the intention.

At 5.30 a.m. the 8th Brigade was ordered to withdraw, but the Gordons did not move till several hours later. They had good fortune in disengaging themselves without loss after some brisk German shelling. They reached Amfroipret, on the northern fringe of the Forêt de Mormal, at 2 a.m. on the 25th. It was a long march and there had been no sleep the previous night, so that the men were very tired. Later that day they marched again, halting at Audencourt, six miles west of Le Cateau.

The German First Army, though it had been so long on the march, had pressed the pursuit of the British II Corps with great energy. The corps commander, General Sir H. L. Smith-Dorrien, decided to halt on the 26th and strike his pursuers a blow which, he hoped, would enable him to resume the retreat in less danger. The position allotted to the 1st Gordon Highlanders was about 1,000 yards in length and just north-west of the small village of Audencourt. The 2nd Royal Scots was on the right and on the left, between the Gordons and the large town of Caudry, was the depleted 2nd Royal Irish.

All that need be said of the battle in general is that the enemy turned the right flank of the II Corps, unsupported by the I Corps which had marched east of the Forêt de Mormal, and made a penetration at Caudry, and that his rapid progress south of Le Cateau rendered a further retreat imperative. The 1st Gordon Highlanders, in a good position with a large field of fire, was not hard pressed to begin with because the Germans saw a better opportunity at Caudry. During the morning fire was opened on German troops on the main Le Cateau-Cambrai road, but it was not called for continuously. Just before 2 p.m. the enemy advanced against the right of the battalion, but its fire and that of the 2nd Royal Scots stopped him before he had gained any ground. Again, at 5 p.m., when withdrawal had begun, the Germans surged forward in close formation, but the rapid fire of the Gordons mowed them down, and though they displayed great bravery and persistence they once more failed to make progress.

The order to retire had reached the 8th Brigade headquarters at 3.30 p.m. Great difficulty was found, however, in communicating this order to the infantry battalions. The 2nd Royal Scots

—less a party on the immediate right of the Gordons—and 4th Middlesex received the order and withdrew without excessive trouble, but it was not received by the Gordons and two companies

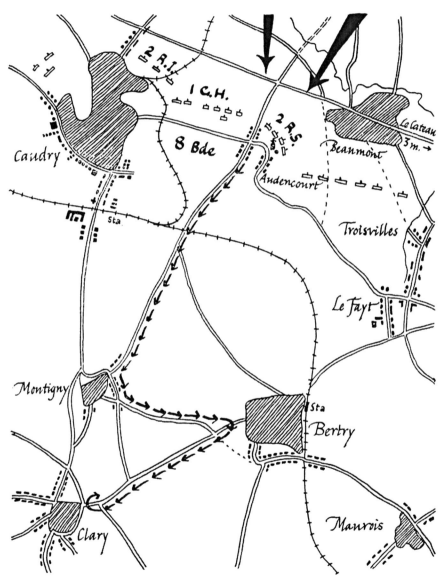

ACTION OF LE CATEAU · 1914

Role of 1ˢᵗ Gordon Highlanders & Attempted Withdrawal Aug 26

German Attacks ▶

of the 2nd Royal Irish. Later in the afternoon B Company got verbal instructions to retire from the brigade major and did so, though even in this case one platoon could not be communicated with and was left behind.

After dark, when the firing had died down, Lieut.-Colonel Neish learnt that hours earlier a signal to retire had been seen by one of his officers. Why it had not been reported to him cannot be discovered. Here then was the battalion, having suffered relatively small loss, left behind by the retreating B.E.F. with two companies of another battalion and a small party of a third. A complication which only the British service could have produced now occurred. The second-in-command, Colonel W. E. Gordon, V.C., held the brevet rank of Colonel and was therefore senior to Lieut.-Colonel Neish in army, though not regimental rank and entitled to take command of a mixed detachment. He decided that the force was now such and assumed command, apparently to the displeasure of the commanding officer. Colonel Gordon did not, however, get the troops assembled until about midnight, and in the interval Lieut.-Colonel Neish sent an officer towards Trois-villes to try to find brigade headquarters; but this messenger was caught by the enemy.

Though the Germans were close at hand, the force, marching off at 12.30 a.m. on August 27th, passed through Audencourt unmolested. An hour later the head of the column reached Montigny, a little over two miles south. The village was in com-plete quietude, but one cottage showed a light. The family within said that British troops had moved through Bertry. A man then guided the detachment through Montigny on to the Bertry road.

So far, so good. At 2 a.m. however, the head of the column was heavily fired on south-west of Bertry. The column—certainly its advanced guard—extended and returned the fire. As it appeared to be suicidal to attempt to fight a way through in darkness and against opposition of unknown strength, thoroughly on the alert, the troops were ordered to fall back along the Montigny road. Instead of turning off right-handed by the way they had come, they kept straight on south-westward to Clary, a mistake which, even in darkness, seems inexplicable except by extreme fatigue.

Suddenly they found themselves facing a field gun trained to fire down the road, which was nearly straight. The gun was seized before it could be discharged, but the rear of the column at once came under fire from the south. It extended and returned the fire, while the head made a desperate attempt to force a way out of the trap by breaking through Clary. A ferocious fire-fight followed, lasting an hour, but it was so one-sided that the end was inevitable. The Germans not only had superiority of numbers but were for the most part firing from cover from all sides. The detachment was overpowered and surrendered after suffering very heavy loss.

Various little parties of stragglers must have joined the column at one point or another, for a German account states that ten regiments, including artillery, were represented among the 700 prisoners taken. Of these approximately 500 were Gordon Highlanders. A large number, including Captain C. R. Lumsden and Lieutenants A. P. F. Lyon and J. K. Trotter, were killed and a few escaped. It was a tragic catastrophe that had overtaken the battalion and the regiment itself, robbing both of officers, warrant officers, non-commissioned officers and private soldiers who could ill be spared because their professional standard was so high. Death comes to the soldier in such force in war that in a long war it is certain to strike down a high proportion, and the war which was just starting was destined to be exceptionally bloody. In this case a large number of men engaged survived to return to their families at the end of the war. Yet a disaster of this sort, which affects a regiment itself more than individual men, is always deplorable, especially when, as is the case here, it does not appear to have been inevitable. More than a generation later contemplation of this episode arouses sentiments of regret and sympathy. At all events it is clear that the fine resistance of the Gordons after the withdrawal had begun eased the situation of the other troops whose retreat had started.

Apart from the transport, all that remained of the 1st Gordon Highlanders was the company of three platoons which had withdrawn from the battlefield of Le Cateau in time. For a fortnight the battalion remained a shadow, and even a month was not long enough to restore it to its full strength.

It reached the Somme at Ham at 9 a.m. on August 28th. After a rest it marched on another twelve miles or so to bivouac beside the village of Genvry, north of Noyon. It crossed the Oise here on the 29th and moved five miles south-east to Cuts, where it was given only four hours in bivouac before marching on to the south bank of the Aisne at Courtieux, half way between Soissons and Compiègne. Then it plunged into the magnificent country of forests and rivers stretching away to the Seine and beyond— magnificent but close and stifling in this weather, when hooves, marching feet, and wheels threw up clouds of dust and the shade of the trees did not seem to compensate for the stagnant atmosphere they created. This was indeed a depressing march, away from the enemy. Men who took part in it have related that they moved in a daze of fatigue, staggering and swaying for want of sleep towards the end of each march.   Yet all evidence points to the fine spirit of the troops despite their exhaustion and to a grave error on the part of G.H.Q. in taking the view that the B.E.F. would have to be withdrawn from the line to rest and refit.   Fortunately, Lord Kitchener ruled otherwise.

South of the Forest of Compiègne the Gordons marched on Meaux, where they crossed the Marne on September 3rd.   Still they moved south, through the Forest of Crécy, into the wooded and sparsely populated area south of Tournan.   Here, on September 5th, their first reinforcement, the "ten per cent reinforcement", joined : 2nd Lieutenant Monteith and 93 other ranks.

They were nearing the Seine at Melun now, but the retreat was at an end.   Indeed, had the orders been passed through and down a little sooner, the B.E.F. might have turned about on the 5th instead of the 6th.   The German First Army had wheeled south-east and advanced beyond the Marne, leaving a weak right flank guard west of the Ourcq.   On the 5th this flank guard had already been attacked by the French Sixth Army, issuing from the Paris defences over the very ground across which the Gordons had passed in retreat.   On the 6th Kluck had withdrawn forces from the Marne to reinforce the flank guard, creating a wide gap which was filled only by cavalry.   September 5th was the first day of the Battle of the Ourcq, a major subsidiary of the Battle of the Marne. September 6th was the first day of the Marne.   The B.E.F. was moving into the gap, but it must be acknowledged that the German cavalry, with the aid of attached Jäger battalions, manoeuvred with skill to make progress difficult.

The 3rd Division marched on the Grand Morin just west of Coulommiers, passing again through the Forest of Crécy and encountering nothing more than cavalry patrols.   On the 7th it crossed the river, and the Gordons picked up their second reinforcement, Lieutenant G. R. V. Hume-Gore and 120 other ranks, the numbers being swollen by about a score of men who had been sent down sick.   The strength must now have been over three hundred.   This country was now rather different from that of the second part of the retreat, rougher and more rugged, still heavily wooded, but without forests such as those of Compiègne, Villers-Cotterets, and Crécy.

On September 8th the Gordons marched with the advanced guard to the Petit Morin, where the enemy made his first stand. They were ordered to await the attack of the 2nd Royal Irish at Gibraltar and then try to take the Germans in flank.   The Royal Irish were, however, held up by well-placed machine guns which could not be located.   In the afternoon the enemy began pulling back as the result of pressure further west and the Gordons were

able to cross, though under heavy fire. The German cavalry had
fought a good rear-guard action, but at the price of fairly heavy
loss, including 150 prisoners in this neighbourhood. The Gordons
had suffered 22 casualties.

They were not engaged again on this front. They reached
Oulchy-la-Ville, beyond the Ourcq, on September 11th. On the
following day they became Army Troops. It was an unwelcome
transfer, but the reason why they were chosen is clear : they were
too weak to perform the duties of a battalion in battle, and it
did not seem likely that they would be brought up to strength
again immediately. In their new role they were not inactive.
They had to provide guards for German prisoners being sent down
to the base, the largest number being 783, who were escorted to
Saint-Nazaire. Another of their duties was more combatant in
character. It was to round up parties of German cavalry isolated
by the retreat of the German right wing in the Forêt de Fére,
between Fére-en-Tardenois and the Marne. The expeditions were
not as successful as had been hoped, but on September 13th a
party of 48 of the enemy, including 2 officers, surrendered without a
fight to Captain Marshall, who had been sent from home to take a
temporary command.

Meanwhile the strength of the battalion was growing. On the
15th seven officers reported, the senior being Captain F. L. M.
Crichton Maitland. On the 18th the fourth reinforcement of
93 men joined. On the 20th came the third reinforcement of 77
men. The reason for its weakness and delay in joining was found
to be that it had been snatched up and sent into action with the
2nd Seaforths of the 10th Brigade, 4th Division, in the thick of
the fighting north of the Aisne, The officer with the party,
Lieutenant W. F. Murray, had been killed. Both the brigade
commander, Brig.-General J. A. L. Haldane, and the officer commanding the Seaforths bestowed warm praise on this draft which,
straight from the train, had fought in the ranks of another
regiment with courage and enthusiasm. On the 26th the battalion
was reorganized on a basis of headquarters, a machine-gun section,
and three companies. It was well on its way back to normal.
On the last day of the month it rejoined the 8th Brigade.

By this time the Battle of the Aisne was over and the B.E.F.
was about to begin its move toward the coast. The 1st Gordon
Highlanders had got a good start in the war at Mons, but thereafter things had gone wrong. The future was to witness a full
recovery, despite the loss of so much splendid human material
which in the case of other regiments, however heavy their losses,
was available to a far greater extent to maintain old traditions and
inculcate skill in war.

CHAPTER II

FIRST YPRES AND LA BASSÉE

ON August 4th, 1914, the Army Reserve and Special Reserve had been called up. The Territorial Force had been mobilized and was for the time being to provide the garrison of the country, almost entirely stripped of regular troops since the last regular division, the 6th, had joined the B.E.F. Next day it was decided to bring home nearly all regular troops on foreign stations in order to form fresh regular divisions.

This decision was taken the day before Field Marshal Lord Kitchener became Secretary of State for War. It is very remarkable how quickly the Government abandoned British tradition in deciding to raise a large army to fight on the Continent. Lord Kitchener might have proceeded to do so on the basis of a great expansion of the Territorial Force, as Haldane had intended. He preferred to create armies of a new type—doubtless because he wanted a force free from the service restrictions of the Territorials. On August 7th, the day after he took up his appointment at the War Office, he called for 100,000 volunteers to form the first of the " New Armies ", six divisions strong. Numerically the premier division of the New Armies was the 9th, with which the Gordon Highlanders were for a time to be associated. These recruits were found within a few days. They were, however, to be grievously hampered in their preparation for war by the fact that, as mentioned in the last chapter, the military cupboard was bare as soon as the regular forces had been equipped, and the Territorial Force equipped on a lower scale.

Although the main expansion was to be based on Kitchener's New Armies, the Territorial Force was also to be enlarged. It was quickly brought up to establishment by volunteers, and soon far above it. In mid-September the Government called on it to volunteer for foreign service. Units in which 60 per cent. volunteered—practically all immediately and the rest within a short time—were then designated " General Service " and directed to recruit up to 25 per cent. beyond establishment. When this had been done, the unit was duplicated, the newly-formed one being known as " Second Line ". A considerable number of these units also served abroad in the course of the war, though none of the battalions of the Gordon Highlanders. Another measure of Territorial Force expansion was the raising of units which did not exist in time of peace. All this betokened energy and determination on the part of the country, but it did not make possible any early relief of the strain to which the British Expeditionary Force was to be subjected. Not even all the reinforcements for units already in the field were satisfactory. Many were too old—the 1st Gordon Highlanders got men who had served at Tel-el-Kebir in 1882 in a draft which arrived in December—while many of the younger men were almost untrained.

After signs of deadlock had appeared on the Aisne, French and Germans both attempted outflanking movements to the north. Corps by corps, forces of either side extended the opposing flanks and clashed in battle or combat. For the most part they fought each other to a standstill and went to ground. As the front extended towards the Channel ports, Sir John French represented to General Joffre the vital interest of the British in their safety and begged that the B.E.F. might be moved northward before the " race to the sea " was over. This was arranged as soon as possible. By the night of October 4th the first British troops were entraining for Flanders.

Meanwhile the fate of Antwerp and of the Belgian Army within the fortress was causing anxiety. So long as the enemy could not employ the heaviest artillery against the forts it seemed relatively secure, but this state of affairs would last only while his siege train, engaged at Maubeuge, was not available. When these heavy guns arrived it would be only a matter of time before the forts were destroyed. It was vital that the Belgian field army should not be trapped. On the other hand, these six divisions might provide invaluable aid to a strong force operating on the coast before the German force engaged in the race to the sea had reached it. Here was a region where a telling blow might still be struck. Unhappily, no such intervening force was available. Britain could send the 7th Division and 3rd Cavalry Division, and did so in the first week of October, at the same time as the Belgian Army left Antwerp. The French promised a Naval division. With the Belgians these forces might have succeeded in driving away the German besiegers and launching an offensive against the German right wing, though it must be doubted whether the Belgians were of high enough quality. Anyhow the concentration was too late. By the evening of the 6th only the 7th Division had arrived on the scene and a German cavalry corps, likewise bent on an outflanking movement, was approaching Ypres. All that the 7th Division could do was to cover the withdrawal of the Belgian Army and help it to make a junction with the rest of the allies.

The 7th Division included the 2nd Gordon Highlanders. In infantry it was possibly the best division in the British Army. If this statement appears unjust to others, the explanation is that not only were all the battalions which came from foreign stations —eight out of twelve, two of those already in the United Kingdom being Guards battalions—seasoned troops with very few reservists, but that they came mostly from healthy stations. The 2nd Gordon Highlanders had been in Egypt. It formed part of the 20th Brigade, the other battalions being the 1st Grenadier Guards, 2nd Scots Guards, and 2nd Border Regiment. The commanding officer was Lieut.-Colonel H. P. Uniacke.

The battalion embarked at Southampton on October 5th and landed at Zeebrugge on the 7th. The whole brigade at once moved to Bruges, infantry by rail, the rest marching. It received the warmest of welcomes from the citizens. Wine and fruit were provided in plenty, and no payment was accepted. Alas! many warm welcomes were to be given to British troops in the early stages of this war, and of others, to be followed by disillusion when our slow-starting country's forces were compelled to retreat by superior strength.

On the 8th came sudden orders to march to Ostend to cover the landing of the 3rd Cavalry Division. No enemy was encountered and at night the Gordons took up a position on the Bruges-Nieuport Canal. On the night of the 9th the battalion was ordered to entrain for Ghent. It left its drums in the custody of the burgomaster and did not see them again till the year 1933, when the Colonel of the Regiment, General Sir Ian Hamilton, fetched them from Berlin. The confusion and misery which always attend the invasion of a thickly populated country were already evident. Ostend station was choked with refugees and wounded Belgian soldiers. Ghent was not reached till 1 a.m. on the 10th. There the battalion detrained and took up a position east of the city. Its job, part of that of two brigades of the 7th Division, as well as a French Marine brigade and some Belgian troops, was to cover the retreat of the Belgian Army. It was not well equipped for this to start with, as it arrived without horses, machine guns, or ammunition, except for 200 rounds on the man. The rest of the night was depressing. Rain fell unceasingly. The field kitchens not being up and open fires being banned because the enemy was believed to be close at hand, the troops deployed or in bivouac were unable to cook. However, the British were not disturbed, except for some spy-hunting, though the French Marines on the Alost road drove off parties of Germans of unknown strength.

Nor was there any pressure on the 10th, but bursts of fire kept most of the troops awake all night. The Belgian Army being more or less clear, it was time for the flank guard to withdraw. Late on October 11th the battalion marched through Ghent, moving at first north-west, halting for some hours at Somergem, then heading south-west to Thielt. The march of the 13th was checked by the report that a German attack was imminent, but the enemy did not appear and Roulers was reached by 10 p.m. On the 14th the Gordons arrived at Ypres and took up an outpost position to the south at Voormezeele. First class though the infantry of the 7th Division was, the men were not in the hardest condition. They had had long marches on the notorious Belgian *pavé* which had swollen their feet, while wet had shrunk their shoes, and very little sleep. Yet their exertions were only the beginning. So fast had disaster moved that they found the handsome and prosperous little city of Ypres engaged in its normal affairs, ignorant of the horrors impending.

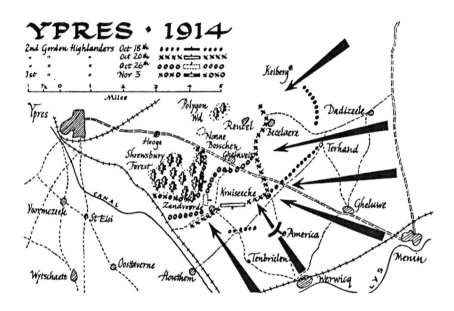

By this time the Belgians were preparing to hold the Yser Canal. The main body of the B.E.F. was arriving on the scene. The left of the III Corps was on the outskirts of Armentières, twelve miles south of Ypres, and between this corps and the 7th Division the gap was filled by the British cavalry.

On October 18th the 7th Division began a deliberate advance on Menin. It was fortunate that the advance was deliberate; for if the IV Corps Commander, Sir Henry Rawlinson, had interpreted in a highly aggressive sense a loosely worded order from G.H.Q., the division might have been crushed, because both the Cavalry Corps and most of the II Corps were stuck. As it was, the 20th Brigade on the right found itself on an ugly front with the right bent back to Zandvoorde. The 2nd Gordons pushed forward to the hamlet of America, where both their flanks were in the air.   G.H.Q. ordered the advance on Menin to be pressed next day.   As his right was outflanked and enfiladed, the divisional commander, Major-General Capper, opened the attack on his left with the 22nd Brigade.

It began well, but it had been based on false information about the enemy's movements, and the operation had to be abandoned as the result of a German attack further north.   The 2nd Gordons and 2nd Scots Guards were moved into divisional reserve at Reutel behind the 22nd Brigade, now withdrawing under pressure.   On October 20th they were ordered to make a reconnaissance towards Gheluwe, two miles west-north-west of Menin, and found it held in force.   The 20th Brigade now faced almost due south between Zandvoorde and Kruiseecke.

Neither Sir John French nor General d'Urbal, the new commander of the French forces north of Ypres, had as yet a clear understanding of what was happening in front of them.   They underrated the quality of the four fresh German reserve corps which had been identified.   They realized neither that these troops were the flower of the youth of Germany, thousands of them volunteers from the educated middle classes, burning with ardour, nor that the enemy had established superiority of strength and was about to launch one of the great offensives of the war, from La Bassée to the sea.   The Battles of Ypres had begun.

The attack of October 21st fell more heavily upon the other two brigades of the 7th Division than upon the 20th, and on the refused right flank it was never pressed home, though parties of Germans dug themselves in very close to the firing line.   The same was generally true of the following days.   Whereas on the 22nd and 23rd the 21st Brigade in particular had to withstand assaults in mass and almost continuous shelling, the 2nd Gordons on the south side of the Kruiseecke salient were called on to face minor attacks, repulsed by straight shooting.   They were also subjected to occasional bursts of artillery fire, and vicious and accurate sniping. On the 23rd Drummer William Kenny rescued 5 wounded men in succession in the most fearless manner under heavy fire.   He was awarded the Victoria Cross for this and previous heroic conduct in saving machine guns and conveying urgent messages over fire-swept ground.

On the night of October 25th, when the Germans broke into Kruiseecke and attacked the 1st Grenadier Guards from front and rear, and next day when they rolled up the 2nd Scots Guards, the Gordons knew little of what was going on.   They were close pressed, but held the Germans off.   Their line remained unchanged and after the loss of Kruiseecke the new front of the brigade formed on their left flank.   So far they had been lucky, and whereas the other three battalions were sadly depleted, they were still strong in numbers. Their losses numbered about 100. The men, despite fatigue, were confident and in good spirits.

October 27th was quiet on the 7th Division's front. It had now been shortened on the northern flank. The 20th Brigade could actually move back a couple of miles behind the firing line. That afternoon, however, came a warning that the Germans intended to attack the division's front next day. The 20th Brigade was brought up again, the 1st Grenadier Guards taking station immediately south of the Menin road, with the 2nd Gordon Highlanders on its left.

The morning of October 29th was foggy. The heavy German bombardment was not at first followed by an infantry attack, and Major-General Capper drew back the two supporting battalions, 2nd Scots Guards and 2nd Border Regiment, because they had no cover and would, when the light improved and the fog cleared, be at the mercy of the German artillery. Then, at 7.30 a.m. the German artillery began to pound the 1st Grenadiers. Almost immediately a swarm of Germans swept down on their left flank, broke through, and attacked them in rear, while simultaneously the enemy assaulted frontally. The Grenadiers were almost cut to pieces and the remnants, with the left flank company of the Gordons pushed back toward Gheluvelt. But the Gordons sent aid in the shape of the reserve company; the Borders and Scots Guards hurried back into action; and a counter-attack north of the Menin road somewhat eased the situation.

At the worst moment, when a counter-attack had failed and the defence had seemed to be on the edge of disaster, the heroism of Captain J. A. O. Brooke had done much to restore it. Brooke was killed, and received the posthumous award of the Victoria Cross. Another contribution came from the 2nd Gordon Highlanders. "C" Company, commanded by Captain B. G. R. Gordon, had remained in its trenches and had been inflicting heavy loss on the enemy. Early in the afternoon it was given a great opportunity when the Germans appeared in mass only a few hundred yards away. On the front of one platoon alone 240 dead were counted later. The lost trenches at Gheluvelt were not recovered, but the front was otherwise restored with little change.

Besides Captain Brooke, the 2nd Gordons had lost Lieutenant the Hon. S. Fraser, and 2 officers attached from other regiments, killed, and 3 officers wounded. The only figure given for the casualties of the rank and file is "about one hundred", but its strength seems to have been lowered by more than this estimate would indicate. It was withdrawn for the night, but by 10 a.m. next morning was again on the move up.

2

Despite the heavy punishment meted out to them, the Germans were not giving up. They had made some progress, though not very much. Falkenhayn had not yet abandoned hope of a break-through on a big scale, leading at least to the capture of Calais.

It must be acknowledged that the allied commanders in the north—General Foch, who had a co-ordinating mission, Field Marshal Sir John French, and General d'Urbal—were equally optimistic and with less cause. They were not aware that the enemy had brought up further strong reinforcements, and they therefore stood by previous orders for the continuance of offensive action, though at no point had more than trifling progress been made for some time and, as has appeared, ground had been lost. However, this policy did not affect the 7th Division because the I Corps Commander, General Sir Douglas Haig, realized that no advance worth counting was possible, in view of the fatigue of his troops, unless the Germans showed signs of weakening under the strain. His overnight orders to his divisions were to dig in and reorganize; he informed them that further orders regarding a resumption of the offensive would be issued on the 30th when the situation had become clearer. It became only too clear at an early hour, so that such orders were not issued.

The German bombardment, one of the most powerful yet experienced, including that of 260 heavy or medium pieces, started at 6.45 a.m. on October 30th, and fell with greatest weight on the Household Cavalry of the 7th Cavalry Brigade in front of Zand-woorde. The trenches had been obliterated and the front line squadrons virtually annihilated when, at 8 o'clock the Germans advanced in strength and overran the position. The battalions of the 7th Division east of Zandwoorde beat off a frontal attack, but that nearest to the village, the 1st Royal Welsh Fusiliers, was then taken in flank and, but for a handful of survivors, destroyed.

Such troops as were available were set in motion to close the breach and if possible recover Zandwoorde. Among these, the 2nd Gordon Highlanders was directed to support a cavalry counter-attack. It went forward in artillery formation, but found the enemy in force in the woods. It stopped him west of the Basseville stream, but could make no further progress and indeed soon found the maintenance of the line reached more than it could well manage. About 2.30 p.m. it gave some ground—how much is not clear from the scanty reports—and finally dug in " in a wood ", actually that later known to the British as Shrewsbury Forest.

The result of the day's fighting was the loss of some useful ground—that on which Zandwoorde stood qualifying as a ridge in this flat country—and heavy casualties, but a gain to the Germans by no means commensurate with their efforts or their sacrifices. The Gordons had suffered severely, and their commanding officer, Lieut.-Colonel Uniacke, had been wounded.

Next day, Saturday, October 31st, was more dangerous still. The official history describes it as " one of the most critical days in the history of the British Expeditionary Force, if not of the British Empire ". Its main incidents were the establishment of a German foothold on the Messines Ridge, the loss of Gheluvelt, and its recapture by a counter-attack which has become immortal and in particular the proudest memory in the annals of the Worcester-shire Regiment.

General Haig, who now had at his disposal a French detachment at Kleine Zillebeke, sent across from the north side of the salient, had issued orders for a force of five battalions under the command of Brig.-General E. S. Bulfin to counter-attack with the object of recovering the gains made by the enemy in the front at Hollebeke the day before. Whether, and if so when, the 2nd Gordon High-landers was also placed under his orders is not clear. The point is, however, immaterial, because the battalion found itself in the midst of his line as a result of the confusion of October 30th. The diary of its own brigade states that it had been ordered to report to him on that day.

All that can be said here is that the Anglo-French counter-attack never really got started, and that the Germans, attacking astride the Menin Road, seized Gheluvelt at about 11.30 a.m. At the earliest possible moment Brig.-General Bulfin organized a counter-attack. It was high time, for the Germans were moving in force across the road from Gheluvelt to Zandwoorde, though more cautiously than in their previous attacks and sometimes apparently in doubt as to their direction. They were probably feeling their heavy losses in officers. Still, they continued to advance and forced their way into Shrewsbury Forest.

The 2nd Gordon Highlanders had suffered heavily and about 2.30 p.m. had been driven back in some disorder. It had then been ordered to prepare a new defensive position three-quarters of a mile in rear. Bulfin now ordered it forward again. He let the 2nd Royal Warwickshire of the 22nd Brigade and the 2nd Royal Sussex of the 1st Division know that reinforcements were coming up and bade them, as soon as they heard cheering behind them, give the enemy a minute's rapid fire—which the troops called " the mad minute " in which a well-trained unit could average fifteen rounds a man—and when the reinforcements drew level attack him with the bayonet. When the Gordons appeared, a mere handful, it is said only some eighty strong, he ordered them to advance in one line cheering.

The plan worked. The slenderness of the reinforcement was hidden from the enemy by the trees. When about 300 yards in rear of the firing line the Gordons began to cheer. At once the troops in front opened independent rapid fire. Then, at the moment when the Highlanders reached the firing line, the men in it jumped to their feet and all went forward together. All victories are of course largely moral victories, but this was an example of an almost entirely moral victory. It also confirmed the old lesson that troops who turn their backs when at close quarters with the enemy are likely to suffer worse than if they had held their ground. The Germans, who had fought very hard, as all through the battle, turned and ran. They were chased, shot down, and bayoneted in large numbers. The counter-attack pressed on for well nigh half a mile, and its effect was strongly felt further north. General Bulfin was indeed anxious lest it should go too far and expose the depleted units, since joined by others equally diminished, to destruction. It was stopped on the eastern fringe of Shrewsbury Forest, within little more than a stone's throw of the position lost in the morning.

This was a grand achievement. For the 2nd Gordon Highlanders, however, it resulted in terrible losses to add to those of the preceding days. These losses were inevitable sooner or later in fighting so ferocious against odds of at least three to one in numbers and the same in guns. The Gordons' luck had held a little longer than that of others. On October 28th their strength had been 26 combatant officers and 812 other ranks. After Captain J. R. E. Stansfeld had been wounded on November 1st they were left with 3 officers—Lieutenant J. M. Hamilton, Lieutenant H. M. Sprot, and 2nd Lieutenant W. J. Graham, Colonel of the Regiment at the time when this volume was written—and 205 other ranks, including battalion headquarters, cooks, and transport men. Among the wounded was another officer destined to be Colonel of the Regiment, Captain J. L. G. Burnett, whose gallantry won him the D.S.O. On October 29th he had twice led his company in desperate counter-attacks alongside the 1st Grenadiers. His servant, Private Christie, found him lying helpless and carried him back to safety, thus saving him from death or capture by the enemy, within whose reach he lay.[1]

Fortunately, pressure was less severe during the next four days. On Messines Ridge to the south heavy fighting occurred, but between the Menin Road and the Ypres-Comines Canal the German attacks, though frequent, were feeble by comparison with those of

---

[1] Private Christie, who received the M.M., remained with his officer all through the war and was still his chauffeur when he was Major-General Sir James Burnett, Bt., of Leys.

the last days of October. The records of the 2nd Gordon High-landers merely note that all were repulsed. Either on November 1st or next day the battalion came under the command of a sub-altern officer, Lieutenant J. M. Hamilton, in place of Captain Stansfeld. On the 3rd it was temporarily reorganized as a single company. November 5th was the worst day. Intense shelling blew in lengths of trench and at some points troops were withdrawn in order to keep down casualties. However, the enemy's attempt to exploit the situation was fruitless. The abandoned trenches, such as they were, were reoccupied, and the Germans were quickly stopped. At one point they brought up a field gun to within half a mile's range, but the Gordons shot down the team and kept the gun out of action all day.

This day saw the arrival on the scene of two brigades to begin the relief of the 7th Division. The shortage of troops which had hitherto made the Battle of Ypres a nightmare was being remedied by the arrival of French reinforcements and of the Indian Corps, which had taken over the La Bassée front. It chanced that one of these brigades was the 7th, which temporarily included the 1st Gordon Highlanders.

The 2nd Battalion marched through the night of November 5th to Locre and on the 7th reached Meteren. There it refitted in peace and absorbed two drafts, each approximately 100 strong. On the 13th the Commander-in-Chief, Field Marshal Sir John French, visited the battalions in their billets and complimented officers and men on their magnificent defence at Ypres.

The appearance on the scene of the 1st Battalion is a suitable moment at which to return to its fortunes, which have been recorded up to September 30th, the date on which it gave up its role as Army Troops and rejoined the 8th Brigade. It now took part in the B.E.F.'s move north, entraining at Pont Saint-Maxence, near Senlis, to the Abbeville area, and then moving by road again, afoot or in buses provided by the French, in the direction of Bethune.

In the early days of October the extension towards the north of the opposing armies, which has already been described, had made considerable progress.[1] By October 8th the French had established a line of battle as far north as Vermelles, four miles south of the La Bassée Canal, on which Bethune stands, while two cavalry corps next day fanned out to hold a front northward to Estaires, on the Lys. The British II Corps, of which the 3rd Division formed part, was ordered to move up on the left of the main French line of battle, that is, with right on Bethune. There appeared to be grounds for hope that the German flank could be

[1] See p. 15.

turned here. The fighting in which the 2nd Gordons were involved, already described, shows that this hope was destined to be
cheated. It has been said that in the race to the sea the Germans
were usually " a day and an army corps ahead ".

In this case there was only German cavalry, with the excellent
Jäger battalions which formed part of each division, opposing the
3rd Division to start with, but these troops, as in the Battle of the
Marne, fought stubborn delaying actions.

On October 12th the 1st Gordon Highlanders came under fire
for the first time since the action on the Petit Morin on September
8th. It was ordered to seize the bridge over the Lawe at Fosse.
The enemy was found to be holding not only the bridge but houses
in Fosse on the far side and a wood close by. It took two battalions
besides the Gordons to turn him out. The advance was resumed
next day over country flat as a tablecloth and intersected by
dykes. Movement was rapid at first, but was checked within two
miles, and the left of the Gordons was counter-attacked. The
machine-gun officer, 2nd-Lieutenant D. R. Turnbull, continued to
serve one of his guns when all the detachment were wounded. He
himself was later wounded in two places and his gun was damaged,
but he carried it out of action on his shoulder. He was awarded
the D.S.O.[1] If today's soldiers are disposed to criticize the pace,
they must realize that dykes had often to be bridged with boards
and that smoke shells or bombs to cover such work were not available.
Indeed, the whole British ammunition supply was already low.
On October 15th the main La Bassée-Estaires road was reached.

On the 16th the 9th Brigade relieved the 8th, which moved
into reserve at Croix Barbée. Its losses had amounted to 32
officers and 601 other ranks killed, wounded and missing. The
figures for the Gordons in these five days are not known, but
probably amount to about a quarter of the total. The 9th Brigade
continued the advance and captured Aubers on the 17th. Yet,
though no one at the moment realized it, this was virtually high
tide. A new German corps had come up.

On the 20th occurred a famous and tragic incident when the
2nd Royal Irish, which had captured the village of Le Pilly with
great gallantry, was surrounded and virtually exterminated, only
twenty or thirty men managing to escape. The 1st Gordon Highlanders was sent up to hold Grand Riez. Sir John French decided
that the II Corps should halt its wheel and "strongly entrench" itself.

It was fortunate that the corps did not further expose itself,
for on October 21st the enemy attacked the 3rd Division in great
strength. From right to left the brigades of this division stood in

---

[1] This outstanding officer was killed on October 1st, 1917, aged 25, in command
of a battalion of the Manchester Regiment.

the order 7th, 9th and 8th, and the main weight of the counter-stroke fell on the 7th and 9th. The situation was an anxious one that morning. It was more or less restored by a counter-attack, but to the north of the 8th Brigade the enemy took La Maisnil and reached the eastern outskirts of Fromelles. The 8th Brigade was therefore ordered at 10 p.m. to abandon Grand Riez and fall back to a position about half a mile in front of Aubers, facing west-north-west.

In view of the exposure of the 3rd Division on the left wing of the II Corps a reserve line of defence had been begun, giving up little ground on the La Bassée Canal but more to the north, where it ran east of Neuve Chapelle and through Fauquissart. It was not much of a defence, but since it had been sited at leisure and dug by French civilians under the supervision of the Royal Engineers it was better than the trenches hurriedly scraped out by weary troops wherever they were halted by hostile fire. When, on the 22nd, the French cavalry appeared unable to hold Fromelles, the corps commander, General Sir Horace Smith-Dorrien, obtained leave to withdraw to this line. The retirement was carried out under cover of darkness without interference from the enemy. How depressing would have been the effect if some immortal, like the Sinister Spirit of Thomas Hardy's *The Dynasts*, had whispered that, with small change, this was to be the British front until it was overrun in the Battle of the Lys, three and a half years later !

No attack was made next day because the Germans had to feel their way forward. They did attack on the morning of October 24th, but the British artillery held them off without much need for small-arms fire. The German Army had in its pre-war training paid relatively little attention to night attacks on the ground that they were too difficult to control and too apt to go astray. Consequently, the British and French had had to face relatively few and those few not generally on a big scale. Now, however, finding that their troops were such easy targets in daylight in this plain, the Germans decided to try their fortune in night fighting, not in a single attack but in a series of attacks in battalion and regimental strength. One of these was directed against the 8th Brigade and on the right of the Jullundur Brigade of the Indian Corps which had relieved the French cavalry from Fauquissart northward on the night of October 23rd.

The 1st Gordon Highlanders was on the left of the 8th Brigade's front, and a gap of some 400 yards divided it from the 15th Sikhs of the Jullundur Brigade. It had been promised some barbed wire, a rare commodity at this time—so rare that it was constantly taken from the fencing of the fields—but this had not arrived. Another trouble was that the telephone equipment lost in the early stages of the campaign had so far been replaced only by two instruments and a couple of miles of cable.

The German attack, carried out with great determination, broke through the Gordons' right company. Hearing the German cheers, the commanding officer, Major A. D. Greenhill Gardyne, turned out the right support company and sent it forward with bayonets fixed. It failed, however, to withstand the German onset and was driven through the orchards of Fauquissart on to the main Neuve Chapelle-Armentières road. Two companies of the 4th Middlesex now arrived, and after some confusion a line was established on the road. Some Gordons still held their ground on the left, but in view of the gap between them and the Indian troops on their left, who were themselves under attack, Major Gardyne thought it best to withdraw them also to the road.

Fortunately, the fronts of the 2nd Royal Scots on the right and the 15th Sikhs on the left held firm. About midnight the 4th Middlesex, supported by the Gordons, counter-attacked and regained the lost trenches. Though all ended well, it was an unhappy incident for the 1st Gordon Highlanders, as Major Gardyne made clear in his report to the 8th Brigade. Obviously it had not yet found itself as an almost entirely reconstituted battalion. Its losses were 7 officers and 197 other ranks, of whom 5 officers and 163 other ranks were missing.

The German offensive was not at an end. On October 27th, indeed, it succeeded in capturing Neuve Chapelle and next day successfully withstood a counter-attack. The strain upon the troops of the II Corps, by now nearly all reservists, special reservists, and recruits, was becoming dangerous. The Indian Corps had almost its full strength in France and could be used to relieve the greater part of it. This process was begun on the night of October 29th. If, however, the infantry expected a rest of any duration it was to be disappointed. The 8th Brigade in fact remained with the Indian Corps, but the 1st Gordon Highlanders was detached to the 7th Brigade, which was to move north and relieve even more exhausted troops on the Ypres front. This accounts for its appearance, as already recorded, in the region of Hooge, where the 7th Brigade relieved the 20th on November 5th. It was now commanded by Major A. W. F. Baird, and within the next three days reached a strength of approximately 660.

During the heavy fighting of November 7th and 8th it remained in support in Shrewsbury Forest, on ground which had been trodden by the 2nd Battalion. On the 9th, a comparatively quiet day on this front, it was in the firing line. The 10th was also uneventful for the British, though marked by a fierce onslaught on the French on the north flank of the salient.

Until dawn on November 11th there was no sign that anything unusual was to happen that day. Then a heavy German bombardment began, increasing in intensity until between 8 and 9 a.m. it became the heaviest ever experienced by the British. During these hours the front-line troops, but for their look-out sentries and the artillery observers who now habitually joined them, crouched in their inadequate and soon battered trenches. At 9 a.m. the German infantry attacked from Messines to Polygon Wood, north of the Menin Road, a front of nine miles. More than half this front was held by the French, whose line ran as far north as Hill 60, but the greatest weight was directed astride the Menin Road. The French front on the north side of the salient, which had been so heavily attacked on the 10th and was expecting a further trial today, was left virtually unmolested.

The 1st Gordon Highlanders was on the front of attack of the German 4th Division, a Pomeranian and West Prussian formation considered to be one of the best. Yet it hardly even troubled the Highlanders. All they have to say of it is that it was repulsed. Musketry may have fallen off owing to the losses suffered by the B.E.F., but it was still good; between it and the shrapnel of the artillery the waves of the attack were broken, and every attempt to re-form them failed. North of the Menin Road the Prussian Guard did gain a substantial success and at one moment had nothing in front of it but the British gun-line. This crack division, however, failed to exploit a great opportunity. The Gordons had one sergeant killed and 2nd Lieutenant Monteith wounded.

This repulse—for such it clearly was—decided the fate of the Battle of Ypres, though the British did not know it and were in fact deeply anxious about the future. On November 12th there was the inevitable heavy bombardment. The Gordons, who had come so lightly out of the last, were out of luck on this day. A single shell killed Captain K. B. Mackenzie (2nd Seaforths, attached) and Captain D. O. W. Thomas (4th Argyll and Sutherland Highlanders, attached), and concussed 2nd Lieutenant B. Cooke (3rd Black Watch, attached). Captain W. F. Mackenzie (3rd Seaforths, attached) was wounded. Six of the rank and file were killed and one wounded. The list is proof of a shortage of officers of the Gordon Highlanders, even if a temporary one only. On the 13th the Germans broke in a short distance on the left. Captain Duncan Campbell led up two companies and drove them out, at a cost of only two casualties. The 1st Battalion had done very well in the Salient and already expunged unhappy memories.

No more need be recorded of this great battle, though heavy shelling continued and the 1st Gordon Highlanders was not relieved by French troops until November 20th. It then marched south-west to Westoutre on the French frontier. At Locre on December 2nd it rejoined the 8th Brigade. The move was part of a big reorganization under which the whole of the Ypres salient was handed over to the French and the British took over a compact sector from the La Bassée Canal to a point west of Wytschaete.

Few battles better deserve to be remembered than the First Battle of Ypres, as it is called popularly. It must take precedence over the contemporary Battle of La Bassée not only because it went on longer and the fighting was more continuous, but above all because it was of far greater strategic significance. Its loss would have involved the loss of the Channel ports and perhaps the destruction of the allied left.

Those who follow its course with care are again and again brought up by the inability of the Germans to exploit their gains against the British and French. Every experienced soldier and student of war knows, of course, that exploitation is difficult and that opportunity is fleeting. Yet in this battle it was allowed to escape almost daily by the German Army, which is enterprising by tradition and in 1914 was aflame with zeal to conquer.

One reason is that the enemy was always expecting to be counter-attacked by reserves. Counter-attacked he generally was, but it was often by single battalions brought to the scene from some other part of the front where the need seemed for the moment less pressing. General Haig, the I Corps Commander, in particular showed extraordinary skill and nerve in this patching process. The Germans knew little about our military organization, but they knew we had a Territorial Army and had heard Haldane spoken of as a great war minister. Why should not the Territorial divisions be arriving on the scene as their own reserve divisions were ? They did not realize that Haldane had not ventured to ask the Liberal Party or the taxpayer for money for the Territorial Army or that it was virtually untrained and not even bound to serve outside the country.

While, therefore, the famous attacks of the German reserve divisions were carried out with astonishing bravery but without sufficient tactical skill, the more experienced troops who appeared later were inclined to hesitate at the critical moment. Mention has been made of the crisis of November 11th, when there was nothing left in front of the Prussian Guard but the British batteries. It is on record that a captured German officer asked what was beyond them and was told : " Divisional headquarters ". His comment was " Almighty God ! "

This does not detract from the achievement of the defence. The most astounding feature of it was the endurance of the troops. They hardly ever tasted hot food and in some cases lived for days on end chiefly on rum and the ration biscuit of those days, indistinguishable from dog-biscuit. The battle began in good weather, but from about November 5th it was vile, with constant rain, sleet, and snow. The vast majority of the men had to sleep, if sleep they could, in the open, without any protection. They were alerted at short intervals and sometimes faced attack three or four times in the course of a day.

Small individual weaknesses appeared from time to time—the troops would not have been human if this had not been so. But they responded to every call made upon them. Again and again they rose to the occasion, even when their own officers thought they had given all they had to give. This ought to be one of the proudest memories of our country.

It had, however, a black side. The old British Army, which had already lost heavily, virtually disappeared in the Battles of Ypres and La Bassée. It is no consolation to say that the German losses were far heavier still. Only a fraction of the German Army was present in this killing-ground, whereas all we had was there ; besides, the Germans had at their disposal a far greater number of capable reserve officers than we had. The losses suffered at Ypres, especially those of officers and non-commissioned officers, were to dog us. They were to involve us in far heavier future losses than we need otherwise have suffered and probably to prolong the war. We could produce armies of wonderful gallantry thereafter, but never armies with such skill in minor tactics and musketry.

But let us not forget the men of Ypres. They fought a defensive battle unexcelled in the annals of the British soldier, who has had to fight all too many.

CHAPTER III

THE first winter of the war was comparatively quiet. Both sides had fought themselves almost to a standstill and all the nations involved were experiencing a shortage of munitions. This winter had, however, depressing features. The B.E.F. began it on low-lying ground, so water-logged that at some points trenches had eventually to be replaced by breast-works. It took time to learn how to keep trenches drained, and sometimes this was a sheer impossibility. Thus, to begin with troops in trenches were virtually always standing in water, and the large-scale issue of " gum-boots thigh " afterwards made in such circumstances had not yet begun.

What had happened had been foreseen by few, though the Russo-Japanese War might well have prepared the minds of the British who had watched this so closely. The opposing armies had gone to ground behind barbed wire from the sea to the Swiss frontier. At some points they were so close together that they could hear each other talking, but the country through which the front ran appeared empty of human life. From an observation post and with the aid of a telescope it was indeed possible to see Germans moving about, though generally in twos or threes only, but for thousands of infantrymen six months might pass without their laying eyes on a hostile soldier. Henceforth there were to be no more attacks undertaken on the spur of the moment. Preliminary arrangements of various kinds were necessary, and these increased in complexity as time went on. Above all, the wire had to be cut.

The life of the infantry ran to a strict programme. At regular intervals, which might be as long as twelve days in a very quiet sector on dry ground and in summer, and as little as two on an agitated front with trenches knee deep in water, battalions holding the trenches would be relieved. They would then withdraw to rest billets. In these it was possible as a rule in the early stages to put officers and warrant officers into dwelling houses and at least the commanding officer of a battalion into the comfort of a room to himself. For the rank and file billets generally meant barns, often constructed with only one brick wall and three of lath and plaster ; but the men accounted them good billets and were well content if clean straw were available and they were not too " close " or overcrowded. In the mining villages of the large French coal-field, with which the British Army became familiar, the rank and file could generally billet in the miners' cottages. This country was depressing in appearance, but it had in winter the solid advantages of cover and fuel in plenty and pit-head baths. Where a countryside was devastated by prolonged fighting, as in the Battle of the Somme in 1916 or deliberately as by the Germans in the retreat to the Hindenburg line, troops not in the trenches were accommodated in tents or hutted camps. In the later stages of the war the depth of the defensive system was increased, and battalions in support often dwelt in a rearward zone of trenches.

Even in good weather there was generally work to do in the trenches, and in bad it never ceased. When a division made a long stay on one part of the front good troops developed something near affection for their own slice of it. They preferred to hold it alternately with another battalion of their own brigade with which they could work to a programme, and often grumbled, on being transferred to a different sub-sector, that it had been neglected by their predecessors. " This comes of battalions sitting idle in good weather ! " is the sort of phrase often found in a diary when trenches collapsed in rain. Thaw after frost was an even more searching test, often too hard for the best constructed and best revetted trenches. Trench stores were regularly handed over and signed for.

One unfortunate feature of this life was that it created a " trench atmosphere ". Trench existence became the normal. It was punctuated by attacks on a rigid pattern. The technique of open warfare was forgotten, so that when the Germans in their retreat to the Hindenburg line cleared out in the night, troops were seen wandering about in the open at a loss what to do next.

For fighting a way through German trenches or clearing British trenches in which the enemy had got a footing, no weapon was as effective and economical as the hand grenade, or " bomb ", as it was generally called. The Germans gained a start in the construction and tactical use of this weapon, but the British presently succeeded in turning out an effective one and also a good rifle grenade, which had a longer range and could often be used in the attack against machine-gun positions. Soon a bomber section was formed in each platoon. Battalion bomber platoons were the next step, though they were not universal, and it became customary to give every man some training in bombing. It was natural that this should be so, but the time given to the grenade and the importance attributed to it by the troops became excessive. Except for highly trained snipers, for whom steel loopholes were provided and who used special sights and occasionally express rifles, musketry became sadly neglected. As the number of machine guns increased and Lewis guns were issued to battalions, the troops counted more and more on them to do any shooting there was to be done. British musketry deteriorated. As a consequence, when the Germans went over to the offensive they often succeeded in attacks weaker and less determined than those which had been shot to pieces by the rapid fire of the battalions of 1914.

Many commentators on the First World War have noted the weakness of the British on the Western Front in training. Less attention has been given to the strenuous efforts to improve it by the founding of schools for officers, n.c.o.'s and specialists and by the provision of training areas well in rear of the battle zone. Whenever possible whole divisions or brigades were withdrawn to these for spells sometimes as long as a month. The training areas became well equipped. The morning was generally devoted to work, with games in the afternoon. These interludes were delightful, above all in summer, when it gave intense pleasure to officers and men to find themselves in unspoiled, smiling country. At harvest time they helped the old men and women and the boys and girls, almost the only labour left in the farming villages, to cut, thresh, and garner the corn.

What handicapped the training was above all the high proportion of loss in active operations, brought about by machine guns, barbed wire and concrete. Junior officers and men did not often last long enough to absorb the training imparted or pass on the experience of battle. When large reinforcements reached France from Palestine in 1918, it was found that the newly arrived battalions, though they at first exposed themselves recklessly because they had been able to do so without paying the penalty when faced by Turks, were tactically superior to those which had been serving on the Western Front. For the latter it was a vicious circle : heavy casualties made it difficult to raise the training standards, and weak standards increased casualties. However, Sir Douglas Haig, who was the inspirer of training, his subordinate commanders, and the training staffs, did win a reward for their efforts. In the final phase of the war the troops improved in minor tactics and learnt the most important lesson of that war, how to deal with machine-gun nests by combined frontal and flank attacks with Lewis guns, rifle grenades, and on occasion Stokes mortars. Losses were thereafter lightened.

The record of the 1st Gordon Highlanders has been carried to the point at which it rejoined its brigade at Locre on December 2nd. The 2nd Battalion was left resting at Meteren on November 13th. Next day it marched up to the front, crossing the Lys at Sailly, and that night relieved troops of the 19th Brigade, though not to begin with in the firing line. The whole of the 7th Division had moved to this area to shorten the front then held by the 6th. The merits of this front were that it was for the time being quiet, with fair accommodation in buildings close up to the trenches.

But these, bad to begin with, were at once ruined by heavy rain. The first days were uneventful as regards the enemy. Large drafts brought the battalion up to strength. Rain turned to snow, snow to frost. White smocks were issued for use on patrol. On November 25th came a thaw which made the trenches into ditches full of creamy mud. The first rifle grenades arrived; then the steel loopholes mentioned above which, when tested, were not even dented at fifty and a hundred yards. On December 1st King George V, accompanied by President Poincaré, the Prince of Wales, and General Joffre, presented medals of the D.S.O. at divisional headquarters.

At this stage another battalion of the regiment arrived and was attached to the 20th Brigade from December 5th. In view of the desperate need of reinforcements the Secretary of State for War, Lord Kitchener, had decided to send out specially selected Territorial battalions, detached from their brigades. Twenty-three arrived before the end of the year. Among those so honoured was the 1/6th Gordon Highlanders.[1] Having been stationed at Bedford since mid-August, it had crossed to France on November 9th and stayed for three weeks near Saint-Omer as G.H.Q. troops. It went into the line the day after its arrival, December 6th. This was a hard beginning of its apprenticeship, worse for a Highland regiment than any other because the 6th Battalion—like the 2nd—entered the trenches wearing shoes, spats, and hose. The brigade diary describes Highlanders' shoes as " useless " in such conditions because they were dragged off and lost in the dark, fifteen pairs disappearing in a single night. It also remarks that the discipline of the 6th Gordons needed tightening, but this would appear to mean trench discipline rather than conduct.

Neither battalion had any active part to play in a minor offensive carried out on December 18th. This was fortunate for them, for the attack was one of these operations far too popular with the British command in the earlier part of the war, undertaken to " distract " the enemy. They rarely succeeded in doing this, were nearly always failures, and generally costly. This led to a loss of over 700 killed, wounded and missing among four battalions.

Both battalions of the Gordons were witnesses of the Christmas truce which is in the public mind one of the best-remembered incidents of that war. It seems to have begun by mutual consent and spread out to either flank from the first point of contact. On

---

[1] The fractional system of numbering is due to the fact that, as already mentioned (see p. 12.) the Territorial battalions had been duplicated and the second-line battalions were given the prefix " 2 ". Since, however, none of these battalions of the the Gordon Highlanders went on active service, the prefix " 1 " seems unnecessary in the case of the first line and will henceforth be omitted.

this part of the front it was valuable in that it permitted the identification and burial of men killed in the attack of the 18th and in some cases brought information about the fate of men missing. Groups from the opposing forces collected in " no mans' land " and exchanged not only reminiscences but also rations and tobacco. Politeness or caution made them keep at a certain distance from each other's trenches—all but one wag of the 6th Battalion, who, seeing a bell on the German wire, went over, rang it, and demanded luncheon. Men of the 6th Battalion took part in hunting a hare which had been put up, but the quarry fell to a German. Despite orders from above, the truce was continued on the 26th and 27th. The Germans expressed disappointment that it had not gone on longer. Unconfirmed tales have, however, since been told that there were occasional scenes of fraternization up to the first days of January 1915.

So another year began. The life of the 2nd and 6th Gordon Highlanders up to the March offensive at Neuve Chapelle is veiled in obscurity, but if the pencilled sheet of the war diary appears dull, we may be sure that its quietude was welcome after the weeks of strain and death. The troops were learning how to make themselves as comfortable as might be. They obtained ammunition boots, though apparently not enough to go round, and wore them in the line, reverting to their shoes the morning after coming out. They began to experiment with breast-works in place of trenches from which it was impossible to keep the water ; these, when abandoned, had their use as wet ditches. Life out of the line, if monotonous, was not unpleasant, and the Highlanders were always liked by the French. The 6th Battalion appreciated being brigaded with " the Ninety-twa " and maintained the happiest and most friendly relations with it.

The 1st Gordon Highlanders had also begun the month of December quietly. On the 14th, however, it was involved in an operation which was part of a series, the last fighting of the year of any importance on the northern part of the allied front. On the first day it was mainly a French operation in which only the British 3rd Division on the French right, and only its 8th Brigade, was to take part. Later on the attack was to spread southwards, with the ultimate aim of capturing the whole of the Messines Ridge. In retrospect it looks a singularly unsatisfactory plan.

The 8th Brigade attacked with the 1st Gordon Highlanders on the right against Maedelstede Farm, on the Kemmel-Wytschaete road, and the 2nd Royal Scots on the left against a copse known as Petit Bois. The artillery of three divisions took part in the pre-liminary bombardment, but, for lack of ammunition, it lasted only three-quarters of an hour. The advance, begun at 7.45 a.m., was at once met by heavy rifle and machine-gun fire. Some men of one of the leading companies of the 1st Gordons were seen to jump into a trench 300 yards from the British line. Then followed an eclipse of vision common in the operations of that war. No one returned with news ; no one could get forward to obtain any.

At last, at 3.55 p.m. the report came through that a line of men was lying fifty yards short of the German trench. Preparations were made for a renewal of the attack, but finding that the German wire was intact, the commanding officer, Major A. W. F. Baird, had the strength of mind to cancel it on his own initiative. After dark the survivors were withdrawn, including a small party found to have entered an advanced trench. The 2nd Royal Scots did get in and took a number of prisoners.

The losses of the 1st Gordon Highlanders were heavy. Captain C. Boddam-Whetham (3rd Black Watch, attached), who had entered the German trench, Lieutenants W. F. R. Dobie and J. J. G. MacWilliam were missing ; 2nd Lieutenants G. C. Rose (3rd Seaforths), G. B. Smith, W. D. Gillies, and R. T. Grant (the two last 4th A. & S. Highlanders) were wounded. Of the rank and file 51 were killed, 123 wounded, and 69 missing, a total of 253.

The French had failed to make any ground. During the two following days the operations were carried out half-heartedly, degenerating into a demonstration. Later attacks achieved no success. The strongest and most costly was that of the 7th Division on December 18th, of which mention has already been made. The Messines Ridge, lost in the November fighting, was a commanding position and an attractive objective. It was also the case that the Germans had withdrawn troops to the Eastern Front and that General Joffre had called for pressure to be exerted in support of operations elsewhere. Yet this looks an ill-considered and ill-conducted offensive.

Some new light is thrown on it by a personal letter from the commander of the II Corps, Sir Horace Smith-Dorrien, to the divisional commander, Major-General Haldane. Evidently shocked by the losses, the writer pointed out that since trench warfare had set in we had never tried the effect of a heavy bombardment of the enemy's trenches followed immediately by an infantry assault, and it was believed this would allow the infantry to get forward. It had in the case of the Royal Scots, but not in that of the Gordons, whose objective, on a bare knoll, was the more formidable. The power of the defence, the corps commander went on, was now proving so great that the war " would possibly last some considerable period ". We had learnt from the determined attack of the Gordons that in order to break down defensive positions Britain would at once have to set to work to produce more howitzers.

The interest of this letter, apart from the sympathy and appreciation which the writer expresses for the regiment, is to be found in its revelation of the mind of an able and experienced soldier at this time. He is looking at something which has since become a commonplace as regards the First World War, but is to him still a novelty on which he is still only at the beginning of the process of forming a judgment. Everyone was in fact groping for tactics to meet the present conditions. The search was to be a long one, very costly in blood and treasure.

For the three battalions of the Gordon Highlanders now on the Western Front the rest of the winter affords virtually no history. The existence of the 1st Battalion was confined to trenches on the Vierstraat-Wytschaete road, a little north of those from which it had attacked on December 14th, and its billets in La Clytte, some two and a half miles behind them. The 2nd and 6th Battalions led a similarly uneventful life, their trenches being near La Cordonnerie Farm, about a mile north of Fromelles. The 1st described its trenches as wretched, but those of the other two were the wetter. After flooding in the middle of January 1915 the 2nd Battalion held its front by posts 150 yards apart, turning sections of trench into little isolated keeps by walling them up and pumping them out. It is clear that the pumping process had to be frequently repeated. The rate of sickness rose, particularly from an affliction first known as " frozen feet " but actually caused by standing in water a little above freezing point. The more suitable name " trench feet " soon came into use. It was eventually found that this could be fought, even before gum-boots were available on a large scale, by rubbing the feet with whale oil and sending up dry socks nightly with the rations. Such measures became a matter of discipline, and no battalion was counted as well-disciplined and efficient if it suffered what appeared to be unduly high casualties from trench feet.

Another batch of Territorial battalions arrived independently from home. One of these was the 4th Gordon Highlanders, like the 6th Battalion from the Highland Division quartered at Bedford. It crossed to Havre on the night of February 19th, joined the 8th Brigade of the 3rd Division at La Clytte on the 27th, and during the first ten days of March went into the line company by company for instruction in trench duties. Thus the four battalions of the regiment formed part of two brigades, the 1st and 4th in the 8th Brigade, and 2nd and 6th in the 20th Brigade, and in each case the regulars were the mentors of the Territorials. In each warm friendship was at once established. The regimental spirit was strong in the Gordon Highlanders, stronger probably than in those regiments which expanded on a far greater scale.

Battalions were always delighted to meet each other. On several occasions when two could not meet but approached within ten miles or so of each other, excursions of officers and men from one were made in order to visit the other. If one were passing through or near the billeting area of another, the latter would send its drums and pipes to play it on its way.

So we come to the major active operations of the year 1915. It must be said in advance that they will make depressing reading. The enemy's defeat on the Marne and his failure to break through to the Channel ports in the Battles of Ypres had aroused hopes that a series of allied offensives would result in sweeping victories and perhaps even drive him out of France and Belgium. This view was not shared by Lord Kitchener, who was inclined to regard the German lines in France as " a fortress that cannot be carried by assault ", or by the British Government generally. General Joffre and Sir John French were, however, more optimistic, and it was in any event urgently necessary to take some measures to relieve the great and growing weight of German and Austrian pressure on Russia. The complex strategic ideas of Joffre—very much those which inspired Haig when he became British Commander-in-Chief and on which the war was finally won—are to be found in the official history and other works, and hardly require to be examined in a regimental history. In any case Joffre's plans were interrupted by a powerful and unexpected German offensive which owed its early success to the use of toxic gas.

The numerous offensives, French and British, of the year 1915 were to result in disillusion. They brought in little to balance the heavy loss which they involved. They proved of no substantial assistance to Russia. And, whenever they are considered, there must lie in the background of the mind the saddening reflection that another good division from among those which took part in them might have changed the fortunes of the Gallipoli campaign, with immense benefit to the future of the war, perhaps even of the world. The opening of the Dardanelles would indeed have eased the pressure on Russia.

CHAPTER IV

THE British offensive to capture the Aubers Ridge, which started with the Battle of Neuve Chapelle, was originally timed to coincide with a more important French offensive against the Vimy Ridge, further south. However, as the plans were worked out, it was found that the French could not attack unless the British relieved one of their corps north of the Comines Canal, whereas the British could not attack if they did so. The solution adopted, that the British should attack first independently, was, to say the least of it, open to criticism. The place had, however, been well chosen. The Germans were thin on the ground and the British contrived to assemble in secrecy very great numerical superiority. The operations were prepared with skill and care by the staff of the First Army.

The 7th Division was not to take part in the first assault, which was to be made on a frontage of only about a mile and a half, with the village of Neuve Chapelle about the centre. Then was to follow, with the greatest possible speed so that the enemy should not have time to recover and reinforce, the advance on to the gently rising ground dignified in this flat country by the title of the Aubers Ridge.

The attack on Neuve Chapelle on the morning of March 10th was brilliantly successful. The right of the 8th Division swept through the ruins of the village and reached its objective. Hopes soared up because it was believed, and rightly, that there was little in front of the troops at this point. Unfortunately, the left of the 8th Division was seriously checked and suffered heavy loss because two 6-inch howitzer batteries, which had arrived from England only the previous day and had not had time to register or construct platforms, failed to destroy a section of the German trench allotted to them. This caused a hold-up not only of the brigade concerned but also of that which was supporting it and destined to pass through. It also affected the 21st Brigade of the 7th Division, two battalions of which, moving up to their assembly trenches, found them blocked. The divisional commander, Major-General Sir T. Capper, begged to be allowed to push on, but was bidden by the commander of the IV Corps, Lieut.-General Sir H. S. Rawlinson, to wait until an orchard, believed to be a strong point, had been taken. The orchard was actually undefended and there was no opposition to speak of in front of the 7th Division.

So precious time was allowed to slip away. By the day's end fair progress had been made by the 21st Brigade until held up in gathering darkness by a few German strong points. The Indian and IV Corps had taken the German defences to a maximum depth of 1,200 yards on a front of two and a quarter miles, but the tempo had been painfully slow, in part owing to delays in communication, and supports and reserves had been left unemployed. The 22nd Brigade on the left of the 21st had not moved and the 20th Brigade in reserve had stayed there, except that it had moved into the trenches vacated by the 21st and then been withdrawn. The 2nd Gordon Highlanders was placed temporarily under the orders of the 21st Brigade and during the night B Company helped the 2nd Wiltshire to dig a communication trench connecting the British and captured German trenches. The company can have had little rest because it did not get back to the support trenches until shortly before dawn. And it had to be on the move early next day.

Sir Douglas Haig ordered the IV Corps to capture the Aubers Ridge as far east as Le Plouich, some half a mile east of the substantial village of Aubers. The plan was rather complex. Whereas the 8th Division was to advance eastward, the leading brigade of the 7th Division, the 21st, was to advance north-eastward. The 20th Brigade was to fill the gap which would occur between them and then attack Aubers village. The brigade began to move up at 3.30 a.m. on March 14th, the 6th Gordon Highlanders bringing up the rear, and picked up the 2nd Battalion on the rue Tilleloy.

At 7 a.m. the 20th Brigade advanced, the 1st Grenadier Guards (directing) on the right, south of the orchard, the 2nd Gordon Highlanders on the left, moving through and north of it. They came immediately under very heavy machine-gun fire from the left, and the advance was brought to a halt even before it had reached the firing line, both battalions having suffered severely. It now became apparent that the position of the 21st Brigade was quite different from what its headquarters believed it to be, its right hanging back so that its line faced south-east. Thus the left of the 20th Brigade was in the air. No further progress was made that day. At dusk two companies of the 2nd Gordon Highlanders dug and occupied a trench facing north-east, the other two being held in rear.

Before first light on March 12th the battalion was withdrawn under very heavy fire. It was not called on to take part in the attack of this day and was not even called upon to help in repelling a counter-attack along the whole front carried out by the considerable reinforcements which the German command had been given time to bring up. At some points this counter-attack bit into the irregular British front, but nearly always only temporarily and the effort as a whole ended in a bloody repulse.

The 2nd Scots Guards and 2nd Borders of the 20th Brigade then captured a part of the German trench system known as the Quadrilateral with a large haul of prisoners. Unhappily, this

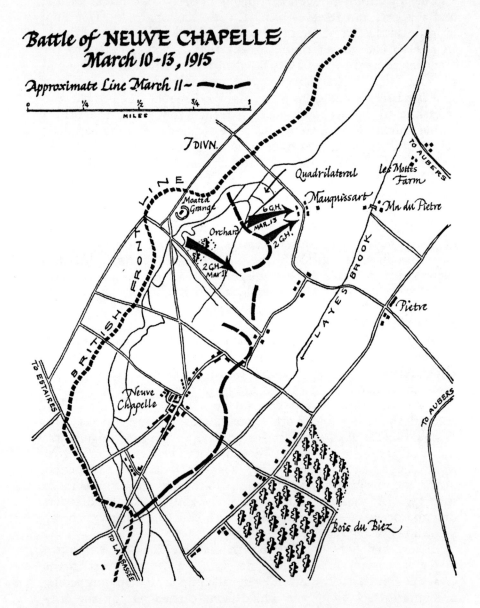

Battle of NEUVE CHAPELLE
March 10-13, 1915

Approximate Line March 11~ — —

0   ¼   ½   ¾   1
MILES

promising start proved deceptive. Attempts to continue the advance broke down. The 2nd Gordon Highlanders, which had been moved up again to the German front line in the hope that the first success might be exploited, did not come into action. The

6th Battalion, which had been standing by in the old British front line, was not called on either, but it was so heavily shelled that it was for a time withdrawn to the reserve line after suffering twenty-five casualties. For a keen but raw battalion, only three months in the country and now in its first engagement, the experience had been so far disappointing. All that it had done had been to wait under increasing artillery fire. Throughout the night practically every available man was employed in carrying up rations and water to the troops in front. This was a valuable service, but one which did not leave the battalion fresh for the morrow.

In the attack of March 13th the 2nd Gordons were to take the place of the 2nd West Yorkshires, 21st Brigade, and at 9.30 a.m. to capture trenches and a few houses at the Moulin du Pietre. The bombardment had quite failed to silence the enemy's machine-guns. The commanding officer, Lieut.-Colonel H. P. Uniacke, who had rejoined only at the end of January after having been wounded in the Battle of Ypres, was killed while examining the ground over which his battalion was called on to advance. His successor, as at Ypres, was J. R. E. Stansfeld, now a major. He in turn was wounded, but remained for some time with his men. He came to the conclusion that it would be suicidal to attack until accurate artillery fire could be arranged—at the moment British shells were falling in his own shallow trenches—in face of the murderous fire. He therefore stopped the assault and as soon as possible reported that he had done so. Command of the battalion passed to Captain J. M. Hamilton.

The 6th Gordon Highlanders had been brought up in the early hours to the old German front line. It was ordered to attack on the left of the 2nd Battalion, and its objectives were pointed out to the officers on the ground. It seems an extraordinary action to send a battalion across the open in broad daylight when the general attack was clearly held up by heavy fire. It shared the fate of the 2nd in losing its commanding officer. Lieut.-Colonel C. McLean was an active and energetic veteran who had commanded since the embodiment of the battalion, which owed a great deal to him.

Captain J. M. Cooke assumed command. He ordered the advance to be carried out by two companies, in lines of half-companies (that is, on a four-platoon front), the other two following at a distance of 200 yards. Artillery, machine-gun, and rifle fire was encountered at the start, but the companies moved at top speed without losing their formation and, though suffering heavily, were not as hard hit as might have been expected. However, as they moved on, the fire grew hotter and hotter, till they came to a halt on a line a little in advance of that of the 2nd Battalion. Captain Cooke received a message from brigade headquarters to the effect that howitzer fire would be turned on to the houses at Moulin du Pietre in order to allow the advance to continue.

Despite this bombardment, the German fire did not slacken. Finally, at 5.45 p.m. orders were received to hold the position already reached. The battalion brought in all wounded men under cover of darkness, and in the early hours of March 14th was relieved by the 2nd Borders. The 2nd Gordon Highlanders spent all that day in the trenches and withdrew after dark to Laventie. The 20th Brigade had been the heaviest sufferer of the three. The losses of the 2nd Battalion numbered 255 killed, wounded and missing, and those of the 6th, 270.[1]

That any further substantial success could now have been gained seems highly improbable, but even if the prospects had been golden no more could have been attempted. The jealously hoarded ammunition reserve had been expended ; it was estimated that the total current production in England would take ten days to replace the 18-pdr. ammunition fired in the first day's bombardment.

The operation had ended in deep disappointment. British leaders have often been reproached with reckless handling of their troops. Here they had proved over-cautious, or rather the commander of the IV Corps, Sir Henry Rawlinson—who was to prove one of the ablest of all British commanders—had checked both divisions engaged when they had such a chance of making a deep advance as was not to recur for two years. This is not wisdom after the event because the British, used to fighting against odds, had a superiority of over ten to one at the outset, and the higher command was aware of the fact. The Germans were now short of reserves on the British front, but it was certain that they would reinforce the threatened sector as fast as possible. They had in fact done so. Another weak point in the attack was unavoidable. It was made initially on a narrow front, which was to be expanded as it progressed. The reason was in part the desire to capture the Neuve Chapelle salient first because it enfiladed the approach to their trenches to the north and south. In any case the ammunition available would not have sufficed to launch the offensive on a broader front.

The Germans had suffered heavily, particularly in the counter-offensive of March 12th, and the official history finds the losses of

[1]		Killed	Wounded	Missing
2nd Gordons	Officers	4	11	1
	Other ranks	49	179	11
6th Gordons	Officers	3	9	—
	Other ranks	29	217	12

The 6th Battalion had 37 further casualties in the first three days, whereas those of the 2nd Battalion are for the whole battle.

the opposing forces roughly equal. On the whole the impression
left by the battle upon the command and even the officers who
went " over the bags " was favourable. This may seem surprising
when we consider the disproportion between hopes and achievement, but those taking part felt that a real trench system—not
just a single trench with odd lengths here and there for supports—
had been attacked with initial success, that it could be breached,
and that the experience acquired at Neuve Chapelle would be of
use to this end.

The operation had been carried out with battalions which cannot have included, counting returned wounded, more than about
20 per cent. of their original officers and men.

In fact the Germans, who were to be much more often on the
defensive than on the offensive for the rest of the year 1915, were
learning too. They began to extend their entrenchments, to dig
switches which would help to seal sections of the system which
had been penetrated. There were to be worse disappointments
than that of Neuve Chapelle.

After a few days for refitting, the 20th Brigade took over
trenches at Fauquissart, just north of the breach made in the
enemy's line in the recent battle. The 6th Gordon Highlanders
remained weak at a time when most battalions in the division were
receiving large drafts. The reason was that 2nd line Territorial
battalions were being reorganized with a view to possible foreign
service, so that those of the 1st line already in the field had to
depend largely on fresh recruiting for their reinforcements. The
battalion received from the brigade commander an exceptionally
high tribute. Brigadier-General F. J. Heyworth remarked that
he found it hard to pick individual battalions for praise, but that
he desired " to note the gallant conduct of the 6th (Territorial)
Battalion the Gordon Highlanders " at Neuve Chapelle. Joining
a seasoned brigade, it had shown itself fully qualified to keep up the
standard ; the 20th Brigade was proud to have the battalion in
its ranks.

At the end of April the 20th Brigade was detached to the 8th
Division. Except for this brigade, the 7th Division was ordered
north in view of the German gas attack at Ypres and the possibility
that the front would collapse. Only the Royal Engineers were
employed in the Salient. During its absence the 20th Brigade
relieved troops of the Indian Corps on the front captured in the
Battle of Neuve Chapelle.

Another offensive to secure the Aubers Ridge was now launched.
This battle, to which the name of the ridge itself was given, was on
a greater scale, more ambitious in aim, and provocative of higher
confidence than that of Neuve Chapelle. Its failure was therefore

a cruel disappointment, a downfall of hopes. The 7th Division, except for its artillery, played no part on the first day, May 9th, its role being to exploit success—which never came—on the second. It narrowly escaped having to relieve the 8th Division on the night of the 9th and repeat its programme. However, Major-General Hubert Gough, who had recently succeeded Major-General Capper as divisional commander, decided that the plan of the IV corps was foredoomed to failure and succeeded in getting it cancelled. The division had cause to be grateful for his strength of mind.

Sir John French felt compelled to do something more in support of the big French Artois offensive. He decided to renew the attack further south on a front of some three miles from the Estaires-La Bassée road. The right flank was allotted to the 7th Division, its right on la Quinque Rue, a road running from south-west to north-east. A village on this road behind the British line gave its name to the operation, the Battle of Festubert. The 7th Division's attack was to be launched at 3.15 a.m. on May 16th, but the Indian Corps on its left was to secure the German front line during the previous night.

The 20th Brigade, on the 7th Division's left flank, formed up with the 2nd Scots Guards on the right and the 2nd Borders on the left, supported by the 2nd Gordon Highlanders and the 1st Grenadier Guards. The 6th Gordon Highlanders was in brigade reserve.

The Scots Guards went forward with magnificent dash. Within an hour, however, an ominous order came to the 2nd Gordons to move forward and protect the Guardsmen's left, because the Borders had been brought to a stop in the German front line by fire from strong points or " defended localities " in the third. Bit by bit, the whole of the 2nd Gordons but for one company was drawn in, since the Scots Guards in the German third line had been reduced to little more than two weak companies. The remainder of the battalion had pressed forward and been overwhelmed by a counter-attack. The Gordons also sent a platoon and their bombers to aid the Borders. It was all of no avail. The later attempts to take the strong points failed.

Orders were issued to renew the attack at 10.30 a.m. on May 17th. It was to be made by the 21st Brigade, supported by the 1st Grenadier Guards and the 6th Gordon Highlanders. This battalion was pushing forward to take the enemy opposed to the 21st Brigade in flank when suddenly a German battalion appeared out of the blue, advancing in a loose mass at the double. The Gordons opened fire. The target could hardly be missed and the Germans were cut down in clumps. An astounding incident then unfolded before the eyes of the Highlanders. The German artillery began to fire on its own troops, as effectively as the Gordons from the other side. At last the truth was realized. The Germans were advancing to surrender. The Gordons thereupon ceased firing. Then 207 Germans out of about 700 who had first come into view, gave themselves up. This surrender, hitherto and for long afterwards unknown among German troops who had not been

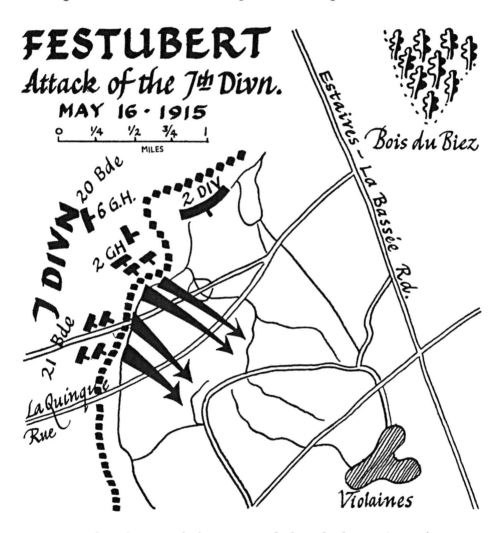

FESTUBERT
Attack of the 7th Divn.
MAY 16 · 1915

0 ¼ ½ ¾ 1
MILES

20 Bde
6 G.H.
2 DIV
2 GH
7 DIV
21 Bde
La Quinque
Rue

Estaires–La Bassée Rd.
Bois du Biez

Violaines

cornered, so impressed the command that the hour of assault was put forward an hour, to 9.30. At this time the 2nd Royal Scots of the 21st Brigade passed through the 6th Gordon Highlanders.

The strong points were captured, and a further advance followed. The rest of this intricate battle would, however, take too much space to follow in detail, in view of the fact that it does not concern the Gordon Highlanders. All that can be said is that it ended

with troops of the 1st Canadian and British 2nd Divisions holding
a front varying from 500 to 900 yards east of the original British
line. Once more the 2nd Gordon Highlanders had suffered
heavily, very heavily seeing that the battalion as a whole had not
taken part in an assault. Its losses amounted to 280.[1] Among
the wounded was the commanding officer, Lieut.-Colonel A. F.
Gordon, and for the second time Major J. M. Hamilton took over
temporary command. The 6th Battalion had scarcely been engaged, though it had had the extreme good luck to make a big
haul of prisoners at a point where the British front was scarcely
under fire. Its casualties amounted only to 32 all ranks.

Festubert was not a failure as thorough as that of Aubers Ridge
on May 9th. It would, however, be stretching complacency a
long way to call it a success, though Lieut.-Colonel Stansfeld,
returning to take command of the 2nd Gordons on recovery from
his wound just after the battle, found the battalion " as pleased as
Punch ". The defensive was, there could be no doubt of it, in
the ascendant. How far the British commanders recognized this
fact it is hard to say. In no case could they have left the French
Arras offensive—which began with wonderful success on a greater
scale but likewise ended in disappointment—to go unsupported.
The quandary was that they lacked the artillery resources to give
it the degree of support required.

While these battles had been waged the 1/1st Highland Division, renamed the 51st (Highland) soon after its arrival, had reached
France. It included the 5th and 7th Gordon Highlanders in the
153rd Brigade. It may be of interest from the point of view of
transportation to note that the transport and details of the 7th
Battalion (3 officers, 103 men, 73 horses, 9 bicycles, 23 vehicles and
2 machine guns) entrained at Bedford in forty minutes on April
30th and crossed from Southampton to Havre. The battalion,
less this detachment, crossed from Folkestone, reached Boulogne
at 3 a.m. on May 3rd, joined the train carrying the transport at
Port de Briques, three miles from the port, and detrained at
Berguette, near Aire in the Pas de Calais, marching thence to
billets at Lillers.[2] It may also be worthy of mention that when

[1]

	Killed	Wounded	Missing
Officers	3	10	—
Other ranks	53	204	10

[2] In the United Kingdom, where passenger coaches were nearly always provided
for the rank and file, a battalion was in such cases divided between two trains. In
France, where far greater numbers had to be carried by train, a single train made up
of the standard *fourgons* or baggage wagons, except for a coach for officers, took the
whole battalion. The *fourgon* was used for either men or animals, and the words
" Hommes quarante, chevaux huit ", painted on it were an endless subject of humour
in the British Army. Needles to say, the speed was not equal to that attained at home.

the battalion moved up in case the 51st Division should be called on in the Battle of Neuve Chapelle, the folk of the village in which it billeted had never seen Highlanders and were inclined to think the kilt an indecorous garment.

One other secondary offensive was undertaken in this area, involving the four battalions of the regiment in the 7th and 51st Divisions. It was trying them highly to send them into action in early June. The diary of the 2nd Battalion records with pleasure a week's training and sport in excellent billets amid lovely country and fields full of stock, though its romantically named village, Bellerive, was not far distant from the front. The infantry of the 7th Division, however, had not had time to absorb drafts under officers who in most cases had little experience themselves. The loss of the 2nd Battalion at Neuve Chapelle and Festubert had been 7 officers killed and 21 wounded. The battalions had not regained their former fighting value. Those of the 51st Division were newly arrived, equally or even more enthusiastic, but unversed in trench warfare.

The operation was, as before, a diversion in aid of the French, but it also aimed at improving a part of the front which urgently needed improvement. This was at Givenchy, a mile and a quarter south of Festubert and lying on the north bank of the La Bassée Canal. In the previous offensive the front had been advanced to the foot of a German-held fortress on high ground known as the Givenchy Bluff. From the summit the enemy overlooked and could even drop bombs into the captured trenches.

As a preliminary operation an attack by two companies of the 6th Gordon Highlanders was made on June 3rd on a strong point at the nose of the German salient. Mining, of which more will have to be written later, had begun in this region, and this assault was preceded by an explosion which caused the enemy serious loss and for the time being shook his defence. The attack was successful, and two barricades were established south and east of the captured work. About 50 prisoners were taken. A party of the 55th Company R.E. put out some wire round the whole position.

Before first light on June 4th the enemy launched a vigorous counter-attack prepared and covered by trench-mortar fire. The defenders quickly ran out of grenades and the German bombers, moving along trenches, could not be reached by rifle fire. After a short, sharp fight the captured trenches were abandoned. Major-General Gough decided to give time for thorough preparation before renewing the attack and that night relieved the 20th Brigade by the 22nd. The 6th Gordons had suffered 142 casualties. The 2nd, though engaged only in burying dead and salving equipment left in the British trenches by its predecessors, lost 41. It was now that this battalion's happy sojourn at Bellerive took place while the 6th was nearby at Robecq.

When the 20th Brigade returned to the front it found the situation unaltered, though there had been more fighting in the area. The main attack was launched on the evening of June 15th with the 1st Canadian Division on the right, 7th Division in the centre, and 51st Division on the left, the 7th Division being represented by the 21st Brigade and the 51st Division by the 154th. None of the four Gordons battalions was involved.

The attack failed, none of the three divisions taking part retaining such slight gains as had been made. It was renewed on June 16th at 4.45 p.m. and was once again a complete failure. On this occasion the 5th and 7th Gordon Highlanders were temporarily attached to the 154th Brigade but, mercifully for them, were not called on to take part in the assault. Projects for further large-scale operations were cancelled, but a minor one was carried out at 9.30 p.m. on June 17th.

The objective was a strong point some 250 yards south-west of Rue d'Ouvert and the trench on either side of it. This faced the junction of the 7th and 51st Division, and the attack was entrusted to the 2nd Gordon Highlanders of the former with a company of the 7th Battalion of the latter on its left. The 7th Battalion complained afterwards that, owing to the haste in which orders were issued, platoon commanders were not clear in their minds what to do. The 2nd Battalion reached the trench first, found the wire uncut, and of course was seen. Such fire was then opened from the trench that the commander of the 7th Battalion's company decided not to advance further and withdrew. His losses were only 10, whereas those of the 2nd Battalion were 147.

At the end of the year 1914 the whole of the Ypres Salient, except for its right shoulder south of the La Bassée Canal, had been held by the French. To set their troops free for offensive action in Artois the British, reinforced by the arrival of two more divisions mainly formed from troops withdrawn from foreign stations and by Territorial Divisions, relieved the French till only two of their divisions remained on the northern flank of the Salient. It was on these divisions—one an African, the other a Territorial[1] —that the German gas attack fell in the late afternoon of a beautiful spring day, April 22nd, 1915.

Shortly afterwards bodies of Algerian riflemen without officers flocked along the roads converging on Ypres, coughing, gasping, pointing to their throats, but otherwise unintelligible. Then

---

[1] It is hardly necessary to point out that the word had an entirely different meaning in French and English. The French Territorial troops were formed of the oldest men liable to military service.

French Territorials were seen crossing the canal north of the city. Finally it was discovered that the whole defence from the left of the 1st Canadian division near Poelcapelle to the canal had not merely collapsed but disappeared. The Germans followed up somewhat cautiously, the command surprised by its own success, the troops nervous about the gas. By night, however, they had penetrated to a maximum depth of two and a half miles.

"Second Ypres" as it is popularly called, "the Battles of Ypres 1915" in official nomenclature, lasted just short of five weeks. The details of the battle or series of battles have, however, nothing to do with the 1st and 4th Gordon Highlanders in the 3rd Division. All that is necessary from their point of view is to describe how they were affected by it, which was to a limited extent only.

The 3rd Division had its right facing Wytschaete and its left a little east of St. Eloi, so that its nearest troops were about seven and a half miles distant from the trenches from which the chlorine gas was discharged on April 22nd. Yet some men of the 1st Gordon Highlanders, which was then holding a narrow front with a half battalion and providing its own trench reliefs, complained of sore eyes. This is not likely to have been imagination on their part because they had not had time to talk about the gas. In all probability they were very slightly affected by leakage from cylinders which are known to have been dug in on this front. Until something better could be procured, the British used wet bandages tied over nose and mouth as protection. Cloth and extra tins of water were sent up to the half battalion of the 1st Gordons.

Nothing more happened until May 12th, when the 8th Brigade left its own divisional front and moved to take over the trenches of the 13th Brigade, 5th Division, in the neighbourhood of Hill 60. The 5th was on the left of the 3rd, north of the Comines Canal, and the most southerly to be involved in the battle. It had lost Hill 60 in a localized gas attack on May 5th and had failed to recover it. The fighting had been ferocious and the losses of the 5th Division had been high. The "hill" was in fact a heap of spoil excavated from the railway cutting. Two others less famous, "the Dump" and "the Caterpillar", lay on the other side of the cutting. Hill 60 was a first-class observation post, unhappily at its best looking north-west towards Ypres. It was by now possibly the most pulverized spot on the battlefields of this war. It could have been recovered, but not held unless a lot of German-held ground, including the Caterpillar, had also been taken. The British, hard-pressed and weary, did not possess the reserves for such an operation.

That evening the 1st Gordon Highlanders took over a section of front facing Hill 60. The scene was ghastly. In the trenches still lay the bodies of many men killed by the gas a week before. The Gordons buried them and retrieved hundreds of rifles, precious at a moment when there were hardly enough at home to equip drafts for the front. Over their left shoulders the troops could see by day the columns of smoke, by night the glow, of big fires burning in Ypres. Shelling was almost continuous, night and day. This spell was not, however, costly. The bombers of the 1st Gordons twice bombed the Germans effectively, in one case crawling up an abandoned communication trench to do so. Otherwise there is nothing to record. The brigade was relieved on May 20th and returned next morning to its own division and its old quarters at La Clytte.

Not for long, however. On Whit Monday, May 24th, in the small hours of the morning the Germans released cloud gas on a far bigger scale than on April 22nd, over a front of four and a half miles from just south of Hooge on the Menin Road. By this time the Ypres salient, though a salient still, had been blunted—from Broodseinde, the middle of the arc, to the extent of three and a half miles. This withdrawal, so far as the British were concerned, had been mainly due to the inability of the French to recover the ground lost in the first gas attack, so that the British had been left with a flank four miles in length facing northward and slenderly defended.

On this occasion there was no surprise. The defence was magnificent, especially when we consider how unnerving must have been the effect of the introduction of lethal gas. Little ground was lost, but the situation looked precarious. The 8th Brigade, out of the line and relatively fresh by the standard of the moment, was first ordered to stand by and later to march. As it approached its bivouac area between Ypres and Vlamertinghe towards the evening it met a number of stragglers suffering from the effects of the gas.

On May 25th the 2nd Royal Scots was detached and sent forward to support the battered front immediately south of the Ypres-Roulers railway. The 1st and 4th Gordons worked on a reserve trench east of Zillebeke. No one on the British side knew that the battle was over and that the Germans had called off their offensive after their failure on the 24th. In any case this did not mean that what remained of the Ypres Salient had become a pleasant front. It was to be highly unpleasant because all the commanding ground had passed into the hands of the enemy.

On May 26th the 8th Brigade marched, happily without loss, through Ypres and took over the whole front from Hooge to the railway. Exactly which troops or fragments of units it relieved is difficult to determine; the 4th Gordon Highlanders records that

its front had been held by a battalion and parts of two others ; the
1st Battalion that there was " no handing over ". On the right
was the 1st Cavalry Division, on the left the 85th Brigade of the
28th Division. Owing to loss of ground the line was a new one
and the trench only half dug.

For a few days the front was relatively quiet. On June 1st,
however, the German fire swelled up again. Little in the way of
reply was possible because the British field artillery was limited to
two or three rounds a gun *per diem*, except in the event of an
attack, and virtually nothing but a little shrapnel was available in
any case.[1] June 2nd was the day of a bombardment which has
become historic. If any day can be said to mark the death of the
old city of Ypres, it was this. Some 500 heavy and medium shells
were fired into it. The trenches of the 1st Gordon Highlanders
were badly damaged and the battalion lost sixty-eight killed and
wounded. The 4th Gordon Highlanders was lucky to suffer only
11 casualties. It must be realized that, though the word " dug-
out " sometimes appears in the records of this period, there was
no such thing in the true sense of the word. Genuine dug-outs
could be made in this region only with the aid of concrete and were
essentially devices of siege warfare. The so-called dug-outs of the
early days were splinter-proof shelters.

On May 31st the 8th Brigade had rejoined the 3rd Division,
which had moved up to the southern flank of the Salient. On
June 16th the 9th Brigade, supported by the 7th, carried out the
action known as the First Attack on Bellewaarde, between the
Menin Road and the Ypres-Roulers Railway. The 4th Gordon
Highlanders and 2nd Suffolk held the line during the attack.

The operation, excellently planned, was a partial success, and
some 200 prisoners were passed back through the Gordons. The
1st Gordon Highlanders and a company of the 4th took over the
captured trenches, which they found full of dead and wounded,
for the most part British. The heavy loss was almost entirely due
to the German artillery bombardment, which the British had
neither guns nor ammunition enough to check. The enemy now
switched to gas shell on a large scale, but the primitive respirators
stood the test pretty well, and, though some men were affected,
no man in the 1st Battalion was overcome. The 4th Battalion had
57 casualties in its single company, but apparently not from gas.
The 8th Brigade was relieved on June 19th.

The 1st and 4th Gordon Highlanders had been engaged only
on the fringe of " Second Ypres ", or when within the area only

---

[1] On May 26th the *total number of rounds* of high explosive for the whole B.E.F.
on the Lines of Communication was : 18-pdr. 272, 4·5-in. howitzer 536. For 6-in.
and 8-in. howitzer the return was nil.

after the battle had reached its end according to the convention accepted by both British and Germans. The two battalions had avoided the shocking losses suffered by many earlier in the Salient and by those of the 9th Brigade at Bellewaarde. They had, none the less, endured a hard enough time. The 1st Battalion's losses between June 15th and 19th numbered 126. Such a casualty list would have been accounted high in some of the British Army's most famous battles—it was 12 more than the 92nd lost at Quatre Bras and Waterloo combined—whereas here it was that of a battalion which did not take part in any attack and was not itself attacked by the enemy's infantry. On June 24th it received a draft of 144 n.c.o.'s and men, with whom came a report from the Deputy Adjutant-General at the Base that it was the finest draft he had ever seen. Half a dozen of these men had served in the United States Army. The 4th Battalion was, on the other hand, very short of men, and on the same date Lieut.-Colonel T. Ogilvie, its veteran Territorial commanding officer, was sent home to use his influence in obtaining a draft and to organize a recruiting campaign.

CHAPTER V

BY the summer of 1915 the Gordon Highlanders were gathering on the Western Front. They were, as has been pointed out in the preface, in this war a Western Front regiment. Not one battalion began its active service elsewhere and one only served outside this theatre of war.

The arrival of the 51st (Highland) Division with two battalions has already been recorded. In the middle of the Battles of Ypres 1915 the 9th (Scottish) Division arrived. It was the senior division of the New Armies and, fittingly, the first to go on active service. It contained one battalion of the Gordons, the 8th, which formed part of the 26th Brigade. The commanding officer was Colonel H. Wright. The battalion, less the transport, which, as in other cases, crossed via Southampton and Havre, reached Boulogne on May 10th. On the 17th, marching through Flètre and Meteren to Bailleul, it passed through the 51st Division and saw a little of its sister battalions, the 5th and 7th. The New Army divisions had gone through hard times at the start of their training owing to lack of equipment and even uniforms, but the 9th Division, which belonged to the first group or " army ", had fared rather better than those with higher numbers.

To anticipate a few events still to be recorded after those related in the last chapter, another New Army division, the 15th (Scottish), arrived in July, 1915. In it were the 9th and 10th Battalions, the former being the Pioneer battalion of the division.

Though Lord Kitchener had by-passed the Territorial divisions by his creation of the New Armies, the former were the better off during their home training. Equipment for their artillery existed, even if it were out of date. The infantry battalions started with rifles, bayonets, and clothing, though recruits joining after the outbreak of war were not always so fortunate. In many cases officers and their friends made generous subscriptions for the purchase of items, such as field-glasses, which could not be obtained otherwise. For some reason water-bottles were particularly hard to obtain.

Lieut.-Colonel Sir Arthur Grant, Bt., of Monymusk, commanding the 5th Gordon Highlanders in the 51st Division, kept a private diary throughout the period of home service. It begins with the mobilization, the arrival of the troops at the drill halls, measures for the defence of Peterhead, all the details with which a commanding officer had to cope in the briefest possible time, with inexperienced officers and non-commissioned officers. One of its main themes is the contrast between this weakness and the enthusiasm of the men. As early as August 21st he writes : " The men improve, but the officers . . . do not know their work." The battalion had then been since the 16th at Bedford, where it remained throughout.

Under September 16th is the entry : " I went out as usual at 6.30, getting up at 5.45, and find that my n.c.o.s give their orders a little better—when I am looking on. I am almost in despair at times. Progress is so slow." And on October 20th : " The authorities have at last awakened to the necessity of having horse-rugs, now many, many horses have died or become ill from exposure." After night operations, Sir Arthur Grant writes : " We did a very successful advance and deployment, and then attack. The men seemed quite to enjoy it, the night being fine and warm."

This particular commanding officer nearly worked himself to a standstill and, according to his own diary, damned right and left. It all seems to have been to good purpose, however. On May 2nd, 1915, leaving Bedford for the front, he noted : " We left at 5.25. Every man sober and there was a very large crowd to see us away from the station, many saying goodbye and God speed to me."

It is impossible to quote further from this record. The New Armies, which endured worse discomforts and frustrations than the Territorials, deserve some space in which to illustrate their struggles. The great value of this diary is that it brings out vividly how hard it is to impart professional skill to amateur soldiers, even when, as in this case, the finest possible human material is available.

The 15th Division was the senior division of " K.2 ", or the " Second Hundred Thousand ". Its troops had undergone greater discomfort and faced more handicaps in their preparation for war than those of the 9th Division. Recruiting swelled to a flood, so that accommodation became hopelessly inadequate. One battalion had, on the formation of the division at Aldershot on September 15th, 1914, one officer—commissioned from the rank of Quartermaster-Sergeant R.G.A.—and 900 men. When the division was inspected by His Majesty King George V on September 26th, only the staff and a few senior officers wore uniform. It being the age of the now almost-forgotten straw " boater ", this headgear was much affected : others wore bowlers or cloth caps. A little later the first uniforms arrived, the jackets being of red serge. The first handful of obsolete rifles for drill were issued in early October.

Troops did not keep war diaries except on active service, and in countless cases the first entry records either the order to mobilize or the order to embark. It is to be feared that much interesting information about the early existence of the troops of the New Armies will die with those who saw it. If so, history will be the loser. A diary is in this case not what the historian wants, because the daily events were mostly of what on paper would appear monotonous routine and triviality. The need is for brief and enlightening summaries of impressions. These are hard to find. In the case of the 9th Gordon Highlanders some notes on the year 1914 have happily been given a place in the war diary. Space permits only limited use of them, but they must be used because they provide rare and precious information.

" K.2 " was given its start by recruits surplus to the needs of " K.1 ". The 9th Gordon Highlanders was formed from surplus personnel of the 8th Battalion, 9th Division, and a draft of 400 recruits from the depot. It formed part of the 44th (Highland) Brigade, the only one in the division bearing that title. Squad drill without arms was the only form of training at the start because there were no arms. The behaviour of the men was good, not so much from natural virtue as because they took their enterprise so seriously. They made no complaints, though all they had was the suit of clothes they had joined in and one blanket apiece.

The 9th and 10th Battalions lay side by side in camp at Rushmoor, so that their experiences must have been practically identical. On September 23rd two horses were issued to the 9th, one for the commanding officer, Colonel W. A. Scott—first commissioned in the year 1874—the other for the adjutant. However, the battalion might have been worse off. Nearly all the tents had floorboards, and it did not take long to provide a palliasse for every man. Other points from this record are : October 7th, greatcoats (civilian) issued ; October 8th, 800 D.P. (drill purposes) rifles issued ; October 9th, four more horses drawn ; November 5th, a note that, though the men looked so well on parade their knowledge was very slight and the simplest military term had to be carefully explained ; November 16th, transport animals now amounted to five pack cobs and two draught ; December 2nd, six bicycles issued ; December 7th, a notification that the battalion would wear drab kilts. Apparently it preferred to wait until its own tartan could be obtained.

Two days before the King's inspection mentioned above he rode about watching the troops at their work. The men had been ordered to fall in in parties or sub-units at his approach and strictly enjoined not to run after him and his escort, as such young citizen-soldiers were inclined to do. As he passed a hill on which a company was drilling an equerry called, " You can come down ". The troops did not await an order. With one accord the company broke ranks and poured down the slope, cheering and shouting with all the strength of their lungs. At the bottom they crowded round the King's horse in red-hot enthusiasm. If any eyebrows were raised, they were not King George's. He was plainly delighted.

In the middle of November the division left Aldershot. The move was made apparently to pass on the facilities to a division more recently raised. It was, however, a fortunate one, especially for the 44th Brigade, which went into billets. The destination of the 9th Gordon Highlanders was the pleasant little town of Haslemere. Battalion headquarters was established in the Spread Eagle, the bar parlour becoming the orderly room.

Billeting, though legally provided for, had long been unknown in England. The Highlanders were received with misgiving by the local people. This soon disappeared. Warm friendships were established and the winter passed happily. In January 1915 the 9th Gordon Highlanders left the 44th Brigade to become the divisional Pioneer battalion. In February it moved to Perham Down, where it remained until it embarked for France.

To recapitulate, by July 1915 the following battalions of the Gordon Highlanders, all those which went on active service, were in France and Belgium : 1st and 4th Battalions in 3rd Division ; 2nd and 6th in 7th Division ; 8th in 9th Division ; 9th (P.) and 10th in 15th Division ; 5th and 7th in 51st Division. The 1st and 4th, the 2nd and 6th, and the 5th and 7th were brigaded together.

Furthest north were the 1st and 4th Battalions. On July 19th the 1st Battalion was involved in a minor operation. Its machine-gunners, bombers and snipers supported the 4th Middlesex in an attack on a little German salient at the western end of Hooge village. One of the newly arrived tunnelling companies had driven a gallery 190 feet long beneath the German support line, and the explosion of the mine, which formed a vast crater, at 7 p.m. was the signal for the attack. It was a determined and successful action, though not all the gains were maintained. The 1st Gordon Highlanders lost 9 killed and 34 wounded. The dead included the bombing officer, Lieutenant T. B. Erskine, a very gallant and capable specialist and a great favourite with the whole battalion. He had been awarded the M.C. only eight days before. A further loss of 44 all ranks was incurred from shell fire during and just after the relief of the Middlesex by the 1st Gordons on July 20th. The 4th Gordons had sent up a company to reinforce the Middlesex ; this aid was found unnecessary, but a dozen bombers were employed. When Lieut.-General Sir Edmund Allenby, commanding the V Corps, inspected the 1st Gordons on August 4th he warmly praised the courage and skill of the grenadiers on July 19th.

On July 24th the 8th Brigade took over a sector between Verbranden Molen and Saint-Éloi, the only one from Ypres to

Wulverghem which it had not previously garrisoned. It was supported by four batteries of Belgian artillery. A little friction caused by the arrest of Belgian linesmen as spies had first to be surmounted. Then the two nationalities got on very well together, all the better because the Belgians had plentiful ammunition, including the precious high explosive of which the British were so short.

No summer season experienced by the British on the Western Front was as quiet as that of 1915. After the June operations near Givenchy that of the 2nd and 6th Gordon Highlanders was exceptionally so. At the beginning of August they bade farewell with regret to the two redoubtable Guards battalions in the 20th Brigade, the 1st Grenadiers and 2nd Scots, which left them to form part of the new Guards Division. They were replaced by two New Army battalions, the 8th and 9th Devonshire. The brigade was still in the Givenchy region.

The 8th Battalion in the 9th Division was close at hand, on a front known as " Festubert, Section C ", where it arrived at the end of June, after instruction in trench duties on the quiet Armentières front. It had had some teething pains. The three Scottish divisions among which five battalions of the Gordons were distributed were all to rank among the best British divisions in France ; some would say among the first half dozen ; some might put it even higher. Their discipline was, or became, as good as their fighting power. An exceptionally candid diary keeper, however, reveals that some characters in the 8th Battalion could not at first withstand the spirit of this countryside, rum, when it was red. Its sale by *bistros* was forbidden in time of war by French law, yet was nearly universal, often in black coffee which disguised it from prying eyes. A certain number of courts martial resulted.

The 9th and 10th Battalions in the 15th Division moved in mid-July to the heart of the coal-mining area south of the La Bassée Canal, the 9th, as Pioneer battalion, at once becoming busy on the construction of trenches and dug-outs. The 10th had the misfortune to lose, as apparently its first casualty, its commanding officer, Lieut.-Colonel Stewart MacDougall of Lunga. His leadership and enthusiasm had served the young battalion well, though his dearest wish, to lead it in action, had not been fulfilled.

The journal of his successor, Lieut.-Colonel H. R. Wallace, is eloquent on the subject of the trenches held by the battalion. He writes in August 1915 :

The best-disciplined regiments live in the best sanitary conditions in trench warfare ; that is to say, given normal conditions of trenches. But those taken over from our allies are not quite normal from the sanitary point of view and they never will be ; for we cannot make them so.

We dig. A hand appears, or a foot, or a head, perhaps six inches from the surface. A French soldier lies there. There are dead a few inches from the surface in and about the trenches; there are dead on the surface a few feet in front and in rear of our parapets—I counted five of these, all French, in front of one bay, yesterday. Dead lie beneath the débris of the houses in Quality Street . . . and they lie skin deep in the back-garden plots of the houses.

The rest billets for these trenches were Mazingarbe, which Lieut.-Colonel Wallace described on his first view of them as the dirtiest he had ever seen, though he managed to clean them up considerably in the course of a long stay. It was an evil part of the line, even when, as then, it was relatively quiet. After the Battle of Loos, which was about to open, it became one of the worst on the British front.

The 5th and 7th Battalions in the 51st Division, after their apprenticeship which had begun so roughly in June at Givenchy, moved furthest south. The division relieved a French division south of the Ancre at the end of July. The 7th Battalion took over a sector at Fricourt on August 1st. This was new country for British troops but was to become all too familiar in the long-drawn battles of the Somme in the following year. The front was quiet above ground, but not below. Mining made it somewhat nerve-racking, though nothing to what the division was to experience in the Labyrinth in 1916.

The Battle of Loos was a major British offensive undertaken on French insistence. The British would have preferred to wait until their recently arrived troops had been thoroughly initiated and others had become available, but the very fact that their force was still so small weakened their position at the council table. Even the battlefield was dictated to them. Sir John French did not want to fight at Loos in one of the most highly developed parts of the coal-mining area, but General Joffre demanded that the effort should be made alongside his own, a renewal of the spring offensive against Vimy Ridge. The French were also attacking in Champagne, in greater strength.

Though for the British it would have been better to await the spring of 1916, if major offensive action in 1915 was necessary it would have been desirable to undertake it in July or August, the Germans being then ill prepared to meet it. This was the original intention. As matters turned out, however, the Allies could not follow a satisfactory time-table from either point of view. Preparation—including that relief of French troops south of the Ancre in which the 51st Division took a share—was found to take so long that the offensive was postponed again and again until finally the date was fixed at September 25th. Meanwhile the

Germans had been put on the alert. From mid-August they started the construction of a second defence system, two to four miles behind the first. At the end of the month four divisions were set in motion from the Eastern to the Western Front. This was the one useful service afforded by the offensive to Russia, now hard pressed.

The British Loos offensive was carried out by Haig's First Army with two corps, IV and I, each with three divisions in line. Another corps, the XI, with the Guards, 21st and 24th Divisions, was held in G.H.Q. (not Army) reserve. From right to left the six first-line divisions were the 47th, 15th, 1st, 7th, 9th, and 2nd. Thus, from right to left five battalions of the Gordon Highlanders were involved : 9th (P.) and 10th, in the 15th Division ; 2nd and 6th, in the 7th Division ; 8th, in the 9th Division. They will be dealt with in that order.

The 15th Division faced Loos, the village which gave its name to the battle. The centre of Loos lay exactly a mile from the British front, but the final objective was over three miles deep and included the second defence system and the Cité Saint-Augustin.[1] The attack was preceded by a four days' bombardment. For forty minutes before the assault gas was discharged from cylinders alternately with clouds of smoke from smoke candles. The gas was provided on a great scale—1,500 cylinders to the 15th Division. It had not previously been used by the British and was believed, rightly as it proved, to have been prepared and installed unknown to the enemy. Much reliance was therefore placed upon it.

The 44th Brigade attacked on the right, with the 9th Black Watch and 8th Seaforth Highlanders in first line, the 7th Cameron Highlanders in support, and the 10th Gordon Highlanders in reserve. Each of these battalions and those of the 46th Brigade on the left had attached to it a section of Royal Engineers and a platoon of the pioneer battalion. The 9th Gordon Highlanders, back at Mazingarbe in divisional reserve, was thus reduced to the strength of two companies.

The leading battalions lost many men in capturing the front system of trenches and again on the western edge of Loos. Going steadily forward, however, with unflinching determination and showing no signs of excitement or nerves, these young troops bore themselves in a way that astonished even the officers who had thought most highly of them. At Loos, first the 7th Camerons and then the 10th Gordons closed up on them. All four battalions of the 44th Brigade took part in the capture of the village, which included hard house-to-house fighting. One of the attached

---

[1] " Cité " in this coalfield stands for " cité ouvrière " and denotes a miners' settlement, with cottages built to a plan and generally to a single model.

platoons of the 9th Gordons was responsible for the capture of buildings which the Germans had organized as a fortress. All the battalions became somewhat intermingled, but were more or less reorganized before they went on towards the final objective.

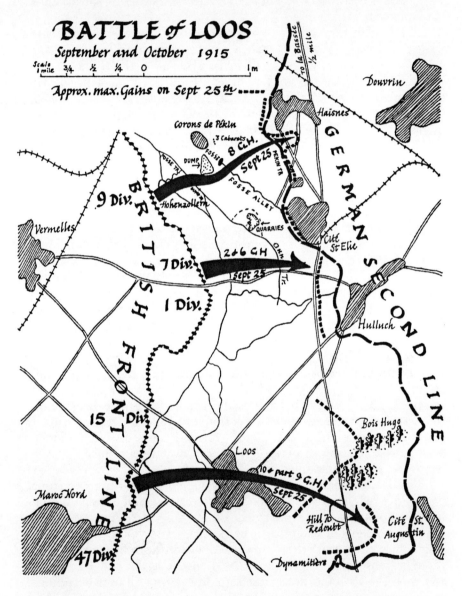

Despite having been drawn into the heavy Loos fighting, the dash of the Gordons was undiminished. Hill 70 was secured, but not Cité Saint-Augustin. On both flanks the division was for some time " out on its own ", especially on its left, where the 1st Division

had been held up. Its own troops, after losing sight of the landmarks familiar to them, had swung right, so that they faced south-
east instead of east on Hill 70. Ferocious fighting took place on
the outskirts of Cité Saint-Laurent, especially at *La Dynamitière*,
a building housing explosives. Parties of the Gordons are known
to have entered this, but virtually all were killed and none returned.
Finally, the senior officer on the ground, Lieut.-Colonel J.
Sandilands, gave the order to dig in on the reverse slope of the
hill. Lieut.-Colonel H. R. Wallace, commanding the 10th Gordons,
assisted him in this and in reorganizing the troops. The survivors of his own battalion seem to have been about the last to be
withdrawn to the new position. The division still had the 45th
Brigade uncommitted, and the divisions to north and south had
got over their difficulties and come up on the flanks. The prospects of continuing the advance looked fairly good. First, however, the 44th Brigade, a very heavy sufferer, had to be relieved.
The brigade of the 21st Division now brought up was, however,
raw, exhausted by long marches and endless traffic-blocks, and
hungry because it had not been able to connect with its transport.
It could not be got forward that evening. As a consequence most
of the troops of the 44th remained where they were all night. The
9th Battalion, with its two remaining companies, was brought up to
Loos to put it into a state of defence. It picked up a score of Germans in the process.

The 26th was a miserable day. The troops of the 21st Division
not only failed in their attack but began drifting, and soon afterwards pouring, to the rear. Worse still, their influence began to
effect troops of the 15th Division unhappily, though those who
gave way were rallied by their officers. Neither battalion of the
Gordon Highlanders was further engaged, though both stood by
at a moment when it appeared that Loos had virtually been abandoned. The calamity was avoided, and the battle ended for the
Division with the front on the western side of Hill 70, to which the
Scottish troops had advanced it.

Very few divisions can have gone into battle with such slight
experience and done as splendidly as the 15th. The Corps Commander, Lieut.-General Sir Henry Rawlinson, said that its feat
of arms could not have been excelled. Both the battalions of the
Gordons had been fully representative of its spirit. Both paid
the price. In the 9th Battalion the losses were for the most part
suffered by the companies providing the platoons which were
attached to the assault battalions. One of these companies, that
attached to the 44th Brigade, lost 2 officers and 119 other ranks.
The total of 225 casualties was exceptionally high for a pioneer
battalion, but then, as has been seen, half this battalion was

employed in a purely infantry role. The 10th Battalion's losses were a good deal higher, but probably included a number of men affected, generally not to a serious extent, by the British gas.[1]

The 7th Division advanced with its right on the Vermelles-Hulluch road. On the right the attack was entrusted to the 20th Brigade, with the 2nd Gordon Highlanders and 8th Devonshire in front line. The 6th Gordon Highlanders was in support to its sister battalion, and the 2nd Border Regiment to the 8th Devonshire. On the left was the 22nd Brigade.

The 2nd Gordons almost at once ran into a belt of British gas, which had drifted on a light breeze from the south-west and in places was blown back into the advancing assailants. The troops had to don their clumsy flannel helmets, but a good many were overcome. Piper Munro piped through the cloud to encourage the men. The German front line was taken without difficulty, but there was more resistance in the support trench, where some fifty prisoners were taken. The battalion had already lost its commanding officer, Lieut.-Colonel J. R. E. Stansfeld, who was mortally wounded—a great fighting man who could ill be spared. Before he died he sent from the casualty clearing station the message : " Well done, dear old 92nd ! "

On this part of the front there was an intermediate line of defence between the first and second systems, taking in a group of quarries, a feature of tactical importance, on the front of the 22nd Brigade. It was called Gun Trench and had been given its name because gun-pits had been observed in it. How often, if ever, they were occupied at ordinary times cannot now be discovered, but it was a bold action on the part of the enemy to bring up guns on this occasion to within 1,300 yards of the British front line. They were surprised by the 2nd Gordons and 8th Devonshire suddenly appearing out of the mist and smoke, and immediately rushed. Four fell to each battalion. Those guns were in due course removed by the divisional cavalry—somewhat rare trophies to be secured in the years of trench warfare.

Though loss had been heavy, the attack of the 20th Brigade had up to this point been a splendid success, and now the 6th Gordons and 2nd Borders were moving forward to provide fresh impetus. Alas ! matters had not gone similarly on the left.

[1]

		Killed	Wounded	Missing
9th Gordons (P.)	Officers	4	4	1
	Other ranks	24	181	21
10th Gordons	Officers	—	5	2
	Other ranks	23	221	130

It must be added that one battalion in the 44th Brigade, the 8th Seaforth Highlanders, suffered almost incredible loss : 49 killed, 372 wounded and 298 missing, reducing it virtually to transport and details.

The 2nd Gordon Highlanders had noted that the 8th Devonshire on its left amounted to little more than a handful, but it can be assumed that up in Gun Trench what had actually happened was unknown. Wire hidden by long grass had stopped the assault of the 22nd Brigade. The attack was renewed with greater success, and finally two large bodies of Germans who had been holding it up were overwhelmed, nearly 200 being captured. By about 9.30 a.m. the Quarries, on the objective reached earlier by the 20th Brigade, had been secured. The forward flow had, however, been considerably disorganized.

Meanwhile the 2nd Gordon Highlanders and the remnant of the 9th Devonshire did not rest from their labours. They pressed on another 500 yards and were brought to a halt by the German second system of defence due south of Cité Saint-Elie. The limit of their advance was the crossing of the two main roads, La Bassée-Lens and Vermelles-Hulluch, the Gordons being to the south of the latter. Here they were joined about 10 a.m. by two companies of the 6th Battalion, the remaining two having been ordered to consolidate Gun Trench. These leading companies had, however, suffered heavily in their passage forward, and two gallant attacks on the defences covering Hulluch, one over the open, one up a communication trench, broke down. The leaders, Captain T. P. Findlay and 2nd Lieutenant I. C. MacPherson, were killed and the survivors fell back to the cross-roads. The supporting battalion of the 8th Devonshire, the 9th, had moved up later than the 6th Gordons and came under still heavier fire because the enemy had brought up fresh machine guns. The achievement of the 20th Brigade had been as brilliant as it had been self-sacrificial, but it could do no more. The capture of the second defence system and of Hulluch and Cité Saint-Elie now depended on the reserve brigade, the 21st.

This brigade failed through no fault of its own. Swept by machine-gun fire as it crossed the open ground, it was brought to a halt at Gun Trench by 1.30 p.m. Cité Saint-Elie and Hulluch remained impregnable because the wire covering them remained uncut, and the afternoon bombardment scarcely damaged it. So the day ended with the 2nd and 6th Gordons digging in south of the cross-roads as well as they could with entrenching tools, a mixed body of the two Devonshire battalions on their left, and no one else near the German second defence system but for a little party of the 2nd Queens of the 22nd Brigade half a mile to the north and facing the north-west corner of Cité Saint-Elie. The main body of the infantry of the 7th Division (including two companies of the 6th Gordons) was in Gun Trench, its northern prolongation Stone Alley, and the Quarries at the northern end of that.

The night was disastrous. Between 11 p.m. and midnight the Germans recovered the Quarries. About the same time parties, mostly Gordon Highlanders, who were returning to the cross-roads with rations, water and ammunition, were attacked in flank, while simultaneously another body of Germans attacked the cross-roads. The carriers, taken by surprise while cumbered with their burdens, were dispersed, and made their way back to Gun Trench. At the cross-roads the men of the 2nd and 6th Gordons had not been idle. They had made a strong point, in which the brigade trench mortar officer, Lieutenant R. W. Carrigan, set up two of his mortars, but the work, for lack of tools, was pathetic as a means of defence. After a sharp fight the position was overrun and the men who had occupied it fell back to Gun Trench. To make confusion still more certain, they were fired on by the garrison, who took them for Germans.

The Germans, in fact, were on their heels. There might have been something worse than confusion had not one of those men who are natural leaders at any time and in any place chanced to be at hand. This was the brigade major, Captain C. C. Foss. He rallied the troops, put an end to all desire to retreat and established them in Gun Trench. Further along it the companies of the 6th Gordons and the 2nd Borders beat off the counter-attack, though some Germans reached the very lip of the trench.

Two counter-attacks to recover the Quarries failed next day. While directing the second Major-General Sir Thomas Capper, the divisional commander, was seriously wounded. He died next day, lamented as a commander and fighting soldier of the highest type, and, if any man deserved the title, one of the victors of First Ypres.

On this, the second day of the battle, the enemy was not very active after his successful counteraction during the previous night. Away to the south at Loos and to the north round the Hohen-zollern Redoubt he was pressing hard and the battle continued to rage. The 7th Division, while it could not recover what it had lost and still less take all that had been allotted to it, could now hold what it had got, at least for the time being. As it turned out, we did lose a section of Gun Trench on September 30th, but at this time the 20th Brigade was out of the line. The 7th Division had to take over another sector immediately, this time immediately south of the La Bassée Canal, with billets at Cambrin. The 2nd and 6th Gordon Highlanders entered the line side by side.

The losses of the 2nd Gordon Highlanders had been catastrophic. They included 117 missing, the majority in the German counter-attack on the cross-roads west of Hulluch. The 6th Gordon Highlanders would have been accounted heavy sufferers in the

battles of most wars—indeed, in the concluding battles of this—
but, largely owing to the fact that only two companies went as far
forward as the cross-roads and the other two stayed in Gun Trench,
its losses in rank and file were less than half those of the senior
battalion. In officers the losses were almost equal and terribly
high, 8 killed, 8 wounded and 1 missing in the 2nd; 3 killed, 7
wounded and 5 missing in the 6th. Both commanding officers,
Lieut.-Colonels J. R. E. Stansfeld and J. E. McQueen, had been
killed. The 2nd Gordons came out with only the following
officers : Major H. A. Ross in command—and he at once went
sick with gas poisoning—Lieutenant G. H. Gordon, 2nd Lieutenants Scoones and MacDonald. Captain L. Carr, an able young
officer of the regiment who was destined to die a lieutenant-general,
took over the command for the next month. Lieut.-Colonel J.
Dawson, succeeded Lieut.-Colonel McQueen in the 6th Gordons.[1]

The 9th Division attacked with the 26th Brigade on its right,
that is, next to the 7th Division. The dispositions were : 7th
Seaforths right, 5th Camerons left, supported by the 8th Gordons
and 8th Black Watch respectively. The brigade was confronted
with the vast and notorious work known as the Hohenzollern
Redoubt. In the First World War a " redoubt " was simply an
entrenched area prepared for all-round defence. Its advantage
was that it did not take very long to prepare and was not always
even recognized for what it was. The role of the Hohenzollern
was, however, obvious. It took the form of a triangle, with the
blunted angle at the apex facing the British and the base formed
by the German front line. Its purpose was to provide extra
protection for the mine buildings and slag heap of Fosse (Pit) 8, in
its rear. The slag heap was enormous, over 300 yards from north
to south and nearly as much from west to east, nearly flat-topped,
twenty feet high, extensively tunnelled to form shelters for observers and machine guns, and commanding the ground about it
in all directions. It was included in the first objective.

The plan of attack was complex and appeared to the battalion
commanders concerned startlingly bold. On reaching Dump
Trench, the main German line behind the Hohenzollern, the 8th
Gordons were to halt and await a report from the 7th Seaforths
that the advance to the Corons de Pékin [2] and the Three Cabarets
was going well. If so, the 8th Gordons and 8th Black Watch were

[1]

		Killed	Wounded	Missing
2nd Gordons	Officers	8	8	1
	Other ranks	73	310	116
6th Gordons	Officers	3	7	5
	Other ranks	37	172	34

[2] " Coron " is a northern dialect term for a miner's home.

to pass south of Fosse 8 and lead the way towards Haisnes. They were to be followed by the battalions originally in the lead, the Fosse then being held by some troops of the 28th Brigade. Haisnes, like Cité Saint-Elie, Hulluch, and Cité Saint-Augustin, was covered by the new German second line. The section which concerned the Gordons, known as Pekin Trench, was not fully dug, but was protected by a formidable belt of barbed wire.

The 26th Brigade's attack went wonderfully well. The 7th Seaforths, advancing with splendid dash and resolution, swept right over the Hohenzollern and quickly secured Fosse 8. The 5th Camerons were a little behind, but their achievement was even more extraordinary. Having waited ten minutes in the vain hope that the cloud of smoke and gas which had come to a stop in front of them would move on, they walked straight through it. The 8th Gordon Highlanders first of all sent a bombing party southward along the German front trench to clear the front of the 7th Division which, as we have seen, began with a dangerous repulse on its left flank. After this improvisation the Gordons carried out their orders to the letter. Crossing the Hohenzollern, they found that the Seaforths in their ardour to get forward had left a number of Germans behind them. They accounted quickly for these, taking about fifty prisoners. At 7.40 a.m., learning that the Seaforths were approaching the Corons de Pékin, the Gordons carried out their manoeuvre. They passed round Fosse 8, pushed on across the thousand yards of open ground separating them from Pekin Trench, somehow or another got through the wire. They were in —that is, through—the last German field defences and on the outskirts of Haisnes.

This was a great feat, of which any battalion, however well trained, might have been proud. It would have been a sheer impossibility had the trench been actually manned. Here the speed of the advance had caught the Germans unready, though the Gordons had to endure artillery and machine-gun fire, mostly in enfilade.

Unhappily, the Gordons alone had been able to follow the original programme exactly. Only one weak company of the 8th Black Watch had come up on their left; the rest had been drawn in to support the Camerons after the hold-up caused by the stationary British gas-cloud. On the left the 28th Brigade had failed: partly owing to the gas, which here blew right through the assembled troops, partly through running into hidden and uncut wire. The left flank of the 26th Brigade being thus open, its other battalions had been held back to defend the vital Fosse 8.

At that time there seemed to be very few Germans in Haisnes. Reduced by casualties though it was, the battalion might have been able to seize the village had there been any sort of prop on its left. As things were, it seemed unwise to make the attempt, since even in the shelter of the trench the battalion was suffering from the enfilade fire. By 11.30 a.m., when the first troops of the 27th Brigade were seen moving up, the Germans had thrown reinforcements into Haisnes.

In all the offensive operations they had undertaken the British had learnt to count upon a German counter-attack as a matter of course, sometimes carried out in surprisingly small strength, but seldom easy to deal with. The growing automatic fire-power of the British infantry did not seem to compensate for the heavy deterioration in that wonderful musketry fire which had time after time stopped the enemy dead at First Ypres and even in the second battle. Now the counter-attacks came, from Haisnes and the railway running just east of it.

Three times C Company of the 8th Gordon Highlanders beat off the Germans, advancing from Haisnes both over the open and along trenches, in which the superiority of their grenades over the " cricket-ball " type then in British use gave them an advantage. Finally the British supply gave out. The defence, though it had been reinforced by companies of the 11th and 12th Royal Scots, 27th Brigade, could no longer endure, and the isolated force began to withdraw. The retirement was carried out in small parties and in good order as far as Fosse Alley, a trench east of Fosse 8. At that point, however, the strain told and the men of the Gordons, despite the efforts of the brigade staff to halt them, continued their withdrawal to Dump Trench. During the night Fosse Alley was lost, but a German counter-attack on Fosse 8 was defeated, though it occurred in the midst of the relief of the troops of the 9th Division by those of the 24th Division from the general reserve.

The 26th Brigade was not engaged on the second day of the battle, September 26th. On September 27th the brigade of the 24th Division lost the Dump. The 9th Division commander, Major-General G. H. Thesiger, at whose disposal this brigade had been placed, hearing that it was shaky, went forward to investigate the situation and was killed in the Hohenzollern. He was the second divisional commander to be killed in the Battle of Loos, a very fine soldier, young by the standard of 1915. There was no hope of recovering Fosse 8 with the strength at the moment available, but the 26th Brigade was ordered to carry out a counter-attack in order to retake Dump Trench and its northward prolongation Fosse Trench.

The brigade had already sent up a party, mostly bombers, about a hundred strong, to encourage the troops in the Hohenzollern. Then, the Gordons' diary states that the order failed to

5

reach six of their platoons—the average strength of a platoon on that day being probably about fifteen—and there was too much need of haste to wait for them. The strength of the brigade assembled for the occasion was no more than 600. Yet it went forward at the double from the British front line into the redoubt and reached its eastern face. The troops could go no further in face of fire which swept the ground beyond, but they saved the Hohenzollern. With bomb and rifle they held up the enemy's advance. That counter-attack was never forgotten in the 9th Division. Small affair as it was by comparison with many later feats of arms, it was a grand proof of mettle and endurance. Late in the afternoon troops of the 28th Division, which had been hurried into action, began entering the Hohenzollern. Those of the 26th Brigade were withdrawn to the British trenches and at 5.30 a.m. on September 28th to the village of Sailly. Late that day the 8th Gordon Highlanders marched back to the comfort of Bethune.

This is a case in which the casualties are not known in detail and are given as 17 officers and " about 500 " other ranks. This was the average for the 26th Brigade, which suffered a loss of 27 officers killed, 41 wounded, and 5 missing ; and a total of 2,074 other ranks in the three categories. Colonel Wright, the commanding officer of the 8th Gordons, was wounded on September 25th and did not return to the battalion. He had taken part in the march to Kandahar in 1880. Like Colonel Scott, who remained in command of the 9th Gordon Highlanders until December 1915, he was one of those veterans whose seniority and ardour sometimes raised a smile but whose work ought to be remembered with gratitude. Some of these officers did jobs in the raising and training of battalions which the young men who commanded those battalions later in the war could not have done, though, having grown up in the war, the younger made better commanders—in the type of war with which they had to do.

Little more need be said about the events of the Battle of Loos except that it ended in mid-October, after a pause from September 28th to October 9th, that the Hohenzollern was lost and partially recovered, and that the maximum depth of ground gained was a mile and three-quarters, just north of Loos.

The terse verdict of Brig.-General Sir James Edmonds on the battle is unanswerable. He writes : " It brought nothing but misfortune and disappointment, for which mismanagement was partly responsible." The mismanagement referred to is the handling of the G.H.Q. reserve, which certainly was mishandled ; but in any case only the Guards Division of the three divisions which formed it was competent to undertake a difficult " leap-frog " manoeuvre. A trained division might indeed have passed through the 9th, which had reached the enemy's second position, early on the first day, but even if the 21st and 24th had had the necessary experience they were released too late and too far from the battle-field and they arrived in the dark in a state of extreme fatigue.

There were also mistakes lower down, as there could hardly fail to be in view of the inexperience of the infantry. It has already been pointed out that the regular divisions, which numbered three out of the six in the initial assault, had been made up hastily by drafts after enormous losses. The young divisions, 9th, 15th and 47th (the last named of which had had the doubtful benefit of fighting at Festubert) were first-class material and destined to become famous fighting divisions. Even at this stage they had done as well as the regulars ; indeed the 9th Division might have claimed to be the most successful. All the battalions of the Gordon Highlanders had given of their best and in many cases those of the Territorial and New Armies had not only displayed bravery but behaved as though they had been mature troops.

The bombardment had been inadequate, especially that of the heavier pieces, for which the ammunition supply was miserably small. The gas was a failure because the wind was too light and fluky. There is no evidence that it inflicted serious loss on the Germans, whereas it incapacitated a considerable number of British. Gas was always capable of doing great damage and worry-ing to the nerves, but once both sides had grown used to chlorine gas from cylinders its terrors were diminished. The admixture of phosgene, first used by the Germans on December 19th, 1915 and then adopted by the British and French, partially restored these terrors. Yet later in the war gas from cylinders was largely replaced by gas fired in shells, both lethal and in the end, on a far larger scale, vesicant, " mustard " gas being used for the purpose. Another gas missile was a steel drum containing compressed lethal gas, fired from a short tube up to a range of 2,000 yards. The new and valuable Lewis gun had been generally issued before the battle, but too late for instruction in its tactical employment, if even in its mechanism.

It will be found that the rate of loss was not diminished at the start of the Battle of the Somme, though by then material, staff work, and tactics had to some extent been accommodated to the conditions. The astonishing feature is the maintenance of the spirit of the infantry. It always expected to be luckier next time. It never lost hope in final victory or determination to achieve it. It remained cheerful and even, in the few good times—a rest in unspoiled country, a Highland festival—happy. The private sol-diers of that generation needed training—more than they could get—but they did not require or get the modern treatment that Americans call " moral endoctrination ". In the best divisions, which included all those in which battalions of the Gordon Highlanders were now serving, the life of the division itself, allied with the older spirit of the regiment, made the morale. Propaganda was not needed.

It may therefore not be surprising that, despite the sharp disappointment and the heavy loss, the majority of the surviving officers and rank and file gained rather than lost confidence at Loos. They felt that such a chapter of accidents and errors could not recur, and that they themselves had proved themselves better men than even in their proudest moments they had claimed to be. In the last respect they were right, but accident and error are an eternal feature of war, which only those who have never fought will mock.

Three subsidiary attacks were carried out on September 25th. The most important was the Second Attack on Bellewaarde. More fighting had occurred in this area since that in which the 1st Gordon Highlanders had been engaged on June 16th. At the end of July the British had lost Hooge and been driven back 500 yards. The 8th Brigade heard the news with indignation, but the troops involved were not to blame. The Germans had exploited a weapon always unsettling but terrifying when used for the first time : the *Flammenwerfer*. Then on August 9th a fine attack by the 6th Division had regained the lost ground from the stables of Hooge Château westward.

The attack of September 25th was carried out by the 3rd Division astride the Menin Road and by a brigade of the 14th on its left. Five battalions, 2nd Royal Scots, 4th and 1st Gordon Highlanders (8th Brigade) ; 2nd South Lancashire and 2nd Royal Irish Rifles (7th Brigade) advanced to the assault at 4.10 a.m. The wire was undamaged and some of it so thick that it defied wire-cutters. At some points, however, the Royal Engineers of the division had cut gaps in it with Bangalore torpedoes immediately after the explosions. The 4th Battalion seems to have been comparatively fortunate in this respect. It was a fine unit now and attacked with the utmost determination. It succeeded in reaching the enemy's third line and inflicting heavy loss on him. The 1st Battalion, on the other hand, had to search for gaps in the dark. Only its right company found one and it did no more than get a footing in the front trench.

About 4.30 a.m. the Germans began a heavy bombardment of their lost trenches. The worst effect was the blocking of the communication trenches, so that bombs, shovels and sand-bags could not be brought up. The men of the 4th Battalion who had reached the third line were cut off and practically all were reported missing.   Between 11 a.m. and noon the Germans attacked both across the open and along the trenches.   After a fierce struggle the 4th Gordons and such of the 1st as had got in were driven out. That was the general pattern of the action, in which no success was gained at any point.   The troops could not have done more.   The battalions of the Gordons suffered heavy loss, approximately the same ; but the 1st had by far the higher proportion of wounded, shot down outside the wire, and the 4th of missing, cut off in the blocked trenches.[1]   In the whole operation just short of 200 prisoners, from three regiments, had been captured, but the German loss must have been light by comparison with the British.   As a diversion the operations had been of no avail because the Germans had been able to contain the attack with local reserves which would in no case have been moved down to the main battlefield, south of the La Bassée Canal.

[1]		*Killed*	*Wounded*	*Missing*
1st Gordons	Officers	6	8	3
	Other ranks	36	232	58
4th Gordons	Officers	2	7	6
	Other ranks	24	148	147

CHAPTER VI

BACKGROUND OF THE WESTERN FRONT

AFTER the Battle of Loos it was decided to exchange some brigades of the old divisions with brigades of the new. The 3rd Division thus lost its 7th Brigade, which was replaced by the 76th Brigade from the 25th Division. The 1st and 4th Gordon Highlanders were transferred to the 76th on October 19th 1915. The two battalions stayed in Flanders for the remainder of the autumn and for the winter. Just before it ended, in the last week of February 1916, the 4th battalion was transferred to the 51st Division. Major-General Haldane, commanding the 3rd Division, an old Gordon Highlander himself, bade it farewell and told the troops how sorry he was to see them go. They were sorry to leave the 3rd Division and to say goodbye to the 1st Battalion, but their transfer did not cause the dismay often set up by such moves because they were returning to their original division which they had quitted when specially chosen to help fill the gaps in the B.E.F. And in that division there were two other battalions of their regiment.

The 1st and 4th Battalions had had a hard and dismal life of it. The winter was wet, and on a rainy day the trenches would collapse like a child's sand castle before the incoming tide. Even the roads became ankle-deep in mud, despite constant repair, except for the paved main routes. The simultaneous development of the use of asphalt on surfaces and of large pneumatic tyres on heavy vehicles has brought about a scarcely-noticed but drastic revolution which has proved as important in war as in peace. Those who have not experienced it have little notion what an effort was required on "mud" roads under heavy traffic. At this stage too the British had made little progress with hutting in places where billets were not available. Men of the 1st Gordon Highlanders declared in November that they preferred the trenches to their quarters in Reninghelst. A couple of months earlier the following angry comment appears in the diary: "No one has yet been able to explain why, after holding the Ypres Salient for over a year, no accommodation has yet been provided for troops who are supposed to be resting."

In February 1916 the Germans carried out some minor operations with objects similar to those of the British which have been the subject of comment: diversionary attacks connected with the Verdun offensive, which was launched on February 21st. In general they were no more successful than those of the British had been. On February 14th, however, a good stroke was dealt on the north bank of the Ypres-Comines Canal. The enemy drove troops of the 17th Division off the Bluff with heavy loss and captured the British front line for 500 yards further north.

The Bluff itself was only a tiny artificial hill topping the terraced spoil bank, but it was an admirable observation post. Next day, February 15th, the 76th Brigade, which had been enjoying a week's rest and training near Saint-Omer, was entrained to Poperinghe, where it came under the orders of the G.O.C. 17th Division. It had been ostensibly chosen as knowing the ground, but the troops felt they had been called on as the men for a big job.

They were not hurried into action. The Second Army Commander, General Sir Herbert Plumer, intended that this should be a careful counter-offensive and that it should lead to the capture of more ground than had been lost. To avoid the confusion of some previous operations, communication trenches were to be one-way and were marked " up " and " down ". Cable was buried. The new steel " shrapnel helmets " just issued on a very small scale, were collected from other units so as to be available for all four battalions of the brigade. The operation was a good specimen of an early " set piece ". The grenadiers, who would have a big part to play, were to carry small black-and-yellow flags which were to be raised to mark their progress. The attack was practised over a representation of the German defences—which could now be obtained from air photographs. The artillery bombardment was to be concluded on the day previous to the assault, and in the course of the night Brig.-General E. St. G. Pratt, commanding the 76th Brigade, was to decide whether to call for a preliminary bombardment or rely on surprise without one. He actually decided on the latter course.

Three battalions attacked in line : 2nd Suffolk right, 8th King's Own centre, 1st Gordon Highlanders left. The *beau rôle*, the recovery of the Bluff, went to the Suffolks, a fine and always reliable unit, but it is not unfair to suggest that the Gordons had an even harder task. They certainly encountered the strongest opposition. The brigade was well served by having as brigade major probably the most celebrated young officer in the Army at that time, Captain W. de la T. Congreve, whom it regarded as " the leading spirit in the attack ".

The right and centre battalions took their objectives. The right company of the 1st Gordons was equally successful, but the left was held up on the enemy's parapet, only twenty men getting in. The supporting company could do no better. 2nd Lieutenant Sanderson then rushed forward alone and bombed the machine gun which was doing the damage, putting it out of action. With the aid of a company and bombers of the 7th Lincolns (17th

Division) the left then swept forward to its objective. 2nd Lieutenant Sanderson received the immediate award of the D.S.O., an
unusual honour for so junior an officer. The losses of the battalion
were 235, many of these from the subsequent German bombardment, including Captain M. S. Robertson, commander of the
right company, killed.[1] We know now that one result of the
action was a feud which lasted throughout the war between the
regiment which had taken the Bluff and the regiment which lost
it, in the first-class 27th (Württemberg) Division. The kilt was
often condemned, perhaps justly, as unsuitable for trench warfare,
but it had its moral value. The prisoners—253 taken by the
brigade—declared with fervour that they wished to give themselves up to " the English " of the 17th Division and by no means
to kilted men.

The Gordons were not directly involved in the fighting round
the St. Eloi craters in late March and the early part of April. A
successful attack was carried out here by the 9th Brigade, and
various battalions of the 8th and 76th Brigades were employed as
reliefs, before the Canadians took over this front. On April 3rd
the 8th King's Own—in brigade reserve at the Bluff—made a fine
attack on a crater in which the enemy still held out. This was
crowned with success when " Billy " Congreve arrived, crawled up
to the crater, and summoned the occupants to surrender. Five
officers and 77 men thereupon came out and gave themselves
up. The Gordons then joined hands with the King's Own and
came in for a lot of the bombardment. They were relieved on
April 4th and taken back in buses to Reninghelst, " the men very
tired but cheerful ". Most of the ground won was recovered by
the Germans.

The 7th Division also spent most of the winter in old haunts.
It stayed for a time on the Loos battlefield. Here on October 24th
the commander of the 20th Brigade, Brig.-General the Hon.
J. F. H. S. Forbes Trefusis, was shot dead by a sniper. He had
held his appointment little more than two months, but had proved
his worth at Loos. His successor, then a substantive major, was to
become a field marshal and Chief of the Imperial General Staff,
Brig.-General C. J. Deverell. On October 26th Major B. G. R.
Gordon, who had already commanded the battalion for a few
days in December 1914, was appointed to the command of the
2nd Gordon Highlanders. The battalion's losses in commanding
officers had so far been as follows : Uniacke wounded, then
killed on March 13th, 1915 ; Stansfeld wounded, then killed on

[1]

	Killed	Wounded	Missing
Officers	3	4	—
Other ranks	71	145	12

September 25th, 1915 ; A. F. Gordon wounded May 16th, 1915.
During the rest of the war it was to lose three more : its new
commander, B. G. R. Gordon ; Major R. D. Oxley, three days after
taking over ; and Lieut.-Colonel H. A. Ross, a fortnight before
the Armistice.

At the beginning of December 1915, the 7th Division moved
south on transfer to the Third Army. The 2nd Battalion went
into billets at La Chaussée and the 6th at Picquigny, in the valley
of the Somme. Then began the most enjoyable period, for the
2nd Battalion lasting about seven weeks, that it had seen since its
arrival on the Continent. Two ranges were constructed in the
valley by the troops under Brig.-General Deverell's direction, the
smaller, at Picquigny, for the two battalions of the Gordons with
ranges of 100, 200 and 300 yards. Platoon and company training
was followed by battalion training and in January 1916 the 2nd
Battalion took part in two brigade field days. The troops were
comfortably housed and time was found for sport.

Since the arrival of the specially selected Territorial units, a
number of brigades had consisted of five or even six battalions.
They were now all to revert to the standard pattern. The 6th
Gordon Highlanders was the battalion which had to go and was
selected for a spell on the lines of communication. Brig.-General
Deverell made a strong plea for its retention. " The battalion is a
fine one in every respect ", he wrote. " It has proved its worth in
active operations, in the trenches, in billets and on the march. I
can always be certain that any duty demanded will be carried out
in the most thorough manner. The offensive spirit is high in the
battalion. . . . The dash and spirit of this battalion is accentuated
by its close connection in this brigade with the 2nd Battalion."

This was a pleasant compliment to both, but the plea had no
success. The brigade commander went at midnight on January
5th, 1916, to see the 6th Battalion off on its short railway journey
to Abbeville.

It remained on the L. of C. until the end of May, five months.
From time to time it was split up, detachments being stationed as
far away as Rouen. The main duties which fell to it were the
provision of guards and road control. Then it returned to the
forward zone and joined the 51st Division. Thus by June 1916
the 51st Division had the four Territorial battalions of the Gordon
Highlanders, 4th, 5th, 6th and 7th, forming one-third of its infantry
strength, in its ranks. The 6th was in the 152nd Brigade, the 5th
and 7th in the 153rd, and the 4th in the 154th.

The 51st Division saw its full share of mining activity. About
La Boisselle, in the Ancre sector to which it moved after its service at
Festubert, it found this going on, and the French miners remained

with it for some time.   When, in March 1916, it moved further
north and relieved a French division west of Vimy Ridge, it experienced mining at its worst.   The ground was honeycombed by
tunnels and, the Germans having got the better of the subterranean
war with the French, mines were constantly being blown below
British trenches.   It was highly unsettling and yet not as destructive to life as might be supposed.   Even before the introduction
of the geophone, trained listeners without special instruments
learnt to detect and to a fair extent locate the enemy's working.
So long as he dug there was no danger—unless indeed he was
approaching a British gallery—but directly he began to tamp it
was necessary to stand ready for a blow, though this might not take
place for a long time.   Over and over again casualties were avoided
or diminished to very small numbers by the timely evacuation or
thinning out of threatened posts.

The British soldier became fatalistic about danger but he never
brought any sort of philosophy to bear on the subject of work
which he loathed.   Mining increased the work because the soil
from galleries could not be dumped near the shaft without giving
away its position.   Except in the driest summer weather and in
chalk this shifting of soil was also the dirtiest and most arduous
kind of work.

Not all the mining was offensive.   Much of it had the object
of boring below a dangerous gallery and cutting it by means of a
reduced charge, which created what was known as a camouflet.   In
some regions, including that of Vimy, where they were on higher
ground, the Germans made small craters close together near their
own front line to provide observation and as an extra measure of
defence.   In the Vimy area it was known that this enabled them
to see into the British trenches, but the full extent of their vision
was not realized until the capture of Vimy Ridge in 1917.   Then
it became apparent that they had at some points been able to see
the duck-boards in the bottom of the trenches.

Apart from mining, work was very hard, especially in wet
weather and in preparing for an offensive.   In November 1915 the
7th Gordon Highlanders on the Ancre, when not holding the front
line, was finding 300 men each night for trench construction and
repair, road maintenance, and machine-gun posts.   In March
1916 the 4th Battalion in the Vimy area provided 200.   This
labour was very tiring to troops in a bad sector, who came out
needing rest after their trench duties.   Yet the Germans certainly
worked harder than our men and profited by gaining more security
and comfort.

The 9th Division, after a brief rest on emerging from the Battle
of Loos, moved north into the Ypres Salient.   The 8th Gordon

Highlanders held trenches near Hill 60 to start with and later in the winter a little further north. The trenches were good or bad according to the weather. On the whole, the men were better off in them than in the camps. Though the Second Army, which held this region throughout the greater part of the war, had a good reputation for administration, for some reason the hutted camps in the Salient—some were of tents, and aged tents, as late 1917—were always abominable. Who that ever resided in it will forget the squalid and aptly-named " Dirty Bucket Camp " ? A little further in rear the country was pleasant, but this the troops saw only at rare intervals.

The appointment of commanding officer had not been permanently filled since Colonel Wright had been wounded at Loos, but on October 27th Lieut.-Colonel A. D. Greenhill Gardyne, who had commanded the 1st Battalion for a few weeks in 1914, took over. Overcoming difficulties due to the primitive equipment of Canada Huts, he arranged that the battalion, on coming out of the line, should find awaiting it hot water for foot-washing, clean shirts and stockings, and soup. The battalion was all the time weak in numbers ; in fact, the New Army battalions of the Gordon Highlanders were now feeling the man-power pinch which Territorial battalions had experienced earlier.

The 15th Division was the only one containing battalions of the Gordon Highlanders which remained on the battlefield of Loos all through the winter and spring. The life of the 10th Battalion during this period could hardly have been less eventful. It had two welcome spells of rest and training, in each of which it was billeted in the village of Allouagne, near Lillers. Each lasted a month, the first being from December 14th, 1915 to January 14th, 1916, and the second from March 25th to April 25th. This latter was a period of strenuous and interesting training, which included an exercise by the whole division with its transport, all too rare an occurrence.

The 9th Gordon Highlanders, as Pioneer battalion, looked on work from a point of view differing from that of other battalions. Work was its life and career. Work brought a number of compensations : fewer losses, better quarters occupied continuously—and skill and material to make them comfortable—a higher proportion of activity in daylight, though much had to be done by night. Yet some work that came the battalion's way may have seemed excessive. Between October 8th and 16th it was " lent " in turn to the 1st and 47th Divisions and accomplished great improvements in their defences. An average night's work involved leaving billets about 5 p.m. and returning to them at 5 a.m. After the battle was over there was no lack of activity on the old battlefield. Though a historian hesitates to say so for fear of ridicule, there are signs that many in the battalion hankered after a more martial role.

Work took many forms, the most agreeable being tree-cutting and timber-shaping, the least so installing gas cylinders and fusing piles of the new Mills hand grenades. Communication trenches were dug, with boarded sides, gratings on the bottoms, and sumps at intervals beneath them. Some old German trenches were re-opened. Buildings were demolished to afford a field of fire. In the rear defences machine-gun emplacements were roofed with steel girders, the spaces between them filled with brick and concrete, with an air cushion and an upper roof laid on rails from the railway and earth banked on top of all. In May one company was put at the disposal of the Tunnelling Company in the area.

The outstanding work carried out by the battalion was spread over four weeks, from mid-January 1916, when the division took over the Loos-Hulluch sector. On this front there was a section a mile and a half long where no support line existed and the front line was bad. The German front line being some 500 yards distant, it was decided to make a new front line in front of the existing one and convert that into a support line. The normal method of doing such work was to sap forward, make T-heads to the saps, and eventually join them up. This seldom resulted in the construction of good trenches and in this case, owing to the length of front involved, the time involved might well have been twelve weeks instead of four. The method adopted was to work in two shifts of half the battalion, completing one section of trench after another. In each case as a new section of trench was opened the pioneers had of course to start work in the open, without any protection until they had got deep enough to afford some cover for themselves.

Time after time the work was interrupted by the enemy's artillery, machine-gun, and rifle fire, but this did not generally continue for long. When bursts of fire became unpleasant the line of men along the trench would sink to the ground and lie flat. As soon as it ceased the troops, without order from officer or n.c.o., would get up and quietly resume their work. In all the battalion dug 1,500 yards of first-class fire-trench, covered by a double apron of wire, in addition to a communication trench 800 yards long and half a dozen of the narrow communication trenches which the French called *boyaux*, connecting the front and support lines. All was done methodically, without fuss. Casualties were very slight.

A blow which had for some time seemed probable now fell. Recruiting had always been at a high rate in Scotland, and the losses had been very heavy. Now there was a serious shortage.

It was decided to amalgamate the 8th and 10th Gordon Highlanders. The 8th, handing over animals, vehicles and Lewis guns,
quitted the 9th Division area for that of the 15th. Three pipe
bands played it out of its billets on May 6th, 1916, and the divisional band played it into its entraining station next day. The
amalgamation parade took place on the 11th. As the senior of the
two the 8th provided the headquarters and the transport personnel
of the new battalion, designated the 8/10th, but neither Lieut.-
Colonel C. W. E. Gordon (who had succeeded Lieut.-Colonel
Greenhill Gardyne in March) nor Lieut.-Colonel W. MacGregor
of the 10th received the command. The new commanding officer
was Lieut.-Colonel H. Pelham Burn, a young officer of the Gordons
who had been commanding a battalion of another regiment. The
8/10th now contained two companies up to full strength from each
of the original battalions. The surplus went to a battalion of a
new type, the 11th Entrenching Battalion, with an establishment
of 500 only, of which Lieut.-Colonel MacGregor took command.

At the moment of the amalgamation Lieut.-Colonel Burn had
not arrived and the second-in-command, Major D. MacLeod, was
asked on the parade ground how soon he would be ready to move as
a fighting unit. He had to confess that a few days for reorganization
had been in his mind. Next day the battalion learnt why the
question had been asked. The Germans had captured a salient
known as the Kink, just south of the Fosse 8 Dump, notorious in
the Battle of Loos. The battalion was not called on to fight here,
but had to move up to the front again very soon. Later it moved
a little further south to the Hulluch area. The trenches here were
in a very bad state and littered with rusty bombs. Commanding
officers did not commonly write the battalion diaries, but the
entry here looks as though it had been dictated or inspired by
Lieut.-Colonel Pelham Burn. It describes the trenches as " in a
most disgraceful condition, clear evidence of gross idleness and in-
efficiency on the part of battalions who have recently occupied this
sub-section ". It must be added that the Gordons were relieving
troops of another brigade of the 15th Division. When, after only
two months with the 8/10th, Lieut.-Colonel Burn commanded a
brigade in the 51st Division, the youngest brigadier in the army at
the time of his appointment, a Jock remarked of him : " They a'
have their fads, and his fad is effeeciency."

What were the relaxations and the anodynes of troops in France
and Belgium then and later ? Among the foremost were the
divisional concert parties, some of which were excellent. The
Expeditionary Force Canteen had started early in 1915, but took
some time to reach its full development. Starting by selling only
food and drink, it became a universal provider, stocking articles

such as footballs and football boots and running a number of clubs. Leave for the rank and file, and indeed junior officers, did not come as often as once a year. A little Paris leave was granted, but generally to officers only. No city or town worth a trip was to be found near the front until in 1917 the British zone was extended to include Amiens, though a certain amount of leave to the city had been arranged earlier. The soldier got most satisfaction from games, especially association football, in which most of the battalions of the Gordon Highlanders were proficient and successful. They had also a number of good boxers and runners, who won many prizes.

On the whole, the infantryman liked more than anything else a quiet time between battles. Two neighbouring sectors were popular in this respect. The Bois de Ploegsteert (Plug Street Wood to the troops) was a delightful spot in spring when the birds were singing and one might imagine oneself a member of the Swiss Family Robinson in one's little hut amid the trees. A little to the south, over the French frontier, the attraction was quite different. Armentières, though very close to the enemy, was rarely shelled, at all events seriously. Its breweries continued to work. Its cafés sold the favourite luxuries of the troops, eggs (" oofs " in the local lingua franca) and chips, white wine (" ving blong "). There was a good restaurant popular with officers. Presumably there was an original " Mademoiselle from Armentières " or several.

Some other features of the period may be briefly mentioned. An improved gas helmet was issued in November 1915. It did not, however, provide adequate protection against phosgene gas, though the troops could not be told of this fact. In August 1916 it was replaced by the satisfactory small box respirator, in use for the rest of the war. Horns and bells were installed in the trenches to give a warning of gas, and when the wind favoured a discharge by the enemy a " gas alert " was ordered, during which the respirator had to be worn under the chin.

The ingenious Germans instituted means of overhearing telephone conversations, regarding which the British were extremely careless. This led to greater insistence on the use of codes, which were wasteful of time. More practical was the introduction of the " Fullerphone ", which rendered overhearing practically impossible. Telephone cable in the forward zone was now commonly buried in trenches five feet deep—more work for the infantry !—as it was inevitably cut by shelling and traffic in battle. Where a line was urgently required across heavily-shelled ground a form of armoured cable in a ladder pattern was sometimes used. Pigeons were issued to divisions going into action and sometimes brought invaluable information. Thomas Atkins was, however, occasionally guilty of cooking and eating a pigeon entrusted to him.

"Paper war" increased. Senior officers often condemned it and tried to reduce it, but the only level at which it can be said that no blame could lie was the battalion. No military head-quarters has ever been responsible for instituting correspondence or starting returns in an upward direction. They are always initiated from above.

Two machine guns per battalion had been increased to four in the summer of 1915. In January or February 1916 brigade machine-gun companies of sixteen guns were formed, the personnel being withdrawn from their regiments. The infantry was now armed with the more portable Lewis gun, the original four being gradually increased to sixteen, one per platoon.

Much more might be written about the background of the soldier's existence in the period of nine months between Loos and the Somme, but space will not permit. The B.E.F., which had landed four divisions strong, now numbered fifty-eight divisions and was preparing to make its greatest effort so far.

CHAPTER VII

THE Battle of the Somme has an evil reputation, not only because of its frightful toll of the finest British youth but also because it developed into a sheer battle of attrition, a form of strategy and tactics which does not arouse enthusiasm. The British Commander-in-Chief would have preferred an offensive in Flanders, but this would have had to be carried out by the British in isolation because the French had no intention of operating in that region. On the Somme front the forces of the two nations would fight side by side. Another factor to be taken into account is that the demands of the defence of Verdun progressively diminished the strength which the French could assign to the Somme offensive. The French participation on the first day was finally reduced to an attack by five divisions in first line as against eleven British divisions. Verdun had another effect, that of making a major offensive on the Western Front a necessity. The pressure was not only military but also political. It would have been politically and morally impossible to allow the French Army and people to suppose that after just on two years of war the British would refuse to make a great effort, something on a scale far bigger than that of Loos.

This is not the place to discuss at length the argument of the " Easterners " in favour of operations outside the Western front, of the policy of " knocking out the props ", in the phrase of the day, or of seeking a " soft under-belly ", in that of more recent times. It must be noted, however, that a relatively soft under-belly had been found at the Dardanelles and that the attempt to pierce it had failed ; that operations against Turkey elsewhere affected Germany and Austria to but a very limited extent ; and that the Germans could transfer forces to Italy as fast as Britain and France could send them and much faster to the Macedonian front. Neither the Italian nor the Macedonian victory in 1918 would have been overpowering had not the main German forces been first heavily defeated in France and Belgium.

All the battalions of the Gordon Highlanders were to take part in the Battle of the Somme. On the opening day, July 1st, 1916, however, one only was present, the 2nd Battalion in the 7th Division. This division was attacking with its three brigades in line, the 20th in the centre. The chief tactical feature on the brigade's front was Mametz, and the 2nd Gordon Highlanders on the right was directed against the westward half of the village. Mametz was a miniature fortress. On most of the front the

Germans had two main lines of defence, but here there was an intermediate line, Cemetery Trench, south of the village, and the so-called second line ran well north of it.   Machine guns were posted

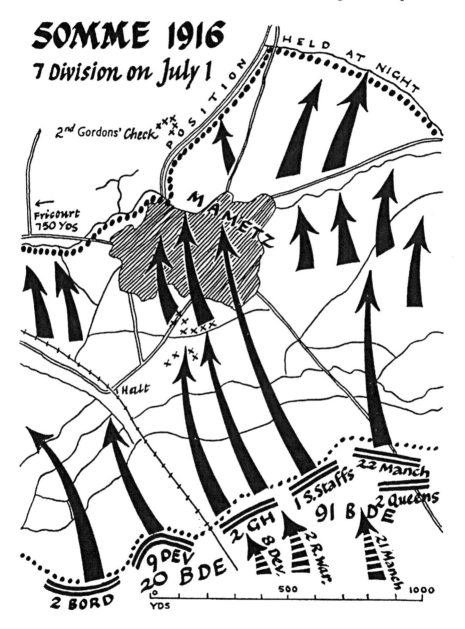

in the village, their detachments being provided with deep dug-outs.   Three battalions of the 20th Brigade were aligned for the assault, the 9th Devonshire in the centre and the 2nd Border on

6

the left, leaving only the 8th Devonshire in reserve. The Gordons were to attack on a frontage of 400 yards in four " waves " at a hundred yards' distance, with two companies abreast in the first and second wave and two in the third and fourth.

The mental and moral excitement of troops going into battle was even higher than usual in the British ranks on the first day of the Battle of the Somme. The desire to excel was keen, and the more intelligent the man the more strongly did he experience it. The Army was being tested before the eyes of the world. The troops had been impressed by the magnitude of the preparations and the power of the ceaselessly-thundering bombardment, though in truth it was slight by comparison with what was to come in 1917 and 1918. As the Gordons marched up past camps of Royal Artillery, Army Service Corps, and infantry in reserve, men poured out to the road to greet them with wild cheering.

The last item of the artillery preparation was a hurricane bombardment by Stokes mortars. At 7.30 a.m. the 2nd Gordon Highlanders advanced, rapidly but steadily. The German artillery here was now virtually out of action. Nearly all the opposition came from machine guns, but that was tough. The first wave assaulted with such speed and violence that the Germans in the front and support trenches had no time to use the grenades they had stacked on the parapets—they, like the British, had become " bomb-minded "—and some that they did throw had the pins undrawn.

The right companies then pressed on with unslackened resolution. The left, however, ran into a length of uncut wire. Here, and further west on the front of the 9th Devonshire, appalling loss was inflicted by machine-gun fire down a narrow valley through which ran the permanent way of a light railway. The consequence was that the right companies of the Gordons for the most part came to a stop in Cemetery Trench, south of Mametz, though a few men crossed the trench and entered a sunk road connecting the village with a halt on the railway. Heavy fire was sweeping in from the left, in part as a result of the failure of the 9th Devonshire. A long hold-up followed.

The commanding officer, Lieut.-Colonel B. G. R. Gordon, received from the right companies a demand for reinforcement timed 9 a.m., but the unhappy fate of the 9th Devonshire had absorbed most of the slender brigade reserve and only one company of the 8th Devonshire was available. A second message, timed 1.45 p.m., was in rather excited terms. It described the situation as grave and reported that the Germans were counter-attacking with the grenade. Lieut.-Colonel Gordon replied firmly that there must be no yielding ; the position gained must be held at all costs ; reinforcements were on the way.

In the early stages of the Somme artillery programmes were apt to be so rigid and difficulties of communication and control so great that, immediately after a hold-up, a satisfactory re-bombardment followed by a well-organized renewal of the infantry attack was a rarity. Here, to the credit of all concerned—including one on the best brigadiers in the Army—this was brought off in ample time. After half an hour's re-bombardment, a force put by Brig.-General Deverell at Lieut.-Colonel Gordon's disposal, two companies 2nd R. Warwickshire of the 22nd Brigade and two platoons of the 8th Devonshire, together with all the men of his own left companies who could be collected, advanced northwards. The sight of them was enough. Before they had even reached the position of the right-hand companies of the Gordons, the enemy gave up. Many men were seen fleeing from the north side of the village. Hundreds more advanced to surrender. It was proof that an enemy who has been under prolonged bombardment and possibly in difficulty with the transport of rations and water may be on the point of moral and physical collapse though he appears to have scored a defensive success. It was also a pointer to the missed opportunities which must have occurred in great numbers.

It may be that one occurred on this evening. The 2nd Gordon Highlanders secured its objective north of Mametz. The 9th Devonshire was enabled to pass on to its objective, in the centre, and the 2nd Border on the left had done so earlier. The 91st Brigade on the right flank of the 7th Division had been equally successful. On the left the 21st Brigade was some way short of its objective on the south-eastern side of Fricourt, which was to be pinched out later. There was still a German garrison in this strongly fortified village. To the north, however, as the troops of the 20th Brigade, including the Gordons, organized the defence of Mametz, all was quiet, even peaceful. Not a sign of movement could be seen in the bright evening light of a perfect summer day. It is true that the British did not know what we know now, that the German defence had been overwhelmed, that the division covering this front had had practically every one of its guns put out of action by the bombardment, or that there were hardly any reserves on the spot. The battalions did, however, report that they were not in contact with the enemy and could see no movement on his part. No orders to exploit were received from above. It seems certain that more ground could have been gained without fighting, perhaps even Mametz Wood—outside the German second defence line but destined to be a thorn in the British flesh later on.

The 2nd Gordon Highlanders was relieved on July 3rd. Its loss numbered 461, 16 officers and 445 other ranks out of a total of 24 officers and 783 other ranks who had gone into action. It had now been made the rule that a nucleus of officers, n.c.o.'s, and specialists was kept out of the offensive battles, so that the task of rebuilding battalions afterwards was less difficult.[1]

By July 5th the 7th Division's front had been pushed forward to the southern end of Mametz Wood, an advance at the maximum of two miles. The achievement of the 2nd Gordon Highlanders has to be measured by the fact that, though the French south of the Somme had gone beyond their objective and north of the river had reached it everywhere, though the XIII Corps between them and the 7th Division had been equally successful and the 7th Division nearly so, the whole centre and left of the great British attack had been a bloody and tragic failure. Granted that a greater measure of surprise had been obtained on the right and that the bombardment and counter-battery fire had been more successful, it still remains a fact worth remembering and an honour to have been one of the assault battalions which reached the whole of its objective on the first day of the Somme.

The 7th Division was given a very short rest. The artillery got none. It had, however, suffered only from fatigue because the enemy had devoted such guns as were able to fire to shelling the British infantry. Even the divisional commander had an almost continuously active job. The troops which had relieved the division failed to take Mametz Wood, not through want of will, but through rawness, and so much confusion followed that Major-General H. E. Watts was sent forward with his two senior staff officers to take over and untangle it. The wood had to be taken before a general attack could be made on the German second line. It was virtually cleared on July 11th. The 7th Division was then ordered to take part in the attack on the second line on July 14th.

This second phase of the battle brought the other regular battalion of the regiment, the 1st, on to the scene. The 3rd Division, of which it formed part, came down from the north to fight

---

[1]

	Killed	Wounded	Missing
Officers	7	9	—
Other ranks	119	287	39

It must be added that the casualties returned for July 1st have been checked by the Part II Battalion Orders by the official historian, who reduces the total for the whole attacking force by about 7 per cent. The difference is attributable to the large number of missing who rejoined after the battalions had made their returns. On the other hand the proportion of " killed " is greatly increased in the corrected casualty list, mainly because most returned as " missing " were found to have been killed, and to a smaller extent because a number previously returned as " wounded " actually died of wounds in casualty clearing stations or hospitals. The figure for " missing " in the return of the 2nd Gordon Highlanders is so small that the correction here is not of much importance, but it should be noted that battalion returns are nearly always over the mark in the total of casualties given and under it in the number of " killed ".

alongside the 7th. On July 6th the 1st Battalion marched through the village of Treux, where the 2nd was in billets licking its wounds. This was the second occasion on which the two had met since the Second Boer War, fifteen years earlier—the first having been for a bare half hour near Ypres—and the fifth in their whole history.

Hopes of obtaining quick and ample successes which could be deeply exploited now looked less rosy than on the morning of July 1st. The British Commander-in-Chief was, however, determined to maintain his effort. The immediate task, as he saw it, was the capture of the seven-mile ridge rising out of the plain between Guillemont and Thiepval, where it is broken by the valley of the Ancre. As they fought their way up the slope the British would be overlooked, but from the crest they would survey a wide vista, the Bapaume plain. Soldiers of this war got into the habit of attributing exaggerated importance to commanding ground—and here the maximum rise, from the valley south of Mametz crossed by the 2nd Gordon Highlanders to the crest north of Bazentin-le-Grand, was less than 400 feet—but it counted for a good deal in slow-moving warfare and for a great deal on a stationary front. On the forward slopes and spurs of this ridge ran the German second line of defence. Near the foot of the reverse slope was the partially completed third line.

The first objective of the 7th Division was Flatiron Trench, covering Bazentin-le-Grand Wood. This was allotted to the 20th Brigade. The Germans had withdrawn to this trench, leaving about 1,100 yards between the opposing fronts, and did not appear to be patrolling actively. The Army Commander, General Rawlinson, decided on the bold plan of an advance under cover of darkness. There was a risk if the move were discovered, but, on the other hand, an advance in daylight invited destruction. Still, to move fourteen first-line battalions of four divisions abreast such a distance in the dark was not easy.

The 20th Brigade's attack was carried out by the 8th Devonshire and 2nd Border. They were led forward in file and aligned on a tape 500 yards from the German front-line trench. The further advance to within assaulting distance was made largely by crawling. As the British artillery opened with a terrific crash, they charged. The extent of the surprise and the resistance varied, but the brigade's objectives, the second line and Bazentin-le-Grand Wood, were taken by 5 a.m. The 22nd Brigade went through and after hot and fluctuating fighting took the village of Bazentin-le-Petit. The 2nd Gordon Highlanders had expected to be called on early, as was usually the fate of the support battalion, but it had no work to do until this phase. Then it sent forward one company in the centre, between Bazentin-le-Grand Wood and village.

This company retook the original objective, which the enemy had recovered, and captured over twenty prisoners in the north end of the village.

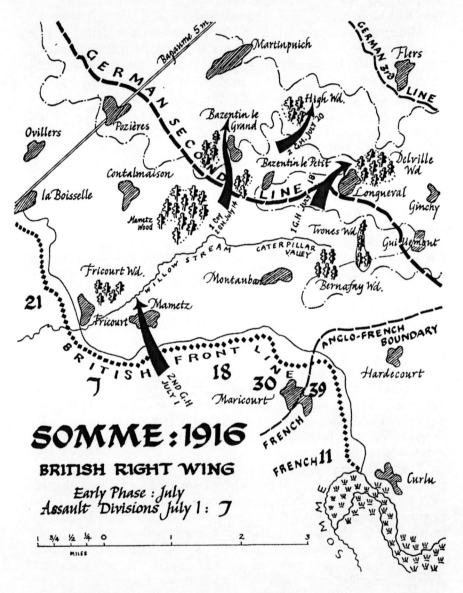

SOMME: 1916

BRITISH RIGHT WING

Early Phase : July
Assault Divisions July 1 : 7

The achievement was brilliant, particularly for a division engaged in its second major offensive within a fortnight, with many recruits in its ranks.   Now, however, a second opportunity seems to have been missed.   Major-General Watts had two-thirds of his infantry uncommitted and ardently desired to put the 91st Brigade through at once. Precious hours went by before he was given a free hand, and it was 7 p.m. before the advance started on High Wood, three-quarters of a mile away on the skyline. The Germans would not have been Germans if they had neglected to make use of the delay. A footing in the wood was secured, but after a bitter struggle the defenders were withdrawn by order of the Corps Commander during the night of July 15th. Rightly or wrongly, it was felt that not only the wood but the main part of the ridge would have been taken by speedy exploitation.

The story of High Wood, like that of its neighbour, the equally notorious Delville Wood, was to become gruesome. It had to be taken if the advance was to continue, and the 20th Brigade was brought back to go into action for the third time. It had had scanty rest in bivouac, and one company of the Gordons had re-mained in the line all the time. On this occasion the capture of the wood was entrusted to the 33rd Division, the task of the 20th Brigade being to clear its eastern edge, with two parallel roads running south-east from it as successive objectives. This was a truly abominable job. It does not need much military knowledge to realize that, bad as fighting a way through a wood full of fallen trees, to say nothing of machine guns, may be, to walk along its fringe with flank exposed to its unseen dangers is more forbidding still. The task of moving on the left of the advance, that is, next to the wood, went to the 2nd Gordon Highlanders.

The battalion advanced on a four-platoon frontage at 3.45 a.m. on July 20th. It reached the first road. A single platoon got to the second, 500 yards beyond, but was destroyed by fire from the wood and Switch Trench, directly ahead, only the platoon com-mander and five men escaping. The 33rd Division had gained some ground, but not enough to stop the enfilade fire. That directly from the front was almost as fatal and, though here the machine guns were in the open, they were hidden in standing corn. The men of the 2nd Gordons and 8th Devons tried again and again to reach Wood Lane, the second road, but all who passed the crest just their side of it were shot down. Finally the survivors, on hands and knees, or even creeping on their bellies, returned to the first road, which was being consolidated by the supports. A renewed attack was discussed, but Brig.-General Deverell, after consulting the commanding officers, gave his voice against it, and the divisional commander concurred.

. The attacking battalions were relieved that night. As the Gordons were starting to move back to Dernancourt, on the Ancre, their commanding officer was killed. Lieut.-Colonel B. G. R. Gordon had taken over command after the Battle of Loos and had shown himself a master of one of the hardest of the soldier's tasks, the rebuilding of a shattered battalion. He was keenly regretted. The adjutant, Captain C. E. Anderson, was also killed during the relief. The losses of the 2nd Battalion between July 14th and 21st were serious, though not, except in officers, on the scale of those of many previous engagements.[1]

The record of the 7th Division in the first three weeks of July 1916 can hardly be surpassed in the war, certainly not in the annals of the Somme, a story of courage and suffering written in blood. The 2nd Gordon Highlanders had played a full part in this splendid achievement.

It has seemed convenient to finish with the 2nd Battalion's participation in this phase, though this involves retracing steps to the record of the 1st. As already mentioned, the 1st Gordon Highlanders had moved up to take part in the battle. The 3rd Division was first ordered to capture the German second position. Its attack on July 14th, on the right of the 7th Division, was successfully carried out by the 8th and 9th Brigades, after a night advance similar to that of the 7th Division, already described. Further to the right half Longueval was taken by the 9th Division on that day, and the greater part of Delville Wood, which overhung the village, on the next.

On July 18th the 76th Brigade of the 3rd Division was put in to clear the northern part of Longueval and the orchards further north. The atmosphere was ominous: during the night the enemy had scourged Delville Wood with an exceptionally fierce bombardment. However, as the hour for the British assault drew near this slackened. The assault was launched at 3.45. The 1st Gordon Highlanders assaulted from the south-west. It did not secure the orchards, but it did succeed in capturing all the buildings. Its losses had, however, been high, and two companies of the 8th King's Own were sent forward to reinforce it.

About noon the bombardment leapt up to an intensity not yet experienced in this battle. The German command, in fact, had determined to win back all the wood and village on the same day that the British planned to extend their grip on them. The wood was capped with clouds of black smoke from the heavy howitzer shells and the houses of Longueval were set aflame or reduced to rubble. There was nothing for it but to withdraw the troops of the 76th Brigade to the trenches from which they had assaulted, at a windmill 500 yards west of Longueval. They had clung to their gains for some eight hours and the 1st Gordons would have been destroyed if it had tried to do so any longer. As

[1]

	Killed	Wounded	Missing
Officers	2	9	—
Other ranks	27	174	50

it was, its losses amounted to 322, including 4 officers killed and 7 wounded. The German infantry, advancing soon after 2.30 p.m. was at first broken up by the British barrage, but in the end reached the southern edge, though the heroic survivors of the South African Brigade (9th Division) held on to some ten acres in the south-west corner.

The 1st Gordon Highlanders was relieved on July 19th and marched back to the mediocre comfort of Carnoy, just inside the old British front, but even this was not enjoyed for long. On the 20th—the day on which the 2nd Gordons attacked east of High Wood—the only two battalions of the 76th Brigade not yet engaged failed in yet another attempt to clear Delville Wood and at night relieved the handful of South Africans remaining in it. Amid all the loss and suffering one man's death was regretted by all. The brigade-major, Major Congreve, who had come forward to clear up confusion resulting from doubt about the front, was shot dead by a sniper. He was awarded the V.C. posthumously. His father, Lieut.-General Sir Walter Congreve, himself a holder of the V.C., was commanding the XIII Corps on this very front.

The impressions of the 1st Gordons may be summed up in four points: mud, gas hanging in the trees, uncertainty about the situation, and disorganization. They found a front held only at what were euphemistically called strong points, which had been formed only because groups of soldiers had rallied there. A kindly mist enabled them to organize rather better defences.

The offensive had started in perfect summer weather, the only disadvantages of which were that the heat was at times oppressive and that maggots appeared in the wounds of men left lying on the ground during the light of a single day. Then had come a change. On July 18th, when the 1st Gordons attacked Longueval, the rain had been extremely heavy. Now mud, one of the outstanding characteristics of the Battle of the Somme, had come upon the scene. It was to increase until by November it had become all pervading and indeed covered practically the whole once green and smiling surface of the band of territory in dispute.

In the most fiercely contested woods, Trones, with which no battalion of the Gordons was concerned, Delville and High, with which the regiment became but too well acquainted, the conditions of the battlefield were at their worst. Artillery on both sides had made of them gigantic abatis. When all the problems of the British command are allowed for, it must be concluded that the relatively isolated assaults on the woods, of which there were several, were bad tactics. It was not enough to pound the German defenders into demoralization because the same fate then lay in store for the British in their place. The best hope of securing them lay in general attacks which prevented the enemy concentrating fire on them because he had to spread it over wide fronts. Now, however, strong German reinforcements had arrived, and deep advances which would have left the woods behind were harder than ever to bring about.   Of this last spell in line the 1st Gordon Highlanders records that friend and foe, living and dead, lay side by side in Delville Wood.

Behind the lines the horrors were equally prominent.   Caterpillar Valley, only a mile in rear of the fighting line at Longueval, was crammed with field artillery.   It was the only possible site for the more forward batteries.   The main reason why the Commander-in-Chief insisted that Longueval and Delville Wood must be taken at all costs was his anxiety lest a German counterstroke at this point should put all this artillery in peril.   The enemy could not see into the valley here, but he knew the guns were there and took the obvious action, shooting up ammunition parties and littering the area with dead horses.   Further west, where it was known as the Happy Valley, this depression carried an indifferent road which was the supply route of several divisions.   In fine weather a cloud of white dust hung over it.   Here the Germans did even more damage.   They dropped a heavy curtain of fire along it at irregular intervals, using shrapnel and high explosive mixed.   The dead animals could not be buried, or, if they were, were soon unearthed again.   The appalling, sickly stench of carrion put some men off their food.   The dense swarms of flies were an equally loathsome feature of this polluted world.

The 51st Division, which now arrived from Artois, did not come in under a lucky star.   To begin with, it was ordered to secure High Wood, with hardly any time to have a good look at it or to think out a plan.   In the second place, it was not warned about the Happy Valley barrage, which came down on its 152nd and 153rd Brigades bivouacked in it.[1]   The 152nd was moved to Fricourt and the 153rd dispersed to avoid serious loss.   During the night of July 21st the 51st Division relieved the 33rd, the 154th Brigade taking over the whole front.

General Rawlinson had good reason to be satisfied with the result of the night advance and dawn attack on July 14th.   It was, in fact, the only satisfactory event in the battle since the success of the right wing on the first day.   For his next general attack he decided on another night operation, and this time a night assault. The objectives were the whole of Delville Wood, the orchards

---

[1] So the divisional history states, the reflection on the XV Corps staff work being of course grave.   Yet the incident is puzzling.   Surely some artillery brigade or battery commander would have told the nearest commanding officer what was in store for him if he could not find a better bivouac.

north of Longueval, High Wood and the " Switch Line " just north of it and running on south of Martinpuich.

The bombardment preceding this offensive began at 7 p.m. on July 22nd. Delville Wood does not on this occasion concern us, though the attack was carried out yet again by the 3rd Division and the 1st Gordon Highlanders was on the spot. The battalion was in the southern fringe of the wood, whereas the attack was made from the west. Again a failure resulted.

The 1st Gordon Highlanders was relieved on July 25th, one company not getting away until the following dawn. On the 28th the battalion moved back to Mericourt-l'Abbaye for a rest. It had gone through an evil experience in the battle, with no success such as had been gained by the 2nd ; indeed, but for that one thrust into Longueval, its fate had been mostly that of lying under bombardment. Yet on August 9th it carried out with great enthusiasm a forced route march for the express purpose of visiting all four Territorial battalions in the 51st Division, which had then been withdrawn from the battle.

The objective of the 154th Brigade was High Wood, of which only a small proportion at the southern end was in British possession and 600 yards of the Switch Line which passed through the northern end. The 4th Gordon Highlanders had been assailed by lachrymatory gas shell on its way up, and the men had to wear the goggles provided for occasions when this, but not gas of more dangerous types, was encountered. Lieut.-Colonel S. R. McClintock was informed personally by the brigade commander, Brig.-General C. E. Stewart, that the attack would take place during the night of the 22nd. He had no opportunity for reconnaissance.

The operation began with an attempt by B Company to seize a German strong point in the eastern part of the wood, of which all that could be seen was the tops of the stakes bearing a wire entanglement. There was never any sign or chance of success. The main attack by the 4th Gordons and 9th Royal Scots was launched at 1.30 a.m. on the 23rd. Fallen trees, undergrowth, wire, and countless shell holes made it difficult in the extreme to force a way through the wood, apart from the enemy's fire. Direction was quickly lost. Exactly what happened in the depths of the wood will never be known, but a German account reveals that there was ferocious close fighting, in which the enemy lost heavily. However, the two Scots battalions were back where they had started by 3 a.m.

In fact, the whole night operation on the Fourth Army front had been a failure. The one success had been gained on the left flank, where Australian troops of the newly formed Reserve Army (renamed Fifth in October) of General Sir Hubert Gough had taken nearly all the village fortress of Pozières.

The 4th Gordon Highlanders was withdrawn on the night of July 23rd as far as a support position near Bazentin-le-Grand. The 154th Brigade remained in line until the 26th, when the 153rd relieved it on an extended front, now running about half way from High Wood to Longueval. The new brigade was already strained and weary. Conditions south of High Wood have already been described, so far as words can describe them. One of the worst features of this front was that ammunition, food, and water for the foremost troops had to be man-hauled over a considerable distance, so that most men in the support brigade had to make a journey once every twenty-four hours from Mametz Wood to the advanced dumps behind High Wood. It was heavy labour over constantly shelled ground, and there was little protection during the hours allotted to sleep. In four days the 7th Gordon Highlanders in this brigade suffered 60 casualties. On the night of July 26th and the three following nights it lost 82 of all ranks, though not in front line.

On July 30th, at 6.10 p.m. the 153rd Brigade attacked. The objective of the 5th Gordon Highlanders was Wood Lane, the more northerly of the two roads to Longueval, which had been the second objective of the 2nd Gordon Highlanders on July 20th, ten days before. The mind balks at contemplation of the sacrifice demanded by these attacks and, it must be added, of the tenacity of the defence. The task was even more difficult this time because a trench had been dug along the road.

The usual blast of fire met the 5th Gordons and 6th Black Watch on their left, not only from the front but from the strong point in the wood, which the 7th Black Watch was unable to take. If valour could have stormed the trench, the two battalions in the open would have done it. A few men of the Gordons actually reached the wire, previously cut but now found to have been hastily repaired. The trench did not appear to be damaged and its garrison was determined and defiant. One German officer jumped out and stood upright, waving a grenade and jeering. In the end the two battalions dug in on such gains as they had made, about 250 yards.

The 7th Battalion in the same brigade was not put in as a unit, but within little over an hour it had sent forward six platoons, mostly in aid of the 7th Black Watch. Of the ten remaining, three formed carrying parties. The corps commander demanded a renewed attack, but there was no time to organize it in the dark. A new trench was dug along the line reached, just short of the crest of the ridge. The 5th Battalion was withdrawn on July 21st and the 7th on August 1st, in the latter case as part of the replacement of the 153rd Brigade by the 152nd. The battalion which relieved the 7th Gordon Highlanders was the 6th.

The losses of the 5th for July 30th and 31st were 245. The officers suffered heavily, especially in the two leading companies, one of which came out under the command of A/C.S.M. Cowie, who was himself wounded. Twenty officers, including battalion headquarters, had gone into action under the new regulations, and half were killed or wounded.[1]

Fortunately for the 6th Gordon Highlanders, attacks on High Wood were discontinued and the 152nd Brigade did not go " over the top" during its front-line spell of duty. In other respects this was as unpleasant as that of its predecessors, and possibly even more arduous. Contact in the wood was not close, and the brigade was directed to gain as much ground as possible by stealthy means. The prospects of stealth looked indifferent, since if the front were to be advanced, digging would be necessary, and it could not be done quietly in a wood. Fortunately, however, the Germans paid little attention. Steadfast as they were in defence, they were not in the best of spirits. Who was, in High Wood ?

The 6th Gordon Highlanders held the front in the wood from August 1st to 5th. The battalion carried out its orders by digging saps with T-heads, then linking the latter so as to form a new continuous fire trench. It was very hard work. Fallen trees, branches, and undergrowth had to be cleared and roots to be severed. The men used axes and billhooks in addition to the usual picks and shovels. A strong defensive position comprising about one-third of High Wood had been established when the Highlanders departed. The 51st Division, after a brief rest, moved north and in mid-August took over a front in the valley of the Lys.

The three battalions of the regiment in the 51st Division and the division itself had to look back upon a thoroughly unhappy experience in its first intervention in the Battle of the Somme. Its one objective had been High Wood—and the neighbouring defences—and the wood was a fortress at the apex of a British salient. The losses suffered were over 3,500, high, though less than those of a number of other divisions ; but in this case there was hardly anything except duty done to show for them. It was to prove next time that its spirits had not been blunted and to show what it could do under better auspices.

1	Killed	Wounded	Missing
Officers	3	7	—
Other ranks	81	137	17

CHAPTER VIII

THE SOMME—AUGUST TO MID-SEPTEMBER 1916

THE events of July had been bitterly disappointing to the British Commander-in-Chief. On the first day, it is true, the success on the right wing had been substantial, but this had occurred on little more than a quarter of the front. On the other three-quarters there had been failure, with devastating losses. Since then the only good day had been the 14th, when the bold night advance and dawn attack secured the German second line on a front of three miles and the two Bazentins beyond it. At the end of July the crest just beyond had still not been reached and some of the German buttresses had been assaulted again and again, without success and at fearful cost.

The prospect of an early break-through into open country, for which he had hoped before launching the offensive and which had once or twice looked possible since, had faded. General Joffre considered that the German resistance could be broken only by a period of attrition. Sir Douglas Haig came round to his view. His hope now was that a succession of powerful though local blows would so weaken the enemy that in about six weeks' time, by mid-September, another grand assault would break through his lines. This view was unduly optimistic. It must be added, however, that Haig, though his intelligence service could as yet provide him with no evidence of the state of mind of the German command, had divined its anxiety. It actually considered the offensive to be " the most serious crisis of the war ". The German losses for July were 160,000 men. Thenceforward they were to exceed those of the British and French combined. The Verdun offensive was brought to an end. The Chief of the General Staff, who was the real Commander-in-Chief, General von Falkenhayn, was dismissed by the Emperor in late August and replaced by the Hindenburg-Ludendorff combination.

Haig translated his idea into a programme. August and the first half of September were devoted to the capture of the fortified localities, including Bouleaux Wood, Guillemont, Ginchy, and the hateful Delville Wood, lying in front of the German third position between Morval and Flers. The assaults were only partially successful. They were, however, followed in mid-September by another great offensive aimed at a break-through, known as the Battle of Flers-Courcelette.[1] It is these attacks which now lie before us.

[1] Officially, there is no such title as " Battle of the Somme ", the popular name. The offensive is known as " The Battles of the Somme 1916 ". These battles have their own titles, Albert, Bazentin Ridge, Delville Wood, Guillemont, Ginchy, Flers-Courcelette, etc.

On August 1st no battalion of the Gordon Highlanders was in or near the line in the battlefield. The 15th Division, with the 8/10th Battalion in the 44th (Highland) Brigade and the 9th Battalion as Pioneers, had not yet been engaged. Now its time had come. It marched the whole way to the battlefield, over sixty miles for nearly all units. A good many men fell out during the first two days' marches, but few afterwards. In fact this march in fine weather was a tonic to the division, which had held for a long time a wide front in the Loos area. The last line held by the 8/10th Battalion was in the Hohenzollern sector, notorious from every point of view. The astonishing performance of the 15th Division on the Somme, when it carried out a successful attack after having been continuously in the line for over five weeks, was certainly influenced by the fitness produced by this long summer march.

Shortly before the start the 15th Division was represented at the annual Presidential review at Longchamps by a party of 2 officers, Major Lord Dudley Gordon and Lieutenant G. Figgis, and 50 other ranks of the 9th Gordons. On the way down the 8/10th Gordons, who had a day's halt at Dieval, played through the village successively the battalions of the 9th Division, coming out of the battle. The 9th Gordons spent one day getting in hay for the commune of Beaumetz. On August 8th the division entered the line south of Martinpuich, the 44th Brigade being in divisional reserve. The pioneers quickly got to work burying cable.

On August 10th the division received orders for one of the limited attacks characteristic of this period of attrition. It was allotted to the 45th and 46th Brigades, and the 8/10th Gordon Highlanders, the only normal infantry battalion in the division, took no part in it. The 9th, however, had a role, more active than often came the way of a pioneer battalion, though involving only a small proportion of its strength. For quick consolidation and especially for opening communication trenches under fire a method had been evolved which depended on the use of metal tubes filled with explosive. These were driven into the ground and then touched off, forming the rudiments of a trench which could then, at least in theory, be completed with pick and shovel. Such was the job allotted to the 9th Gordons on August 12th. It was certainly safer than attacking as the infantry did, but not attractive. The explosive pipes did not always wait for the sapper n.c.o.'s to touch them off.

This was a night attack, at 10.32 p.m. On the right the 12th Highland Light Infantry suffered very heavily while forming up and failed in its assault. Two platoons of the 9th Gordons were to dig two communication trenches begun by the explosion of a line of pipes or tubes in the way described. The right platoon was commanded by a n.c.o., Sergeant G. Henderson, " admirably commanded ", as the report afterwards put it. Almost immediately after the waves of the assault had gone by men began to come back. Sergeant Henderson strongly suspected that the so-called Switch Line in front had not been taken. He therefore kept his men as far as possible under cover but gradually deepened the new trench. When it had reached a point within thirty yards of the German front line a machine gun opened fire straight in front. This confirmed his view that the assault had not got in, so he prolonged the trench no further. To have finished it properly he would have had to get men extended on the surface. He did not do this, but deepened the trench to five feet in case it should be wanted later. Then he took his platoon to the empty British trench, manned the parapet, stopped all stragglers who came through, and made them do likewise. He remained until 6 a.m. when a relieving battalion appeared.

This is a small incident, which does not find a mention in the history of the 15th Division, but seems worthy of description in that of the Gordon Highlanders. It shows how, even in that war, where circumstances so often seemed to control men rather than men circumstances, a sergeant who used his head could save lives while carrying out his orders to the extent that they remained practical. Sergeant Henderson was awarded the Military Medal and at a later date an Italian decoration.

Lieutenant C. L. MacGregor, in command of the left platoon, apparently got no warning of the failure of the assault and was severely wounded in trying to prolong his trench right up to the German front line. In the case of the next trench further west, the work was held up when it was found that the German front opposite had not been taken. A little later the platoon moved 150 yards further west, where it faced German trenches which had been carried. The communication trench was then dug through to them without loss. The 9th Gordons got off lightly, having only two officers and ten rank and file wounded, with three more remaining at duty. The ground won on the left gave useful observation and on the evening of August 13th fire directed from it stopped German troops trying to advance from Martinpuich.

On the 17th the Pioneers did more good work, in support of the 7th Camerons of the 44th Brigade, which entered the German trenches. The enemy grenadiers counter-attacked, and the situation was for some time doubtful. The Camerons ran out of bombs. Two platoons of the 9th Gordons, which had brought up boards for the construction of strong points in the captured trenches, formed themselves into a chain to deliver a fresh supply of bombs, with the aid of which the gains were held. The commanding officer of the 9th Gordons, Lieut.-Colonel E. H. Gordon, received a letter of warm appreciation of the services of his men from Brig.-General F. H. Marshall, commanding the 44th Brigade.

Some, but not very much, fighting occurred on this front between the events already recorded and the " big push " of September 15th. The 8/10th Gordon Highlanders had several spells in front line but was never actively engaged. The 9th Battalion was mainly occupied in the endless job of digging cable trenches.

Before the major offensive, beginning on September 15th, the 3rd and 7th Divisions returned. By a coincidence—so far as the two regular battalions of the Gordon Highlanders were concerned —General Deverell, the outstanding commander of the 20th Brigade, 7th Division, in which the 2nd Battalion served, had now become commander of the 3rd Division in which was the 1st Battalion. On the night of August 14th, the 3rd Division took over trenches on the British right up to the junction with the French and near the village of Guillemont. It was at once put into an attack—one of those " preliminary operations " which so often failed and which later experience generally condemned—to capture the spur south of this village. This was successful only to a very limited degree, leaving the more to be done in the bigger attack of August 18th.

A preliminary bombardment, at a regular rate of fire all the time because the enemy had previously obtained warning from the quickening of fire in the latter stages, lasted thirty-six hours. Zero hour was 2.45 p.m. On the right the 76th Brigade attacked on a narrow front, with two companies 1st Gordons in first line on the right and two 10th Royal Welsh Fusiliers on the left. The first objective was approximately the Hardecourt-Guillemont road ; the second ran north from the northern end of Angle Wood (to be taken by the French) which lay in a ravine between two spurs of the main ridge. Admittedly it was an awkward piece of ground and to advance in one stage 1,500 yards on to the high ground beyond the ravine and attempt to storm the strongly defended Falfemont Farm would have been to court trouble. Yet an objective along a gully looks odd from the tactical point of view.

The 1st Gordons, shoulder to shoulder with their allies, were on their mettle. Owing to the shape of the ground, the assault was visible to countless British and French eyes—and it is to be feared to too many German. It was a remarkable spectacle, which deeply impressed onlookers. The contrasting tactics of the two nations in the attack were clearly illustrated. The French division, the 153rd, was a good one. The infantry swept forward, moving at high speed in irregular formation, often in little groups.

7

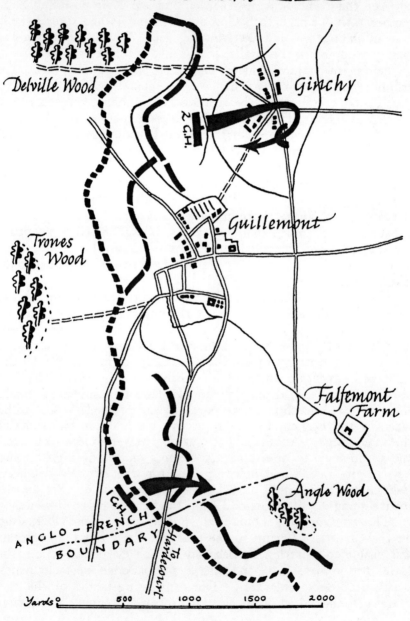

GUILLEMONT AND GINCHY 1916

Ist. Gordon Highlanders Aug 18th. 2nd Gordon Highlanders Sept 6

FOURTH ARMY GAINS - AUG 18

Delville Wood

Ginchy

2. G.H.

Guillemont

Trones Wood

Falfemont Farm

Angle Wood

CH.

ANGLO - FRENCH BOUNDARY

To Hardecourt

Yards 0   500   1000   1500   2000

The 1st Gordons, moving behind the "creeping" or "rolling" field-artillery barrage which had gradually developed in the past six weeks and was by now established, advanced at a steady pace in dressed lines. It can hardly be doubted that the French method was the more effective and the less costly, but the British had its advantages. In the first place, the best means of avoiding the German barrage, which sometimes came down very quickly, was to get the troops moving at once in regular lines. In the second, the French were apt to arrive dispersed on their objectives and were not easily controlled by their officers. Thus the fruits of great feats of arms were often lost, for the average French soldier, though he had more tactical sense and did more thinking for himself than the British, was less of a " sticker " when counter-attacked. At all events, the representatives of each army, here fighting side by side, on this occasion upheld in noble and friendly rivalry the honour of its country's arms.

The Hardecourt-Guillemont road was unrecognizable owing to shell-fire, but the objective was indicated by the shape of the spur which it followed. At once the right company came under hot machine-gun fire from Falfemont Farm across the ravine. Though suffering very heavily, it reached the first objective in touch with the French. The left company did even more, one of its platoons pursuing the enemy for 250 yards beyond the objective and then digging in. Both companies were reinforced by Lieut.-Colonel S. G. Craufurd.

The French had dashed into the ravine, but there they were sharply counter-attacked and driven back. The 9th Brigade on the 76th Brigade's left had made hardly any progress and in consequence the 10th Royal Welsh Fusiliers was taken in flank and forced to withdraw. The 1st Gordon Highlanders was in trouble on both flanks and had to refuse both. An attempt to continue the attack to the second objective was now out of the question. Brigade headquarters, in fact, appears to have believed for a time that practically all gains had been lost. This was by no means the case. The line of the Hardecourt-Guillemont road was eventually consolidated. The losses of the 1st Gordons were 4 officers killed, 3 wounded and 257 other ranks, killed, wounded and missing.

The 3rd Division was relieved and sent north to the coal-mining area. It had at least scored a valuable success at a time of frequent failures. Before it began its march the 1st Gordons received two drafts, amounting in sum to 345 other ranks, and on the road 9 2nd Lieutenants joined.

The battalion had covered about half the march when, on the night of August 26th, the 7th Division took over the front a little north of that on which the 3rd Division had been operating. The right of the 7th faced Ginchy and the left held the eastern side of Delville Wood, all but a small corner of which was now in British possession. The 22nd Brigade at once started bombing attacks to improve the position, in particular to clear German trenches running to the outskirts of the wood. The 91st Brigade took over from it, but little was achieved. On the morning of August 31st, however, the whole of the notorious wood was held by the 91st Brigade and the 24th Division on its left.

This was no longer the case that night. " Devil's Wood ", as the troops called it, was to be still a source of trouble. A German counter-attack obtained a footing in it, deepest in the north-east corner, in the sector of the 91st Brigade. The 22nd Brigade was brought back again, made a little progress in the wood, and on September 3rd took and lost Ginchy. On the 4th the 20th Brigade failed in another attack on the village.

The 2nd Gordon Highlanders was in brigade reserve on this date. That night it moved forward to two parallel trenches facing Ginchy, at respectively 500 and 750 yards. The guides were late ; the route was muddy and slippery ; and the trenches were congested. It proved impossible to get into position for an attack on Ginchy on the morning of September 5th as ordered. It was postponed until 3.30 a.m. on the 6th. The early hour was due to the belief that there were still some troops of the 22nd Brigade in the village. A further bombardment having been forbidden for this reason, the best course was to rush it before dawn.

Lieut.-Colonel H. A. Ross, the officer commanding the 2nd Gordons had gone sick on the eve of the attack. Major R. D. Oxley took command. The delay brought a fearful bombardment on the battalion and by zero hour it had lost three of its four company commanders and suffered numerous other casualties. " Rushing Ginchy before dawn " looked less easy on a dark morning with two rather weak companies in the lead spread out over a frontage of some 750 yards. Direction was lost. It is easy to say this ought not to have happened, but who is to know how many of those carrying compasses survived an action in which 5 officers were killed and 15 wounded ?

Major Oxley reorganized the troops, having to bring them back to their starting point to do so. This time matters went better to begin with, but the advance was checked by heavy fire about fifty yards short of the trees on the fringe of Ginchy, the survivors somewhat scattered on their wide front. Up came the devoted Major Oxley to reorganize once more, but only to be killed.

The 9th Devonshire now worked two companies up to the Gordon's right. Captain D. R. Turnbull, who had assumed command on Major Oxley's death, reorganized the survivors and bade them take a third effort. Wonderful to relate, these high-hearted men made a very fine one. With the Devons they broke into Ginchy.

Alas that a tale of so much heroism and endurance should have to end in defeat ! The Germans bombarded the place viciously. To add to the effect, the Gordons had edged and bombed forward —all credit to them, but it often brought frightful consequences in village fighting with communications what they were on the Somme—well beyond the line which they had reported themselves as holding. British heavy howitzer shells now began falling in their midst. One shell from our own side is more demoralizing than two from the enemy's and sometimes more damaging physically because men contrive to get some shelter from frontal fire, but seldom have any against fire from their rear. It was in these circumstances that the remnants of the Gordons and Devons abandoned their hold on Ginchy in face of a counter-attack about 200 strong which they might otherwise have withstood. The Gordons' report attributed their failure to the following combination of influences : the haste with which the operation had been mounted ; the excessive breadth of the front; the early loss of three company commanders, replaced by less experienced officers ; and the moral and material effect of being shelled by their own guns.

The 7th Division regarded this phase of the battle as one of the most unsatisfactory of its career. It had shown courage, drive, and endurance both in the attack on Ginchy and in the almost ceaseless fighting in Delville Wood, but had little to show for its efforts and sacrifice. The only consolation was that on September 3rd it had contributed to the capture of Guillemont by the 5th Division on its right. Its commander, Major-General H. E. Watts, was strongly of the opinion that the attacks had been too fragmentary and piecemeal and that better results might have been looked for from a more concerted effort. Clearly, too, his division had been brought back to the battle without having been given sufficient time for rest or for the instruction of newly-joined officers and the large drafts of rank and file which had replaced the losses of the earlier stages of the offensive.

After a ten days' rest behind the front the infantry of the division moved north to Flanders, leaving the artillery to fight on in the big battle of mid-September, and took over the Le Touquet and Ploegsteert sectors between the Lys and the Douve brook. Major R. A. N. Tytler took over command of the 2nd Gordon Highlanders.

CHAPTER IX

THE SOMME—LAST PHASES

BY pure chance the Gordon Highlanders, which took a big part in the Somme offensive, took little part in the Battle of Flers-Courcelette, one of the greatest efforts made by the British and one of the most historic. Of the five divisions in which battalions of the regiment were at this time incorporated one only, the 15th, was present, and it launched its attack with its 45th and 46th Brigades, whereas the 8/10th Battalion was in the 44th. Nor is there much to be said even of the event which made September 15th, 1916, historic, the first use of the tank in war.[1] Only four tanks were allotted to the 15th Division ; only two were available ; only one got into action ; and it was so late that it accomplished little or nothing. Its appearance is said to have scared the Germans.

The final objective of the division was the large village of Martinpuich, the better part of a mile long. A maze of trenches lay between its south-eastern end and the British front. The final objective was taken with a large haul of prisoners and—what was rarer—four guns. Losses were not high by the standard of the Somme. This operation was one of the 15th Division's finest achievements.

Overnight the 8/10th Gordons had marched to Contalmaison, captured in July. On September 16th they were detached to the 46th Brigade and moved up to Gunpit Road, a sunken road running north-west from Martinpuich, and to the village itself. On the following day an artillery officer visiting the front line reported that some trenches which lay outside the objective were neither wired nor occupied. Patrols from the Gordons and the 10/11th H.L.I. of the 46th Brigade went forward, but came under heavy fire. Whether wired or not, the trenches were occupied. Further loss was caused by a German bombardment in retaliation for the reconnaissance. The Gordons were angry with the 46th Brigade, as troops are when things go wrong under a strange command, but it is probable that divisional headquarters was responsible for the order. The brigadier of the 46th wrote : " I am under the impression that the artillery officer had not read his map correctly." That night the Gordons were relieved, but moved in the first instance only to reserve trenches where they had no shelter from shell-fire.

---

[1] " Tank Supply Committee " was a " cover " name for the Admiralty Committee —a strange undertaking for the sea service due to the enthusiasm of the then First Lord, Mr. Winston Churchill—co-ordinating effort, experiment, and design. The incongruous name " tank " has stuck ever since to this armoured fighting vehicle.

The 9th Battalion was busy. These Pioneers were great diggers. They continued on that day and just afterwards a British communication Trench, Welch Alley, on the right flank, up to the outskirts of Martinpuich, a distance of 360 yards and to a depth of five feet. Gordon Alley on the left was continued right up to Gunpit Road, about a thousand yards, but had been dug only to a depth of from two to four feet when the battalion was relieved on the 18th. It had had 4 officers wounded and 125 other ranks killed or wounded during its duties on this front.

The first day of the Battle of Flers-Courcelette had been a heavy blow for the Germans, but had not fulfilled British hopes by a long way. The German third position had been stormed on a front of 4,500 yards. The Fourth Army had taken Flers and Martinpuich and the Reserve Army (later named Fifth), under General Sir Hubert Gough—who had once commanded the 7th Division—Courcelette ; but Morval, Lesboeufs, and Guedecourt, within the final objective, which was at one point a mile beyond the line reached, had not even been approached. The enemy had certainly been severely punished, stretched to the utmost, and thoroughly alarmed. As he put it, " the defence was as good as completely broken " by the tanks, and they had seriously affected the spirit of the troops. But the secret of the tanks was out, and they had been used in small numbers, prematurely as many thought, just because the Commander-in-Chief was striving after a decisive success.

The way in which the battlefield had been cut up, and the shortage of fresh troops, made it questionable whether an equal effort could be developed for some time to come. A number of divisions remained in line. The 15th had been released only because it had been there so long. Showers during the evening made the ground even more difficult to cross.

Yet what followed certainly seemed to support the Commander-in-Chief's moderate optimism. The Germans really were shaken now. The Battle of Morval between September 25th and 27th was a more successful offensive than that of Flers-Courcelette. Combles (jointly with the French), Morval, Lesboeufs, and Guedecourt were captured by the Fourth Army. In the overlapping Battle of Thiepval Ridge the Reserve Army took the fortress village of Thiepval, a name of dread owing to the losses that had been suffered around it. It was not highly satisfactory, but it was very different from the " attrition " period of August and the first half of September. General Haig now instructed the Army Commanders to prepare for another big attack, both east of the Ancre and to the west of it where the German front had remained intact since the terrible failure of July 1st. Once again, preliminary operations, gravely hampered by a deterioration in the weather, lasted longer than expected, with the consequence that the programme had to be revised by being spread over a longer period and in some respects restricted.

The 15th Division began its return to the battlefield in the first days of October. The greater part of it had passed a full three weeks in training. Billets in the Franvillers area had been good, but the weather turned cold after September and straw was not plentiful. However, it was elysium by comparison with the front which the 8/10th Gordon Highlanders took over on the night of October 8th. The guides from the 23rd Division must have been good; otherwise the battalion would not have reached its trenches before daylight. One battalion of the 15th Division spent nearly an hour digging three men out of the mud in which they were gripped so tightly that they could not move by their own exertions. In a normal world we find it hard to believe that strong and fit young men can be helplessly trapped in mud, short of a quicksand; but then we do not create such mud. Some trenches held water up to the height of thigh-boots. The surface of the ground was a quagmire. Few of such landmarks as were left could be discerned in the dark. The tracks, established at random, wound like corkscrews.

When the Gordons worked out their position in daylight they found it even worse than was to be expected. An offensive, the Battle of the Transloy Ridges, had begun. Success had been limited, that of the 23rd Division on October 7th having been the most striking. It had captured Le Sars, a long village on either side of the Amiens-Bapaume road, but to the east of the place the attack had broken down. The Gordons thus formed a flank guard, with their backs to Le Sars. In the trenches the dead lay unburied. The battalion was relieved on the night of the 10th. It could not quit its position until 3.30 a.m. on the 11th, and then small parties lost themselves and wandered about till daylight.

More heavy rain fell while the battalion " rested ", and on October 18th it described the countryside as " awash ". Next evening it set off again for the line, a matter of some three miles as the crow flies, but this was small consolation to men who did not possess wings. The mud in the communication trenches was now two to three feet deep. Again and again men had to be dug out. The relief took ten hours. Lieut.-Colonel D. MacLeod made up his mind that in future the battalion should move over the top, whether coming in or going out, and carried out this policy, virtually without loss. Moves were in fact frequently postponed owing to heavy rain, an unhappy event for the battalion awaiting relief.

In rear the congestion of the roads, few in this agricultural area and deep in mud, caused periods of chaos. Constant traffic blocks occurred, horses and mules standing patiently in the rain while road control and transport men relieved their temper with profanity. A hard struggle was required to get up the immediate needs of the troops, food, water, and ammunition, often at the cost of postponing the movement of stores such as timber, steel shelters for dug-outs, and road-metal, which would have alleviated their trials. As usual the Pioneer battalion, the 9th Gordons, worked like Trojans, on roads, a light railway—one of the greatest possible contributions to the saving of toil, the strengthening of the defence, and the mounting of future offensives in such circumstances—communication trenches, and huts.

No active operations took place during the period of just on a month in which the 8/10th Gordons were in the firing line, in support, or close up in reserve. The conditions have been described at more than usual length because they are not familiar. Those of the Ypres battles of 1917, lumped together under the unsuitable title of " Passchendaele " in the popular mind, are much more so because they have been dealt with by popular writers to a greater extent. Many soldiers of all ranks, however, who served in both campaigns, found those of the Somme the worse and the chalk mud of the Somme nearly as tenacious as, and more slippery than, the clay mud of Flanders.

The 8/10th Gordons moved on November 6th to Bresle for a real rest. Their diary records, as one would praise a comfortable hotel bedroom, that the camp was well drained and the tents had floor-boards. To begin with 12 officers and 300 men were detached for work on hutting, but they returned on November 20th, so that the whole battalion could settle down to " solid training ".

Almost simultaneously with the 8/10th and 9th, the four battalions of the Gordons in the 51st Division, the 4th, 5th, 6th and 7th, arrived on the scene. The 6th Battalion, 152nd Brigade, was the first to enter the line, south-east of Hebuterne, on October 4th. It has already been pointed out that the front from the Ancre northwards remained as it had been before July 1st, when the offensive had utterly failed. It has also been stated that the Commander-in-Chief had been contemplating another great offensive astride the Ancre, but that the programme had been modified by rebuffs and delays further south. The 51st Division thus found itself doing nearly six weeks of trench-holding before called on to undertake an attack.

The battalions did some thorough training during this period under the inspiration of the divisional commander, Major-General G. M. Harper. " Uncle " Harper—so called by reason of his white hair, though relatively young—was an exceptional trainer and student of tactics, as well as a vigorous and inspiring leader. He had a touch of showmanship which troops like when it is combined with efficiency. Other divisions, observing his ways, declared that the divisional sign " H.D. " (standing for " Highland Division ") betokened " Harper's Duds ". Had the division been a weak one the joke would have been galling, but since it was well above the average, though not yet as famous as when a German intelligence study put it at the top of the list, the troops could afford to smile.

One feature of Major-General Harper's training was based on the fact that the agricultural population here lived in communities, chiefly owing to a shortage of water supply, which was one of the bugbears of the British Army. Some isolated farmhouses like Mouquet Farm and Eaucourt l'Abbaye became notorious in the battles, but they were rare. Villages were generally fortified by the enemy, and the deep cellars cut in the chalk afforded good cover, which was often actually improved when houses were reduced to rubble above them. The battalions practised the assault on villages on both sides of the line of July 1st and street fighting. They were also trained in dealing with the vast mined dug-outs which the Germans had made on this front, so long inactive.

The 3rd Division was also to take part in the offensive astride the Ancre of the Fifth Army, which took the number instead of the title " Reserve " at the end of October 1916. The division entered the line in the neighbourhood of Beaumont-Hamel (which was within the German front) on October 8th. On the night of the 26th the 1st Gordon Highlanders had to carry out a raid to obtain identifications. This was, according to its own description, "a fiasco". The artillery opened a quarter of an hour " too soon ", at all events that much before the battalion had understood that it would begin. This in itself did not prevent the raid, but the German counter-barrage was so thick that to attempt to penetrate it would have been suicidal.

Two raids were carried out with better fortune by battalions of the regiment in the 51st Division. In that of the 4th Gordons on October 17th, 3 Germans were certainly killed and probably more, but it was impossible to obtain a prisoner. The 7th Gordons took one on the night of the 26th. This man was disarmed by Sergeant Morrison, who had previously killed 4 others and then found himself faced by 2 more, with his magazine empty and no bombs left. Private L. Thompson rushed past him, killed one of the Germans with his entrenching tool, picked up his rifle and shot the second. Germans often said that there was a flaming zeal in " Jocks " in raiding parties which made them very unwelcome troops to face.

After the adjustments called for by the concentration had been completed the front was held by the 63rd (Royal Naval) Division with right on the Ancre marshes, the 51st south-west and south of Beaumont-Hamel, the 2nd as far as a ridge known as the Redan Spur, and the 3rd on a narrow frontage facing Serre. The great offensive formerly projected had been limited owing to the lateness of the season to an attempt to eliminate a German salient astride the Ancre with an arc four and a half miles across, from the neighbourhood of the Amiens-Bapaume road at Le Sars to Serre. The main attack was that of the V Corps west of the Ancre with the four divisions mentioned above. The directions of the 63rd and 2nd Divisions converged, so that if matters went well the 51st, between them, would be pinched out after capturing its second objective, the "Yellow Line", some 1,500 yards deep in the German Defence zone and represented by Frankfort Trench. Even that would be on a very narrow front. The other divisions had further objectives, that of the 63rd including the village of Beaucourt in the Ancre valley.

Though the weather changed for the better after November 8th, the ground remained extremely wet. It was decided that the barrage should move at 100 yards in five minutes instead of three ; Major-General Deverell of the 3rd Division proposed ten minutes, but his superiors considered that would be too slow. Several postponements were made to allow the ground to dry somewhat. Finally, the Army Commander, General Gough, pointed out to G.H.Q. that the postponements were wearing out his troops and demanded that the attack should be fixed for the 13th. Otherwise, he said, he must withdraw the greater part of the troops for a rest. The opinion of the divisional commanders and brigadiers was with him ; they were for "attack or cancellation—no more postponements".

The 51st Division was to attack with the 153rd Brigade on the right and the 152nd on the left. The 153rd had a two-battalion frontage : 7th Gordon Highlanders right, 6th Black Watch left, 5th Gordon Highlanders in support. It was typical of the material development of the war that the fourth battalion of the brigade, the 7th Black Watch, was employed mainly in carrying grenades and stuff needed for consolidation. The brigade had to take only the extreme southern end of Beaumont-Hamel, but a deep gully known as " Y Ravine " formed an awkward obstacle on its front.

The 7th Gordons experienced an abominable approach march. The battalion had only two and a half miles to cover, but its communication trench was deep in mud as sticky as treacle. It took four hours to reach the front line, and this trench was in such a state that the men lay down behind the parados and thus spent the remainder of the night of November 12th. The 5th Gordons were in trenches in rear, a degree better than the front line, but bad enough. The 12th had been foggy all day. Altogether the atmosphere was depressing. Many of the attacks which had broken

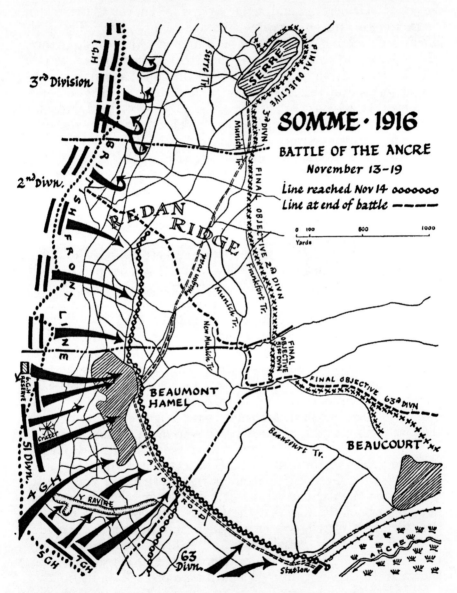

down had been launched under brighter auspices and it must be doubted whether many experienced men felt in their hearts any great confidence in this.

Zero hour was 5.45 a.m. At this hour there would have been little light in any event, but in the fog it was still so dark that the troops had difficulty in seeing their way. Yet the fog favoured the attack, as it nearly always does. In the first place, it allowed the assault battalions to creep forward on to the fringe of the barrage before it began to move, without being observed. In the advance the fog screened the attackers from all but the nearest machineguns. It also prevented the German artillery from observing the signals by fireworks which the enemy normally used with skill and effect.

The right of the 7th Gordons, always hugging the barrage, took line after line of trenches and reached its objective, "Station Road", the sunken road running from Beaumont-Hamel to Beaucourt Station, known as the Green Line. Here there had been no hitch from first to last. Affairs went less smoothly with the left half battalion. It could not keep as close to the barrage, with the consequence that the enemy was able to mount machine guns which held up the greater part of these two companies. In one case the troops were astounded when a machine gun opened fire in enfilade upon them from a trench which they had already cleared. Only when the fighting ended did they realize that it had been brought through a tunnel, one of several, leading from the Y Ravine to nearby trenches. The 5th Gordons were drawn into the fighting, which was slow and stubborn, mainly the work of bombing squads. It took nearly five hours of close fighting to silence the last gun. Towards the end the Germans began to surrender in large numbers.

At divisional headquarters the situation was far from clear, but it was known that there had been a hold-up in Y Ravine. Major-General Harper therefore placed the 4th Gordon Highlanders of the 154th Brigade at the disposal of the 153rd for the purpose of clearing Y Ravine with the grenade. Before the battalion reached the scene the enemy's defence in the ravine had collapsed. It was then ordered to capture the southern end of Beaumont-Hamel within the brigade's objective. This was carried out early in the afternoon with the aid of men of the 5th Battalion, some of whom were carried on by the 4th into Station Road. On arrival there the 4th Gordons learnt that their sister battalion, the 7th, had not only reached this road but had temporarily established itself 250 yards beyond it, capturing 50 Germans. Unfortunately, the delay caused by the German resistance in rear had so far disrupted the attack that this advance proved fruitless, except for the prisoners. The men of the 7th Gordons, with both flanks open, fell back to Station Road.

On the left wing of the 51st Division Brig.-General H. Pelham Burn's 152nd Brigade attacked in the same formation as the 153rd, except that the fourth battalion was not employed as carriers but formed a brigade reserve. This battalion was the 6th Gordon Highlanders. On the front of this brigade the British had blown a mine just outside the German front trench as a prelude to the calamitously unsuccessful attack of July 1st, and the Germans had afterwards fortified the crater. A fresh shaft had been driven below this, and a big charge was exploded at zero hour.

This did great damage and gave the attack a good start.[1] It quickly ran into trouble, however, because the leading battalions could not keep up with the barrage in the mud and came under machine-gun fire when they had lost it. First the support battalion was drawn into the fight ; then the 6th Gordons in brigade reserve were ordered to send up a company to fill a gap. This company forced its way into the German second line, but was there held up by machine-gun fire from the third. Brig.-General Burn then ordered forward two bombing squads to clear the front. By this date German superiority in trench fighting with the grenade was a thing of the past, at all events against trained British bombers of good physique. Those of the 6th Gordons, brilliantly led, quickly opened a way to the German third line by closing in on the obstructing machine guns from both flanks. In the course of this little action they took 53 prisoners.

The advance was then continued into Beaumont-Hamel. An entry was made easily enough, but stubborn work went on well into the afternoon, clearing out the enemy underground. In addition to deep cellars and mined dug-outs, there were in this area certain caves from which limestone for building had been cut. Fanciful tales of the " underground city " of Beaumont-Hamel have been told, but the reality was remarkable enough. In a few cases these underground refuges were of two stories. They were lit by electric light and fitted with bunks, tables and chairs. How many prisoners the 51st Division took here will never be known because a good many were handed over to troops of the 63rd Division, but there were over 2,000 to show at the end of the operations. It is also difficult to apportion prisoners between battalions, which became much intermingled, but the four battalions of the Gordons may justly claim a good half. In most of the Somme fighting booty was represented almost entirely by weapons and ammunition. There were plenty of these here, but other spoil, more practically interesting to the troops, included tinned beef, sardines, cigars and cigarettes, and many thousands of bottles of beer and soda-water. There was also a piano.

---

[1] The German platoon in the crater was naturally wiped out. A party of the 252nd Tunnelling Company took nearly 60 prisoners from a dug-out close by. These men reported that other dug-outs destroyed by the explosion contained similar numbers of Germans.

More bombers of the 6th Gordons assisted the advance to the Green Line, here far east of Station Road. Indeed, the battalion, though allotted only what at first sight seem to be secondary jobs, had played a primary part in the attack. This was the more to its credit because each of the tasks carried out by its detachments was improvised : thought-out minor tactics instead of the rehearsed, tailor-made, drill-tactics so common in trench warfare.

The advance to the final objective would have been possible so far as the 51st Division itself was concerned. The situation was, however, obscure on both flanks. So much was this the case that on the right the 5th Gordons of the 153rd Brigade formed a defensive flank to connect with the left of the 63rd Division in the German front system. The 63rd Division had in fact done finely just further south, where this had been one of the great days in the career of a young lieut.-colonel, B. C. Freyberg, V.C. The advance to the final objective was, therefore, cancelled.

On the left of the 51st the right brigade of the 2nd Division had reached the trench running northward from the eastern edge of Beaumont-Hamel well in advance of the 152nd Brigade, which did not get into the village until the afternoon, and had afterwards consolidated a position beyond it. The left brigade, however, next to the 3rd Division, had failed.

The 3rd Division had a hard task ahead of it. The village of Serre stood on high and commanding ground. Four lines of trenches covered the approach to its western side, at the nearest point 900 yards from the British front line. In addition, it was encircled by a trench and had communication trenches running back to further defensive positions in rear. Serre was the final objective, a deep salient, but one not unfavourable for defensive purposes if once secured.

The 8th Brigade was to attack on the right and the leading battalions were to go through to take Serre. On the left the 76th Brigade had the 10th Royal Welch Fusiliers and 2nd Suffolk in first line, but they were to advance only so far as Serre Trench, the fourth line, and the 1st Gordon Highlanders and the 8th King's Own were to pass through them there.

The attack immediately fell into confusion. The leading battalions found themselves floundering in mud which would seem to have been worse than anywhere on the front north of the Ancre, which is saying a great deal. Delayed also because the wire was insufficiently gapped, they lost the barrage from the start. The support battalions then closed on them and there was much intermingling. Groups of the best men led the way into the German trenches, but co-ordination was lost.

Inevitably, the attack broke down. Parties remained at isolated points during daylight, large numbers returning at 7 p.m. One of the 1st Gordons, which may have represented a fair proportion of the battalion, reached the third line and stayed there till the divisional artillery, unaware that any troops remained so far forward, dropped its barrage on this trench. This party must have been the last, or among the last, to come in. It was a doleful day for the 3rd Division.

November 14th was not a good one for the 51st. Troubles began when the 152nd Brigade, which was to have renewed its attack at 6.20 a.m. received its orders too late to do so. At 7.30 the 7th Argyll and Sutherland Highlanders bombed their way along communication trenches into Munich Trench, half-way to Frankfort Trench, the final objective of the division. Soon after 11 a.m. however, a British heavy battery shelled this trench and the Argylls withdrew from it. During the night two battalions of the Gordons took over the whole of the Green Line, the 4th on the 153rd Brigade front on the right, the 6th on that of the 152nd Brigade on the left. Neither battalion took part in the attack of November 15th by two fresh companies of the Argylls, which ran into their own barrage—the lifts having been shortened to 50 in place of the 100 yards to which the troops were accustomed—after passing Munich Trench, which was unoccupied by the enemy. Only a few parties reached Frankfort Trench. Eventually a trench dug in rear of Munich, known as New Munich Trench, was held. The 51st Division did not take part in the further operations, though it held New Munich Trench until November 17th when its foremost positions were taken over by another division.

The 3rd Division, which had retained no foothold in the enemy's position, did not renew the attack on November 14th. That evening the 1st Gordon Highlanders took over part of the front line, holding it until the 17th when it moved back to Courcelles.

The losses of the regiment in the Battle of the Ancre are not given in the usual detail. In three cases they were low by the standard of the Somme and earlier battles. The 1st Battalion had 141, and this in a division which failed in its attack, the 4th 108, the 5th 244, and the 6th 118. Those of the 7th are not given, but were high.[1]

1		Killed	Wounded	Missing
1st Gordons	Officers			
	Other ranks	141 all ranks and categories		
4th Gordons	Officers	1	6	—
	Other ranks	24	76	1
5th Gordons	Officers	6	8	—
	Other ranks	60	130	40
6th Gordons	Officers	2	1	—
	Other ranks	115 killed and wounded		

The battle was continued until November 19th and resulted in a little more progress on either side of the Ancre. It must be considered a success on balance, though it did not come up to expectations. Ludendorff described the attack of November 13th as " a particularly heavy blow ". He had not believed that on an untouched German front and with the ground in the state in which it was, the British were capable of so deep an advance. The stubborn defence of the Redan Ridge north of Beaumont-Hamel prevented this irruption from being exploited.

The feats of arms of the 63rd Division in the valley of the Ancre and of the 51st Division further north are among the best remembered of the battles of the Somme. The 51st fought without tanks because these could not move. The two which tried to go into action on November 14th were bogged at the German front line. In 1917 and 1918 " Beaumont-Hamel Day " was celebrated, and as far as possible observed as a holiday. It was of course a divisional rather than a regimental occasion. Yet it is a notable and honourable date in the history of the Gordon Highlanders also. No other regiment was represented in the 51st Division by more than two battalions, whereas four of the Gordon Highlanders took part. The regiment probably never fought in less favourable ground conditions. The heavy handicap of the mud made its achievement exceptionally fine. " Beaumont-Hamel " should be a proud name in the regiment.

CHAPTER X

EVERY British division in the theatre but three had been engaged in the Battles of the Somme and one of these three had taken part in the subsidiary attack on Fromelles in July 1916. After the opening of the great offensive no other large-scale operations took place that year. This did not mean, however, that troops on the rest of the front enjoyed a placid existence. On the contrary, they were engaged to exert the greatest possible pressure on the enemy in order to render the reinforcement of the German Somme front as difficult as might be. There can be no doubt that the policy of G.H.Q. was correct in this respect, but it proved trying to the troops.

The strain became progressively heavier. To begin with the majority of the divisions called on to engage in active and aggressive forms of trench warfare were fresh. Then the front was to an ever greater extent held by divisions which had been through the mill, had in some cases not been brought up to establishment, and at best had a large proportion of raw men among their drafts. Their losses in officers and n.c.o.s, often the best of each, was an equal handicap. Artillery support was never strong because the concentration on the battlefield was so great. Ammunition supplies were limited, though the shortage bore no relationship to that of the bad days of 1915 and there was always enough for a minor operation. Cloud gas being plentiful, it was naturally often used, but the installation of cylinders was one of the most arduous tasks of the infantry. Of course, as always, some sectors were preferable to others. Battalions of the Gordons enjoyed those of Armentières and Ploegsteert Wood, south and north of the Lys, though activity was the order and many raids were carried out.

The 3rd Division was so long in the battle or near the battlefield that no more need be said of the 1st Gordon Highlanders during this period. Its experience in the coal-mining area, with billets in places such as Noeux-le-Mines and Mazingarbe, was not unhappy in the circumstances, and it was given some time for training.

The 7th Division also spent much of its time fighting or in rest after fighting. The 2nd Battalion was seldom far from the battlefront until late in September. Its sojourn north of the Lys involved large working-parties. It was not called on to take part in any of the raids and its casualties could hardly have been lower, 24 rank and file wounded during the month of October, though more than twice as many sick were sent to hospital.

The 51st Division carried out a large number of raids. Soon after its arrival in the Armentières area, on August 31st, a big discharge of cylinder gas took place. Each cylinder had to be carried up a communication trench by two men, with another couple accompanying them to act as a relief. Three hundred cylinders would, therefore, demand 1,200 men, about the maximum working strength of two battalions, though the emplacement of such a large number of cylinders might extend over more than one night. The 7th Gordons were almost incredibly lucky on this occasion. They came in for a smart retaliatory bombardment in the small hours of the following morning but did not suffer the loss of a man. No record can be found of a further gas discharge here, but this battalion was carrying cylinders early in September. It must be explained that they were often enough left undischarged for a considerable time, awaiting a favourable wind. The infantry then found them detestable companions in the trenches ; even if they were not hit by the enemy a few would eventually start to leak of their own accord. Therein lay their worst disadvantage, which finally led to their replacement by other means of projecting gas. As means of protection the British " small box respirator " was issued in September and universally welcomed as efficient, light, and handy.

The raids attempted by the battalions of the Gordons achieved only a very limited success, but the failures cost virtually no loss and were due to faulty equipment. Both the 6th and the 7th Battalions sent out raiding parties on the night of September 15th. In the first case, the torpedo, formed as previously described by assembling together short lengths of piping filled with ammonal, proved too weak to be handled in the time available and came apart after being pushed out of reach under the German wire. The other torpedo apparently exploded, but failed to make a gap.

On the following night, that of September 16th, the 5th Gordons mounted an elaborate raid. On this occasion ladders and mats or " blankets " to lay across the wire were used to make an entry. The raiders were divided into a centre party of one officer and 13 other ranks—the real raiding party—with two very small blocking parties to protect the flanks and a covering party of one n.c.o., two ladder men, three blanket men, and a seventh man to carry these men's rifles so that they could form a rear guard in No Man's Land after they had put the ladders and blankets in place. The faces of the raiders were blackened. Fourteen Germans certainly were killed and several more were believed to have been. The raiders had one man slightly wounded. The leader of the centre part, 2nd Lieutenant A. C. Hendry, received the immediate award of the Military Cross. The 6th Battalion tried again on

September 22nd, but had only a half-success. The party could not penetrate the wire but bombed the German trench at three points.

The 15th Division never held a line except on the battlefield of the Somme from the time of its arrival at the end of July. All its time but for two periods of rest was spent there. There is thus nothing to be recorded of the 8/10th and 9th Battalions of the Gordon Highlanders during the Battles of the Somme so far as experience of other fronts is concerned.

After this brief retrospective sketch of trench warfare while the battle was in progress we go on to see what happened to the eight battalions of the Gordon Highlanders during the winter of 1916-17. Part of the story still belongs to the battlefield.

The 1st Battalion in the 3rd Division remained there for some time. Late in November its commanding officer, Colonel S. G. Craufurd, left to command a brigade and was shortly afterwards replaced by Lieut.-Colonel J. L. G. Burnett. It hardly needs to be said that that winter, after all the fighting that had taken place, was uncomfortable in the extreme. The trenches opposite Serre were almost as muddy as ever, and when out of them carrying and working parties, once " practically the whole battalion ", on other occasions up to 300 men, were called for. However, when the battalion came out of the trenches after a spell of four days in mid-December, it recorded that this had been one of the quietest within memory. Returning to the line on the 29th it found and pulled out a man of the battalion relieved who had been stuck in the mud for five hours.

On January 8th, 1917 the 1st Gordons reached Pernois in the Canaples training area near Abbeville. Training lasted a full month, during which there were several moves. It was cold all the time, with up to 12 degrees of frost and generally strong winds. However, in a back area fuel was always to be had—if not always legitimately—and at least there was no mud. Nor had officers to be on the watch for lunatics who in the trenches lit a coke fire in an iron basket, drew the anti-gas curtain to keep out the wind, and were perhaps found in the morning with one man dead and the rest in a stupor, to come to with agonizing and prolonged headaches.

Training over, the 1st Gordons moved with the 3rd Division to the Arras front. It entered the trenches on February 11th and found them in a good state owing to the frost. But, when it took over its front a second time on the night of the 19th, after four days in billets in Arras, the thaw had come and the trenches were everywhere collapsing.

The cessation of fighting on a major scale made it possible for divisions to hold wider fronts and consequently for more to engage

in training. After having done so for a month in January and
early February the battalion then had the whole of March for the
purpose. While it was absent a strong party left behind, consisting
of nearly the whole of C Company, carried out a brilliantly successful raid in a snow-storm. Twenty-one prisoners and a machine
gun were taken and 11 Germans killed. The British casualties
were Captain W. H. S. Grant, the leader of the raid, and 4 other
ranks wounded, all slightly. Raids on such a scale with such
trifling loss on the side of the attackers and loss so heavy for the
raided had been very rare in the past.

The battalion remained in this area until the opening of the
Battle of Arras, in which the 3rd Division took part.

The 2nd Gordon Highlanders combined training with a move
south during the first three weeks of November. On one day, the
11th, the whole division was on the march. On the 21st the 1st
and 2nd Battalions were so close together that numbers of men of
the 2nd were given passes to visit the sister battalion. Next day
they met on the march.

The front taken over by the 7th Division was that on which
the 51st had been engaged and just south of that still held by the
3rd. The diary of the 2nd Gordons, entering the trenches north
of Beaumont-Hamel, described it as " a most irregular front line
in close touch with the Germans ". That of the Germans was the
notorious Munich Trench. Next day comes the inevitable comment on the mud and two days later an equally frequent account
of men being dug out of it is repeated.

At the end of December a new feature appeared in the capture
of exceptionally large numbers of Germans by patrols. The 2nd
Gordons did not share in it until January 2nd, 1917, but then it
was on a large scale. In the early hours of January 2nd a party
of one officer, 4 n.c.o.s, and 25 men blundered into B Company and
were taken. Next morning A Company took an artillery officer and
his orderly, and in the evening B Company got 5 more prisoners.
That made 37. It was unheard of. Fog, the obliteration of
landmarks, and the arrival of different troops in this sector had
something to do with it, but they did not account for the size of
the bigger hauls—two other battalions had picked up 30 prisoners
in four days—or for a marked readiness to surrender on the part of
Germans suddenly confronted by British troops in the darkness.
It cannot be doubted that the incessant pounding and grinding of
the Battles of the Somme was the prime cause.

The British troops took winter in and out of the trenches
philosophically. Early in January the 2nd Gordons heard that
they would shortly move into a back area, pleasant news even in
this season. Then the move was cancelled. The diary records

this without grumbling but with a certain complacency. The cancellation had been made, wrote the keeper of the diary, because the division which was to have carried it out was too raw to hold a front like that of Beaumont-Hamel. However, by January 24th the battalion had reached Terramesnil, in a training area.

The 51st Division remained facing Beaumont-Hamel until relieved by the 7th Division on November 24th. In these few days after the fighting had died down it carried out an immense amount of salvage. The British Army was now setting itself seriously to this task. A much grimmer task was that of the collection of the dead for burial. Besides the bodies of those who had fallen in the recent offensive, there were many skeletons of men who must have belonged to the 4th and 29th Divisions and been killed in the unsuccessful attack of July 1st. Why these bodies had been reduced to skeletons in so short a time does not require explanation. The men of one brigade, the 152nd, buried 669 of these skeletons. The more sensitive men were deeply distressed by this gruesome work.

In his farewell to the division the commander of the V Corps, Lieut.-General E. A. Fanshawe, under whose orders the division had been serving wrote : " It is evident from the newspapers that all the world looks upon the capture of Beaumont-Hamel as one of the greatest feats of arms in the war, and to those who know the ground and the defences it must ever be a marvellously fine per-formance."

It was a change of corps only, not yet goodbye to the battlefield. The division moved almost straight to the Courcelette sector on the other side of the Ancre, taking over from the 4th Canadian Division. The spirit of the men had been good, but this front was a trial too great for it. Major-General Harper, an invincible optimist, said afterwards that he had never seen a man smile east of Pozières. The ground was worse here than at Beaumont-Hamel because it had been the scene of more prolonged fighting. Vegetation had disappeared. So churned was the soil that trenches could not be dug. The foremost garrison of the position lived in shell-holes, sometimes joined together by shallow ditches. Ropes were issued as trench stores, so frequent had burial in the mud become. Illness grew rapidly, and no measures could prevent the increase of " trench foot ".

Rubber thigh-boots were now sufficient for all troops in the trenches, but the tops chafed the men's thighs and these abrasions often festered. Then at last the Gordons and other kilted troops humbled their pride. They had, it will be recalled, earlier gone so far as to exchange their shoes for ammunition boots in bad weather. Now they drew drawers and trousers—which they firmly described as " trews ". It might have been wiser to yield earlier.

Kilts were not suited to the mud of the Somme Battlefield. The 4th and 7th Gordons both mention large sick parades, that of the former consisting of 130 men, and state that swollen feet were the chief ailment. The men became moody and depressed. Whether the film seen by the Gordons after their Christmas dinner cheered them up is not known. It was " The Battle of the Somme ". Highly topical of course, but may it not have been too much so ? [1]

At last, in January 1917, the division escaped from its prison-house of mud. The 4th Gordons note that before entering their buses they changed into kilts. As has been mentioned in describing the experiences of the 7th Division, that January was marked by cold, not wet, the lesser evil, but trying in barns which had been kicked about by many billeters and which there was no labour to repair. The 51st Division records some temperatures lower than those experienced by the 7th, 24 degrees of frost on one night.

It is worth while to set out the items on the training programme of the 5th Gordon Highlanders at Millencourt, omitting dates and times. It shows that the type of warfare had acquired a technique of its own. The subjects are given in the order in which they are set down:

Arms, extended order, and saluting drill ; specialist training for Lewis gunners, battalion bombers, signallers, scouts, and snipers ; cross-country run (for all) ; rifle range, bayonet fighting, grenade throwing ; lectures on tactics, discipline, sanitation, etc.; guard mounting, fire discipline and control, rapid wiring, night patrolling ; siting and consolidation of trenches, map reading ; training for stretcher-bearers ; crossing obstacles.

Besides these subjects, general and special, there were the exercises in which battalions, brigades, and on rare occasions, whole divisions took part. It is pretty comprehensive, but does not include the subject which was about the most important in time of peace : bolt-work, magazine-filling, and rapid firing.

On February 11th the 51st Division relieved the 9th in a region which it previously knew well, the Roclincourt front near Arras, where it had relieved French troops in the spring. Once again the trenches were in a bad state, though not as bad as those on the Somme, while the ground was very much less cut up.

On March 5th the 6th Gordon Highlanders carried out a raid on an exceptionally big scale, the first of several undertaken by the division. These raids were not made merely to obtain identifications or to harass the enemy. They were also preparations for the Battle of Arras. What the enemy could do in the way of fortification in a chalk country had been proved on the Somme.

---

[1] This was the first genuine battle film and is of considerable historical interest.

Here his defences were very strong, all the more so because they were commanded from the crest of Vimy Ridge. The intention was to do damage which could not be repaired before the assault as well as to inflict really heavy loss on the garrison.

The raiding force under the command of Captain Ian G. Fleming numbered 13 officers and 300 men. It was divided into eleven groups which were sub-divided into three or four squads, each group having its own objective. The force was to capture the German first and second lines on a frontage of 485 yards and hold them while the work of destruction was carried out.

Careful preparation was made. Dug-outs discovered on air photographs were transferred to a very large-scale map. Squads were detailed to deal with those located with charges of ammonal to blow in doors, phosphorus bombs, and even Stokes mortar bombs to blow in the dug-outs. The enemy's front was kept under constant observation for ten days. Ladders were made, less for the purpose of getting into trenches than for that of getting out again if they proved deep, as German trenches often were.

After the 51st Division had relieved the French on this ground early in 1916 it had abandoned the French front line as a death-trap and dug a new one in rear of it, which remained as it had been constructed the better part of a year before. The old line could be used for assembly nearer to the enemy than the new, but called for a great deal of hard work. It was by this time hardly more than a trace in the mud and had to be virtually re-dug, as quietly as possible. Then, though the German wire could be cut by artillery—nine lanes were in fact opened—that in front of the old French trench had to be laboriously cut and removed by hand in the dark.

The officers were instructed to obtain S. D. jackets of the type issued to the rank and file. It is astounding to realize today that officers had been allowed to go into action on the Somme wearing the officer's pattern jacket and breeches. The collar and tie, though not worn by other ranks, was a trifling matter. It was the silhouette made by the breeches and skirts of the officer's jacket, longer and wider than those of more recent years, which showed up the officer. In future officers engaged in active operations always dressed in the same clothes as the men.

Zero was 6.10 a.m., the barrage opening at Zero—1. The assault was carried out in two waves, the second passing through the first to take the support line. In some of the most successful raids the enemy was half beaten before the attack went in, but this was not the case here. The defence was stout-hearted and persistent. Bombs were thrown from every occupied dug-out. Mills bombs thrown down the stairways had no effect, and the German grenadiers inside, desperate though their situation was, were not silenced until the ammonal charges had been exploded. Yet after fierce and prolonged fighting the raid was a complete success. The destruction was well up to expectations and 21 prisoners were brought back. How many perished in the dug-outs is unknown, but 66 dead were counted in the trenches. The casualties were not inconsiderable, 54 in all. The raiders did not meet the troops they expected to find, but a Bavarian battalion which had entered the trenches only six hours earlier. Lieut.-Colonel J. Dawson thought that his casualty list would have been very small but for the exceptional quality of these troops. He attributed the success largely to careful arrangements and rehearsals.

The battalion itself was not in the line. The raiders were taken by lorry to rejoin it, and that very afternoon the Commander-in-Chief, with whom was the Third Army Commander, Lieut.-General Sir Edmund Allenby, inspected both, the raiders drawn up separately, at Haute Avesnes. It was sometimes said that Sir Douglas Haig's shyness made him unsympathetic to troops, but he assuredly showed imagination on this occasion. No troops could fail to be impressed, even thrilled, by the honour done them when the Commander-in-Chief, on the eve of a great battle, came to compliment them on their minor operation within a few hours of its taking place.

The 15th Division spent the month of November 1916 out of the line. The 8/10th Gordon Highlanders records that between the 8th and the 20th of the month, when it was " supposed to be training ", it was keeping 12 officers and 300 other ranks at Bécourt for building huts. On November 21st this detachment rejoined. Effective training could then be undertaken, but it lasted only just over a week. Then the division moved to a supporting position on the Somme front and the 8/10th Gordons were set to road cleaning at Albert.

These working parties were a nuisance and a handicap to the infantry. It must be acknowledged, however, that they were of vital importance. The comfort and health of the troops depended on the construction of the hutted camps now springing up like mushrooms in the devastated area and on the repair and maintenance of roads. It is hard to see how the labour of the infantry could have been lightened at this stage. In the later stages of the war it was lightened to some extent by the employment of labour units, but these, largely coloured, could only in a few cases be employed near the firing line.

For the 9th Gordons the problem did not arise. Labour was their role. They often worked when all other battalions were training. Seldom were they more useful than now. On

December 6th the III Corps Commander, Lieut.-General Sir W. P. Pulteney, expressed to the battalion his warm appreciation of the work accomplished in the previous six weeks, despite adverse weather, on roads, railways, and tramways. From the third week in February 1917, after the division had moved to Arras, the work was all concerned with the spring offensive.

While the 15th Division was holding the front at Le Sars, astride the Amiens-Baupaume road, running south-west to north-east as straight as a die, the 8/10th carried out on January 29th, a raid on a scale as great as that of the 6th Battalion on the slope of Vimy Ridge five weeks later. Inside a salient in the German front stood an extraordinary conical mound, the Butte de Warlencourt. It was artificial, the material having been taken from a quarry beside it, apparently to get at good chalk. In height and diameter it measured roughly a hundred yards. It had been temporarily reached during the battle, but now lay 400 yards from the British front line. It afforded a first-class observation post. The mound was believed, and the quarry known, to contain dug-outs and their garrison to be furnished with machine guns. The operation was to be carried out by night, zero hour being 1.45 a.m.

The raid having been entrusted to the Gordons, Lieut.-Colonel J. G. Thom detailed B and D Companies for the task. The raid was well rehearsed and otherwise prepared. As the ground was covered with snow the attackers wore white smocks and white-washed helmets. Black tapes were used for the lines to form up on. The wire was cut by artillery, but there was no preliminary bombardment. The raid differed from that of the 6th Gordons in having a short programme. At Zero+25 the barrage, having lifted to behind the Butte and the quarry, was to return to the German front-line trench.

Three German machine guns, one of them on the lip of the quarry, opened fire. They were, however, relatively ineffective in the dark and were speedily silenced. Otherwise there was not much opposition. Parties moved beyond the Butte to cover the men detailed to tackle it and the dug-outs. One of these parties discovered one post of 6 men, who at once surrendered. On the north side of the Butte several entrances were found. The Highlanders shouted demands for surrender, which brought another dozen prisoners. Where no answer was received Mills grenades and Stokes shells were thrown in. In the quarry also many dug-outs were destroyed.

After the withdrawal the Butte was seen to be flaming. Early next morning there was a big explosion, certainly a bomb-store, and flames rose thirty feet high. And all through the day the Butte continued to smoke.

The prisoners numbered 17 ; the losses 1 officer, 2nd Lieutenant Knowles wounded and missing, 2 other officers slightly wounded, 4 men killed and 10 wounded.   The loss suffered by the enemy is impossible to estimate : it depends on how many men there were in the bombed dug-outs.   The Gordons' estimate, after interrogating prisoners, was fifty to sixty.   The incident closed the record of the division and of the 8/10th Gordons in the Battles of the Somme. It was a highly effective ending.

CHAPTER XI

THE HINDENBURG LINE

IMPATIENCE with the methods and results—as the critics saw them—of the Battles of the Somme had appeared in political circles both in Britain and France. In the former case it was at least partly responsible for the fall of the Asquith Ministry and its replacement by that of Lloyd George. In the latter it resulted in the supersession of the military Commander-in-Chief, General Joffre, by General Nivelle. This brought about a great change in the plans for 1917. Nivelle, on the strength of two fine victories at Verdun in October and December 1916, believed he had a sealed-pattern solution to the problem of turning a break-in to a break-through. He proposed to apply this on a vast scale in Champagne in a tremendous offensive followed by lightning exploitation which would drive the Germans out of France in rout. Thus British operations, which had assumed the highest importance in Joffre's eyes because he saw in them a means of taking the strain off France, became entirely subordinated to French.

Another result of the Somme was the enemy's reaction. The Germans had constructed a vast retrenchment roughly 65 miles long, from south of Arras to east of Soissons. It was a trench system, front and support lines, the most formidable dug in the course of the war. Prefabrication was employed on an un-exampled scale. The trenches were unusually wide, too wide if the designers had been thinking only of the protection of the infantry, but they had in mind also the creation of a tank obstacle. The wire defences were of vast depth. Cutting them by artillery fire was not impossible locally, but to cut them on a very wide front as before the Battles of the Somme was out of the question. This defensive system was known as the "Hindenburg Line" to the British, though practically never to the Germans, who called it the *Siegfried-Stellung*.

Its advantages were a saving of front to be held, the reduction being upwards of thirty miles, which represented an economy of fourteen divisions on an active front, and the substitution of a defensive position based on the tactical features of the country for one where the fighting had come to a stop in the course of the long battle. The Germans, though compelled by the exhaustion of their troops to put their programme into effect sooner than they had intended, had made all the essential preparations. To delay pursuit they had ready a scheme of ruthless devastation of the country. Villages were destroyed by explosives; vast craters were blown at cross-roads. Where roads, as was general, were bordered by trees, these were cut down and made to serve as barriers. And it must be realized that various appliances familiar today which would have enabled such obstacles to be quickly removed had not then been invented. Nearly every large tree had to be sawn through before it could be removed. Wells were filled up or polluted. Booby-traps were left behind, the most deadly being delayed-action bombs in buildings, or cellars left intact. In addition the command was ready to defend suitable rear-guard positions to afford time for the organization of the new front.

Only one battalion of the Gordon Highlanders, the 2nd, was seriously concerned in the operations brought about by this retreat. The episode deserves, however, a certain amount of attention because this was the only occasion when anything like open warfare occurred on the Western Front between 1914 and 1918.

The retreat was to have begun on March 16th, 1917, but the British pressure and German fatigue brought about an evacuation of the salient north of the Ancre at the end of February. The 7th Division, after a rest of over a month, had then just returned to the front, facing Serre, against which the 3rd Division, including the 1st Gordon Highlanders, had dashed itself in vain three months earlier.

On the morning of February 24th patrols found Serre abandoned. Troops had become so used to trench warfare that they could at first hardly believe their eyes, occupied most of the day in patrolling, and by its end had done no more than establish posts south of the ruined village. Next day the advance was slight, the 91st Brigade being held back because it was ahead of the troops on its flanks. On February 26th there was some fighting in Puisieux, but by the following morning the enemy had vanished for the second time. He was found digging in round Bucquoy, rather over a mile to the north, and evidently meant to stand there.

So far the 2nd Gordon Highlanders had been in reserve. On the night of March 2nd its brigade, the 20th, took over the front. Again, however, there was nothing more than patrolling because it was considered that an attack on Bucquoy must await the advance of the divisions on the left of the 7th. As they did not get forward, the 7th Division was withdrawn for a brief rest on March 5th.

The bare record may give the impression of slackness and weak leadership. Let it be admitted that when troops, and officers, sometimes up to an astonishingly high level, found that they could walk about " on top "—the very use of the term suggests that they looked on this as an unknown world—they were nearly always at a loss about what to do. Once again, however, we must keep clear the difference between the equipment of today and that then in use. This was an army dependent on horse transport, but for a relatively small number of lorries of weak performance and slow speed in the third line. The Serre-Puisieux-Bucquoy road was in parts unrecognizable and of no use. The ground had been scourged by shell-fire till it resembled the landscape of the moon. When the guns moved forward they required double teams and every round had to be carried on pack-saddles. The wastage in animals was enormous and was in itself an argument for caution because there was a shortage of both horses and mules and a transport crisis had created a temporary shortage of forage. Vast exertions were needed to get up food and water.

It was in these circumstances that the 7th Division returned to the front and attacked Bucquoy in the early hours of March 14th. The 91st Brigade failed completely with heavy loss. The division was deeply dissatisfied. The brigadier had protested that the wire was uncut and had been supported by Major-General G. de S. Barrow, who had recently succeeded Major-General Watts as divisional commander.

Wire cutting was now resumed, but, as might have been expected, the Germans cleared out before a fresh attack on Bucquoy could be mounted. This time they made a wide and deep withdrawal. Still the 2nd Gordons had not been engaged. Instead they were given the humdrum task of repairing roads at Puisieux and Bucquoy. The enemy was now back in various villages which he intended to use for a time as outposts to the Hindenburg Line, these being represented on the front allotted to the 7th Division by Longatte, Ecoust-St. Mein, and Croisilles, the two former in effect a single village. In addition, small rearguards disputed the approaches to these places, while seeking to avoid becoming seriously engaged.

On March 28th the division began closing in on these outpost villages, but met with a hot reception. The first task allotted to the 2nd Gordons was to deal with a line of posts, containing half a dozen machine guns or more, south of Longatte. The battalion failed to take the two on its front, in the case of one because the platoon detailed for the job could not get into position before dawn. Further efforts on March 29th were no more successful; indeed the whole division was held up. On the 30th the 2nd Gordons were relieved by the 2nd Borders. They at once tried to rush the posts and failed, but secured them after dark.

On April 2nd a full-dress attack was launched. This time the 7th Division had two brigades in line, and other troops were operating on its left. To the 20th Brigade was allotted the objective Longatte-Ecoust: 2nd Gordon Highlanders right, 8th Devonshire centre, 9th Devonshire left. By now the artillery, despite a restricted ammunition supply, had cut numerous lanes in the wire. Some anxiety was felt about an advanced strong point to which the enemy had clung, but he abandoned it when the British barrage fell.

The advance began at 5.15 a.m. The Gordons, advancing on Longatte, veered a little to the right, leaving a gap between themselves and the 8th Devonshire, but they fortunately had two platoons which had been detailed to take the strong point ready to fill the void. Though lanes had been cut, they were not easy to make use of because the defenders trained machine guns on them. The history of the 7th Division describes resistance in Longatte as " desperate ". It was certainly sharp, but the war diary of the Gordons takes a modest line and describes the opposition as typically that of a rear guard. However, the village was not completely cleared until 9 a.m. and the losses were considerable, the Gordons having 6 officers and 92 other ranks killed or wounded and the total of the 20th Brigade being 321. The number of prisoners taken by the Gordons is not given, but the brigade captured 52 men, 14 machine guns and 2 mortars, of which 4 machine guns and the 2 mortars fell to the Gordons. With a little more luck they might have taken some artillery, but it just escaped their clutches. Croisilles had also been taken, and the two villages were consolidated.

On April 3rd the Gordons were relieved and next day withdrew to Logeast Wood, eight miles west of Longatte, with only the protection of some tents, bivouac sheets, and trench shelters against inclement weather, which shortly afterwards produced snow and sleet.

The last operation of the 7th Division, after more than one failure, had been a good one. Few of the attacks on the places which Sir Douglas Haig called in his dispatch " villages and well-wired trenches forming an advanced line of resistance to the Hindenburg Line " had been as strongly or as stoutly resisted.

The advance from Serre to the Hindenburg Line beyond Longatte, Ecoust, and Croisilles had been trying and fairly costly in proportion to the size of the hostile rear guards encountered, but there can be no doubt that it did the troops engaged in it, and not the infantry only, a great deal of good. It broadened their horizon and taught them that warfare in trenches was not the only sort, as was becoming their impression. It might have been more useful still had it lasted longer.

It also opened the eyes of senior officers to deficiencies in minor tactics. Major-General Barrow's appointment as divisional commander had been that of a stop-gap ; he was a cavalryman and returned to his own arm, with which he was to win great distinction in Palestine. Before the attack on the outpost villages he was succeeded by Major-General T. H. Shoubridge. He at once realized that many of the junior officers and n.c.o.s were not at home in the open. They had done well in the attack on Longatte, Ecoust and Croisilles because this was more or less a set piece such as they were used to. Where they had failed had been in long-range patrolling, making use of the features of the ground in daylight, fire control in sub-units, rapid transmission of accurate information, threats to the enemy's flanks and rear when his frontal resistance proved stiff.

Major-General Shoubridge tried to develop these talents. The old handicaps remained: the high losses in battle which made it difficult for a battalion to hold on to the instruction it had received and the amount of time spent on trench work, road work and other fatigues. The first factor was not quite so grave as the casualty figures would suggest, because many sick and wounded returned, a fair proportion of them quickly. The Gordons would appear to have been luckier than many other regiments in getting their own men back. Their war diaries not infrequently comment on the good quality of drafts and state that the majority were old hands and belonged to the regiment. Nevertheless, the personnel of all infantry battalions changed rapidly in this theatre of war.

Moreover, some extremists who wanted all the stress of training to be put on open warfare sinned against common sense. The trenches were there and likely to be for some time to come. They had to be taken or defended by every known skill and appliance. It would have been folly to allow newly-arrived reinforcements to go into action without having acquired as much as possible of the technique of trench warfare. Their success and their lives depended on it. Unless open warfare set in definitely, the object must be to broaden the minds of the troops, especially junior leaders, so that they could acquit themselves well in more than one type of warfare.

CHAPTER XII

AS previously stated, with the advent of General Nivelle and his revision of French plans, less importance was attributed to British operations. What General Nivelle wanted of Sir Douglas Haig was chiefly that he should contain and defeat as many German divisions as possible. Haig decided that he could give Nivelle the maximum of support by attacking in front of Arras, just north of the devastated area of the Somme battlefield. He intended to strike with all his might, and was now better furnished with medium and heavy artillery than when he had opened the Battle of the Somme nine months earlier. He set distant objectives for exploitation of victory. However, if Nivelle's great offensive proved less successful than he hoped, Haig was determined to break off his operations at Arras and open an offensive in the region of Ypres to clear the Belgian coast of the enemy. For the second year he was thinking of the north while he attacked elsewhere to suit the French. However, this time he had at least one objective well worth attaining, the dominating Vimy Ridge.

Like all the major offensives, this required long preparation. One interesting feature of these was the use of the vast caves in the chalk below Arras, formed by quarrying for the rebuilding of the seventeenth-century city. Twenty-five thousand troops could be lodged in them and in a sewer following the ditch of the old fortifications. Two tunnels were pierced up to the front line, 3,000 yards away, lit by electricity and provided with piped water. Further north, where the underground warfare on Vimy Ridge had ended in the defeat of the German miners, a dozen shorter tunnels were dug along which troops could move up to the front line. Apart from the stocking of ammunition and supplies, dumps of road metal were assembled because the only hope of feeding a long advance—twenty-two miles being the distance along the straight national road to Cambrai, a possible objective for exploitation by the Cavalry Corps—lay in quick repair of the roads, especially the Arras-Cambrai, Arras-Douai, and Arras-Lille highways.

The original attack was to be made by fourteen divisions : ten (in three corps) in Sir Edmund Allenby's Third Army ; four against Vimy Ridge in the Canadian Corps, the right wing of Sir Henry Horne's First Army. With the exception of the 2nd Gordon Highlanders, which had been taking part in the pursuit to the Hindenburg Line until a few days before the Battles of Arras opened, the regiment was represented in these assault divisions by all battalions on active service : 1st Battalion in the 3rd Division,

attacking south of the Arras-Cambrai road ; 8/10th Battalion and
9th Battalion (P.) in the 15th Division, with left flank on the
Scarpe, the wide marshy bed of which split the battle-field in two ;

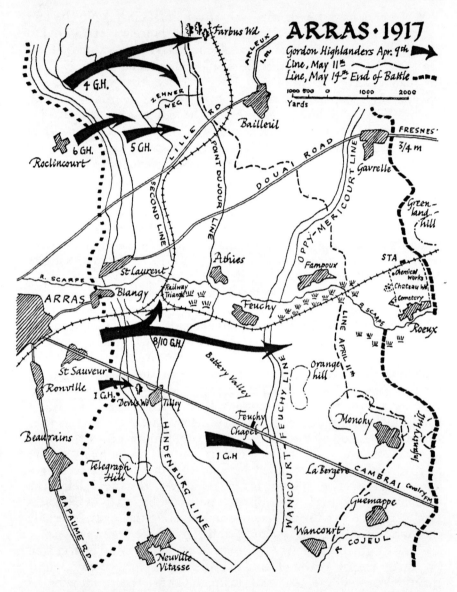

4th, 5th, 6th, and 7th Battalions in the 51st Division, the left-
hand division of the Third Army and next to the Canadians. From
the point of view of the Gordons this was a great occasion, and the
same can be said of Scottish troops in general. In the ten assault
divisions of the Third Army, if we include the London Scottish,

the South African Scottish, and Tyneside Scottish battalions of the Northumberland Fusiliers, there were 44 Scottish infantry battalions out of 120. Arras was an occasion of pride and mourning for Scotland.

The retreat to the Hindenburg Line affected the right flank of the attack because this new system of defence joined the old German front line at Telegraph Hill, two miles south-east of Arras. The right-hand corps attacked later than the rest of the Third Army and in succession from left to right. The 3rd Division on the right of the VI Corps was not touched to as great an extent by the change in the enemy's dispositions. It was, however, attacking on a very narrow front, which was to be doubled on its final objective, known as the Wancourt-Feuchy line. In the first instance it employed only a single battalion because on the right the new German front curved sharply away to the south-east and here the British first objective did not extend to it. This single battalion, attacking on a frontage of 420 yards, with a shallow objective of four lines of trenches close together, was the 1st Gordon Highlanders. It was at this time commanded by Lieut.-Colonel J. L. G. Burnett, one of the best officers produced by the regiment in the course of the war.

The 1st Gordons marched into Arras on May 7th and were lodged that night in the cellars already described. Next day they drew their stock of grenades, shovels and signalling flares. The first company entered one of the tunnels at 6 p.m. and the battalion reached the assembly position without the loss of a man. It was disposed on a two-company front in four lines, the objectives of the first two companies being the first and second German trenches and those of the second two the third and fourth trenches. Parties carrying material for consolidation were found by three platoons of the 8th King's Own.

April often fails to live up to its reputation as a harbinger of spring, but even so the weather of Easter Monday, April 9th, was exceptionally vicious. Squalls of rain, sleet and snow blew up one after another, and night brought a long and heavy snow shower. Sometimes the high west wind blew snow straight into the faces of the German defenders, and then the weather was to the advantage of the attack. On the other hand, assembly trenches and those which formed the objectives were often knee-deep in mud and water.

At 5.30 a.m. the Gordons went forward so fast that the four waves, probably closed up to rather less than the thirty yards distance laid down in the orders, avoided the German artillery barrage altogether. Such fire as there was fell behind them, but the German batteries had been so severely punished that there was not much. Nor was there much resistance left in the German infantry, and the wire was well cut. The fourth objective was reached at 5.50, the scheduled hour. At this time the loss suffered was about sixty, probably the lowest the battalion had ever met with in a great battle. The battalion had behaved with great dash and determination and its light loss so far was a just reward.

The 10th Royal Welch Fusiliers now passed through and cleared Devil's Wood. At 7.30 a.m. the 9th Brigade advanced to the second objective, represented by the ruins of Tilloy-lez-Mofflaines and the trenches of the German second position running through it. There was a slight delay in capturing the village, doubtless due to the bogging of tanks which should have aided the infantry, but it did not prevent the 8th Brigade from taking over the attack, the objective now being the Wancourt-Feuchy line, a mile and a half away. The advance was pushed to within about 600 yards of this system of defence, but was then halted by machine gun fire.

Major-General Deverell issued orders for a renewed attack at 5.30 p.m. by two battalions of the 76th Brigade, the 1st Gordon Highlanders, still virtually intact and comparatively fresh, and the 8th King's Own, which had hardly been engaged. Unhappily, the King's Own did not get the order until 6.35 and, having a mile and a quarter to cover, could not get up in time to assault at 6.45. A second misfortune was a false report that the fortifications at Feuchy Chapel, on the left flank, had been taken. The chapel itself had been taken by the 12th Division, but not the strong outworks of the Wancourt-Feuchy line behind it.

The Gordons attacked alone. They went forward with undiminished gallantry and resolution and carried their assault to within 300 yards of the foremost German trench. They had, however, been steadily raked by enfilade fire from the work beyond Feuchy Chapel, and at this point could no longer endure it. The battalion fell back to the track running from Neuville-Vitasse to the chapel and there dug itself in. Once again, after a successful start, the British had been unable to maintain sufficient balance to overcome a check and drive their advance through to its objective. This was a calamity beyond the ordinary because, though the wire of the Wancourt-Feuchy line was uncut, the German garrison of the trenches had for the most part fled.

North of the Arras-Cambrai road the attack was carried out by the 12th Division. The next further north was the 15th Division, and in the first attack its right-hand battalion was the 8/10th Gordon Highlanders.

The dispositions and methods of the 15th Division differed from those of the 3rd. The leading battalions were to go right through to the second objective, which was here a spur running northward towards the Scarpe valley and known as Observation Ridge. This stage was to be carried out by the 44th and 45th Brigades. Further east the frontage was narrowed by pools and marshes of the Scarpe valley, and the advance to the Wancourt-Feuchy line was to be carried out by the 46th Brigade alone.

Having to advance over 2,000 yards, a distance accounted considerable in trench warfare, the 8/10th Gordon Highlanders was disposed in depth : on a front of two half-companies. Thirty seconds after zero a German s.o.s. signal was fired and the enemy's barrage was almost immediately laid down. The two leading companies followed the British barrage closely and without check to the first objective, as did those of the 9th Black Watch on the left. Here there was a halt of forty minutes for reorganization, during which hardly any shelling had to be faced because the German artillery was withdrawing.

At 7.50 a.m. the advance was resumed by the other two companies. Their experience was very different. Hardly had they moved another 150 yards than they were brought to a dead stop by galling machine-gun fire from a redoubt on the right and the "Railway Triangle" on the left. Both were outside the battalion's frontage. In the case of the redoubt it crossed the 12th Division's boundary and took it. The Triangle was a far more formidable affair, with a base nearly half a mile long and its two other sides embanked, so that it commanded a wide expanse of ground. The Gordons also took part in its capture with the aid of a tank. The two companies then resumed the advance to their objective and reached it without further accident. This was a first-class achievement in view of the interruption of the advance by the resistance in the Railway Triangle. At 2 p.m. the 46th Brigade passed through and advanced on the Wancourt-Feuchy line. Despite uncut wire, it captured the objective on its whole front. On the way it took thirty-one guns in Battery Valley, on the far side of Observation Ridge, but lost heavily from the point-blank fire of some of them. The divisional commander, Major-General McCracken, wanted it to go on, but the corps commander adhered to the original plan of sending a brigade of the 37th Division through to take the dominating village of Monchy-le-Preux. This involved an hour's delay, on top of that caused by the hold-up at the Railway Triangle. The April day was not long enough for the taking of Monchy, though a brigade of the 37th Division did advance 1,000 yards beyond the Wancourt-Feuchy line and consolidated a position on high ground known as Orange Hill.

After fine successes, the Third Army had lost some chances south of the Scarpe on the first day, chances unlikely to be equally good on the morrow. The 15th Division had, however, put to its credit one of the best performances of the day, and the 8/10th Gordon Highlanders had played a fine part in this.

The 9th Gordon Highlanders, the Pioneer battalion of the division, began the day in the cellars in Arras. It was equipped with picks and shovels and with, per company, twenty axes, four saws, twenty wire cutters, whitewashed pickets to mark cross-country tracks for the advance of field artillery batteries, and a drag-rope. At 10.58 it was ordered to begin work on the tracks ; and by about 11.45 one company had started on that to Blangy, the eastern suburb of Arras, and another on a second a little further south. For the first 600 yards the ground was pocked by shell-holes and covered with wire and débris. At 4.30 p.m. Lieut.-Colonel Taylor found the men working hard and well and the supervision excellent. He then went forward and laid out a track from Battery Valley in the direction of Orange Hill, but it could be worked on only up to the east side of the valley that day. The battalion prepared the communications called for by the artillery programme, even though the check to the infantry at the Railway Triangle had caused some delay in starting work.

North of the Scarpe on the XVII Corps front the 4th Division passed through the assault division, the 9th, on the third objective, and captured Fampoux. This was the deepest advance of the day, and the deepest made by any belligerent on the Western Front on a single day since the beginning of trench warfare, a distance of three and a half miles. Further north the 34th Division captured its third objective on the right and in the centre.

The left-hand assault division of the XVII Corps was the 51st. The task was complicated by the fact that the objectives of the 1st Canadian Division on the left did not exactly correspond with its own, so that it had to make two wheels to bring its front level with them.

The attack was to be carried out up to the third objective by the 152nd and 154th Brigades, each with a battalion of the 153rd in support. The 153rd, with the two battalions remaining to it, was later to secure a further objective a maximum distance of only 500 yards ahead.

In the 152nd Brigade the 6th Gordon Highlanders was on the right and the 6th Seaforth Highlanders on the left, supported by the 8th Argyll and Sutherland and the 5th Seaforth Highlanders. The Gordons were fit from training and in good heart, the memory of their wonderfully successful raid in March, partly over the same ground, being fresh in the memory of the men. The battalion was disposed in three double waves, each of five platoons, the sixteenth platoon being organized in three bombing squads. Each wave was to take one of the three lines of trenches in the German front system of defence.

In many cases in this battle the first objective was secured in face of relatively slight resistance and at no great cost. This was not so here. The Germans fought with desperate courage and losses were heavy, but the battalion was at the top of its form in this sort of struggle, and the issue was not in doubt, despite the tremendous explosion of a German mortar-bomb store on the objective, which caused 20 casualties. A chatty prisoner, who said that he had been a head waiter in a London hotel, told his captors that he knew of no troops in rear of the final objective and that if they got this matters would be easy for them. Unfortunately it was not taken on the front of the 152nd Brigade, the support battalions being held up some 600 yards short of it.

On the left the 154th Brigade had the 9th Royal Scots and 4th Seaforths in first line and the 7th Argylls and 4th Gordons in second. In this case the first objective was reached without much difficulty. The two leading companies of the Gordons were sharply checked in front of the second objective. After overcoming hard opposition part of the left company reached it and made contact with the Canadians. The right company, however, was brought to a complete standstill by the enemy's fire. At 9.35 Lieut.-Colonel McClintock ordered the two rear companies to move up and help to take these defences and then to go on to take the third objective on the crest of the ridge, their allotted task. These companies moved at 10 a.m., and the extra impetus did all that was needed. Here, as in many cases, it was a matter of overcoming " island " positions which had deep dug-outs within them. Only by means of these could the Germans hold their first and second systems of defence because the terrific bombardment had bashed in the trenches and the German garrison's sole means of defence was to maintain a few posts close to their shelter. This did not, however, apply to the trenches of the third objective, over three miles from the original British battery positions.

The final advance on the 154th Brigade's front was characterized by a mishap fairly common when a battlefield had been pounded into a featureless desert as was the case here. The 7th Argylls, who had lost their most experienced officers, made a right wheel and veered across the front of the 152nd Brigade—which, as has been seen, was hung up. This battalion ended up in a communication trench named the *Zehner-Weg* which it took to be its objective but which actually ran at right angles to it. The 4th Gordons followed suit, and in their case also got split up. The right company followed the Argylls to the *Zehner-Weg*. The left made a lesser swerve and occupied a communication trench further north. Its left platoon, however, had kept careful touch with the Canadian right flank and was the only part of the brigade front which was not deflected from its true line of advance. It duly entered the front trench of the German third system, but then, finding its right in the air, withdrew.

It has since become clear that these defences, known as the Point du Jour line, could have been had for the asking. A sub-section of the 153rd Machine Gun Company, attached to the 154th Brigade, made its way into the trenches. Its officer made contact with Canadian patrols in Farbus Wood, on the scarped eastern slope of Vimy Ridge, and walked some hundreds of yards along the German front trench, without meeting a soul. Next morning the Germans returned and he had to withdraw. It does not do to give German troops a second chance.

The 5th Gordon Highlanders had been detached from the 153rd Brigade to the 152nd. At 12.15 p.m. the leading companies moved forward in artillery formation and advanced steadily under some long-range machine-gun fire. It found the brigade held up as already recorded, and the trenches in which it sought refuge congested with men. It received orders to attack the Point du Jour line next morning, on the wholly erroneous supposition that north of the *Zehner-Weg* this was already in possession of the 154th Brigade.

The remaining battalion of the Gordon Highlanders, the 7th, stayed in reserve, and its only task was to send up a party of stretcher-bearers.

Only the results of the fighting in divisions containing bat-talions of the Gordon Highlanders have been given, but they afford a pretty fair notion of events in the Third Army front on the opening day of the battle. Up to a point it had been a great success, the greatest so far won by the British, and the casualties of the two armies were about one-tenth of those of the first day of the Somme, with the same number of divisions in the assault. Yet this success would have been far greater and provided far rosier chances of exploitation on the morrow but for accidents, and though these are a part of war they had been too numerous. Now the advance would be faced by reserve divisions which the German Army command had held too far back but were now moving for-ward and in one case had deployed artillery before the fall of darkness.

On April 10th the 1st Gordon Highlanders in the 3rd Division was not employed. It had returned to its own brigade, the 76th, from the 8th. The latter brigade made a successful attack on the untaken Wancourt-Feuchy line and the 37th carried on the advance to within 800 yards of Guémappe and Monchy. The left-hand brigade of this widely-spread division also made an advance of about half a mile between Monchy and the Scarpe. Its left was covered by the 45th Brigade of the 15th Division. The 8/10th Gordon Highlanders, which had spent a night in the snow on its objective of April 9th, was not engaged on the 10th.

North of the Scarpe the confusion was partially rectified, but partially only. The 5th Gordon Highlanders set about obeying the orders received overnight, to capture the Point du Jour line south of the *Zehner-Weg*. Lieut.-Colonel McTaggart was directed to employ only two companies because it was supposed that the 154th Brigade on the left already held that line on its front. Being convinced that this was not so, he put in all four companies and also sent a party of grenadiers along the *Zehner-Weg* to cover his left. No rolling barrage could be provided, but a protective barrage was laid down beyond the objective.

The battalion advanced with great determination, and the defence showed little. It was in consequence possible to cut gaps in the intact German wire. The battalion took all the German defences on the ridge and inflicted considerable loss on the retreating enemy. No touch could, however, be found with the 154th Brigade and constant fire came from the left. There could now be no doubt that Lieut.-Colonel McTaggart had been right. His precautions had been effective and his battalion had responded to his leadership in the finest way.

The muddle on the front of the 154th Brigade was by now becoming a tragi-comedy. The headquarters had not found out during the night that the reports of its troops being on their objective were false. The divisional headquarters was equally in the dark and sent out no orders to capture a position which should have been taken long before because it believed the brigade to be in possesion of it. As late as 9.35 a.m. on April 10th brigade headquarters reported that it was.

When Major-General Harper learnt the truth he sent orders that the objective must be secured by 2 p.m. A first attempt in which the 4th Gordons took part, to bomb a way up the communication trenches failed, largely because it was interfered with by the fire of the British artillery. An attack ordered in the evening led to no advance. At least, however, a line of posts was dug across the crest of the ridge to link with the Canadians. The troops of the 51st Division had distinguished themselves by drive and determination, but no one can pretend that the staff work had been good. A mistake as to their position such as that made by the 7th Argyll and Sutherland and the 4th Gordon Highlanders might have happened with any troops ; but that it should have remained undiscovered for twenty hours by brigade and divisional headquarters showed that something was seriously wrong somewhere.

General Allenby still hoped for big results on April 11th, but the successes gained were limited and the disappointments many. Among them were two attacks by the 76th Brigade, 3rd Division, on Guémappe. In the first of these the 1st Gordon Highlanders was in reserve. In the second it was ordered to advance with the 8th King's Own, but that battalion, dispersed in shell-hole posts, could not be assembled in time. The Gordons were held up by a strong German barrage. This was all new artillery, or nearly so, replacing that which had been virtually destroyed. The German resistance was stiffening. In any case the 1st Gordons were exhausted by exposure. They had been three days in the open in bitter wind and frequent snow and their losses, 13 officers and 263 other ranks killed, wounded, or missing, were far above the average. They now moved back to the underground world of Arras, arriving at 8 a.m. on April 12th in a state of extreme fatigue.

The battalion had started the battle with complete success and made that success look simple by its speed and efficiency. Then, twice in four days, it had been put into hastily-mounted improvised attacks for which the battalion that was to have been its partner could not be assembled and it had, therefore, advanced alone. It had assuredly given of its best.

Further north Monchy-le-Preux was captured by the 37th Division and held against counter-attacks with the aid of the 8th Cavalry Brigade. Tactically, Monchy was a notable gain because it was perched on a knoll dominating the plain ahead. It was, however, a costly prize and the prospect of using it to support a deep advance in the direction of Cambrai was swiftly fading.

The 15th Division strongly supported the capture of Monchy but made no progress in its main task, that of capturing Pelves on the south bank of the Scarpe. The best effort was that of the 8/10th Gordon Highlanders in the afternoon. Having received orders at 3 p.m. to renew the attack, it took advantage of the screen afforded by a long snow shower and gained 600 yards of ground half way between Monchy and the Scarpe. Then the commanding officer, Lieut.-Colonel J. G. Thom, ordered a halt on finding that his battalion was out by itself, with both flanks in air. He was right. Disregard of flanks, which might have been praiseworthy in some cases earlier, was now a deadly risk because the fresh German reserve divisions had arrived in force.

The 15th Division was now relieved by the 17th. The relieving division was held up by traffic blocks and snow so that it could not complete its task until just before dawn on April 12th. Nor could it take over the scattered posts held by various battalions where their advance had been halted. It aligned itself on the Monchy-Fampoux road as a recognizable front. Thus the front north of Monchy was for the most part in rear of that reached on April 10th. The 8/10th Gordons had to fall back 300 yards in order to be relieved. They did not reach Arras until 11.30 a.m. on the 11th, being played in by their own pipes and those of the 9th Battalion. That day the congratulations of Sir Douglas Haig, Sir Edmund Allenby and Sir Aylmer Haldane—Commander-in-Chief, Army commander and Corps commander—were conveyed to them. They had suffered a loss of 253, only 23 less than that of the 1st Battalion.[1]

The 9th Gordon Highlanders (P.) which had on April 10th taken over the construction of a " tramway " in addition to its work on tracks, continued both on the 11th. It was not relieved when the infantry of the 15th Division was withdrawn from the front. The men accepted this as a commonplace. They well knew that their lot was easier than that of the infantry battalions and their losses about a tenth of the average, though when used in an infantry role at Loos they had been very high. On this occasion they had not to lie out on the muddy, snow-swept battlefield and their losses were only 17. They were first-class pioneers, who always worked well and never better than when a battle was in progress. Now they drove their light railway forward at a great pace and laid a boarded track beside the rails. On April 15th they linked it with the German light railway.

North of the Scarpe a little progress was made on the right of the XVII Corps. On the front of the 51st Division there was something like an anti-climax, due to the confusion of the previous day. The division had been ordered to take the left of its original objective, the front of the 154th Brigade, which it had so far failed to secure. In this attack the role of the 4th Gordon Highlanders was to send parties of grenadiers along two communication trenches north of the *Zehner-Weg* to support an attack across the open. The 7th Gordons of the 153rd Brigade prepared a thrust from the right flank to aid it. None of all this was required. The Germans had abandoned the position.

On the night of April 11th the 51st Division was relieved by the 2nd, though not all the battalions left the forward zone till next day. Thus two of the three divisions, the 15th and 51st, in which battalions of the Gordon Highlanders had fought had been withdrawn. The 3rd Division was to come out while the 1st Gordons remained in Arras. The regiment had had its share in both the brilliant successes and the bitter disappointments of the Battle of Arras, but was still not done with it. Moreover, the

[1]	*Killed*	*Wounded*	*Missing*
Officers	4	4	—
Other ranks	47	162	36

2nd Battalion was to take part in the ferocious Battle of Bulle-court, a subsidiary operation officially included in the Battles of Arras. The losses of the 1st, 8/10th, and 9th Battalions have been given. In the 51st Division the 7th Battalion, which was not engaged in an attack and cannot have suffered seriously, does not record its losses. Of the other three battalions in the division the 6th was the heaviest sufferer.[1]

By April 11th Vimy Ridge had been secured, the Third Army alone had captured over 7,000 prisoners and 112 guns, and a number of German divisions had been reduced to shreds. In the light of subsequent knowledge and of past experience it might have been the best policy to shut down the battle at this stage and launch an offensive to clear the coast of Flanders at the earliest possible moment. It is useless to speculate whether Sir Douglas Haig would have done so had he had a free hand—probably not, as there were still some hopeful factors—though it is pretty certain that he would not have carried on the offensive as long as he did. He had not a free hand. His main task was to afford the maximum assistance to the French offensive in Champagne. This was to take place on April 14th, but was postponed until the 16th because bad visibility had hindered observation of fire. In these circum-stances continuation of the British offensive was inevitable. It was a duty owed to the alliance.

[1]		Killed	Wounded	Missing
4th Gordons	Officers	1	6	—
	Other ranks	25	132	10
5th Gordons	Officers	5	1	—
	Other ranks	19	79	1
6th Gordons	Officers	3	12	—
	Other ranks	63	174	—

CHAPTER XIII

ARRAS AND BULLECOURT

ON April 12th progress, including the occupation of Héninel and Wancourt, was made on the right of the Third Army. In the centre an attack on Roeux, on the north bank of the Scarpe, failed. On the left, Canadian and British troops of the First Army completed the capture of the Vimy and Lorette Ridges. On the 13th the Third Army gained no ground, but in front of the First Army the Germans withdrew, to a maximum of four miles from the ridge, from the ground dominated by it and sought refuge in their third line. April 14th was marked by a successful German counter-attack east of Monchy, but the village remained in British hands. Next day the Commander-in-Chief announced his intention to call a halt in order to prepare for a renewed attack on a big scale.

Some fresh divisions were available, but not enough to take the place of all those that had to be rested. Thus the 51st Division, after only forty-eight hours' absence from the front, was brought back to relieve the 9th Division immediately north of the Scarpe. The 7th Gordon Highlanders dug assembly trenches for the coming offensive on April 16th and 17th and found the work very severe, the soil heavy with wet and the German artillery active. Then the battalion was relieved, but only to move to the mediocre shelter of captured trenches. The 15th Division's rest—which, as usual in such cases, did not apply to the artillery, engineers, and pioneers—was longer. The infantry got into Arras and its outskirts on the morning of April 12th and on that of the 19th re-entered the line, this time astride the Cambrai road.

After amendment and postponement the plan emerged as follows: the Third Army was to take the spur beyond the Sensée east of Chérisy; Saint-Rohart Factory, a mile and a quarter east of Guémappe, which was still in German hands; and north of the Scarpe, Greenland Hill, which meant also Roeux and the Chemical Works; the First Army, employing only one division, was to break the Oppy-Méricourt line at Gavrelle. Guémappe and Saint-Rohart Factory concerned the 15th Division, Roeux and the Chemical Works the 51st.

The weather had improved and the ground, though wet still, was less holding than at the beginning of the battle. Thanks to many train-loads of stone and to "tramways"—one, it will be recalled, laid by the 9th Gordons—the ammunition supply was plentiful. On the other hand, the German defence system had been thoroughly reorganized; fresh entrenchments had been dug;

and the heavy losses in guns had been replaced—indeed the number of field guns on the battle front was 30 per cent. higher than on April 9th. And most of the British infantry committed had all too recently gone through the mill and still felt the effects.

Some officers with long experience thought that April 23rd witnessed the hardest fighting of any British offensive since the beginning of the war. Despite the heavy losses and the numerous failures to reach objectives, the majority of the troops were convinced that they had won a victory. They had by no means given up hope of winning another.

During the period of preparation the 8/10th Gordon Highlanders held the front of the 44th Brigade for two days, returning to Arras on April 21st. That afternoon was an occasion unique in the history of the regiment. The bands of the 1st Battalion (3rd Division), 5th and 6th (51st Division), 8/10th and 9th (15th division), played retreat in the Grande Place, now a peaceful spot. That faithful Gordon Highlander, Lieut.-General Sir Aylmer Haldane, commanding the VI Corps, found time to be present. Arras had been close to the front line for two and a half years. It had been constantly shelled and from time to time heavily bombarded, so that a great proportion of it now lay in ruins. The city had not, however, suffered the fate of Ypres and could not be described as having been destroyed. The accommodation below ground was vast, and now that the place was pretty well free from shell fire surviving buildings were being taken into use. It had been cleaned and tidied, needless to say by the exertions of the infantry battalions quartered in it, there being no other labour to be had. As a resting-place in the midst of a great battle it was welcome, far superior to the camps behind the Ypres Salient. It was also invaluable as a meeting-place for the regiment. For the Gordon Highlanders in the First World War it has more associations than any other site. There was within it a genuine if not very comfortable social life. The Gordons were fond of it. Yet the associations include the heavy losses suffered, some of the heaviest of which were, at the period before us, still to come.

April 23rd dawned with mist, thickened by the British barrage and bombardment, especially the smoke shell, to a heavy fog. This was, however, quickly dispersed by wind and sun and the rest of the day was bright and warm.

The 44th Brigade attacked on the right of the 15th Division, its first objective being Guémappe, a tough and so far a defiant one. The 8/10th Gordon Highlanders was in brigade reserve and at this stage employed in carrying ammunition and engineers' stores. This dual function was common. It was hard on the troops em-employed in it and in some cases the fatigue lessened the value of the battalion as a reserve, but it is difficult to see how the practice could have been avoided.

Guémappe, as usual, held up the assault. A two hours' fire fight followed, the men of the 8th Seaforths creeping from trench to trench and shell-hole to shell-hole. Then the enemy gave way and the place was won. But not to be held. The division on the right was counter-attacked and gave way, exposing the Seaforths in Guémappe to terrific enfilade machine gun fire, which eventually caused the battalion to withdraw from the village. The Germans were, however, prevented from re-entering it. The 15th Division was ordered to renew the attack, but for this day the task was modified. Instead of attempting to take the third objective originally laid down, at Saint-Rohart Factory, the division was to confine itself to securing the second, which ran east of a large building with enclosures known as Cavalry Farm, an advance of rather over a mile instead of one of a mile and three quarters. This task was to be simultaneous with that of securing the whole of the first objective. It was allotted to the 46th Brigade, to which the 8/10th Gordons were transferred to act as a reserve.

The 8/10th Gordons got plenty of kicks with no halfpence in this battle. The men constantly stumped forward under heavy burdens, on one occasion Stokes-mortar bombs; they were constantly shelled and suffered serious losses; but they were not put in with a chance to revenge themselves on the enemy. The battle known as the Second Battle of the Scarpe ended on April 24th, though fierce local fighting continued after that date, especially at Cavalry Farm. The 15th Division's second objective was generally attained, but Cavalry Farm itself was untenable by either side. What had been won had been won by sheer grit, individual efforts between the set attacks. The losses of the 8/10th Gordons were exceptionally high for a battalion which had not been engaged in an assault, a total of 153.[1] It had already been recorded that the losses in the early stages numbered 250, making a total of 406 between April 9th and 24th inclusive.

The 9th Gordon Highlanders (P.) wasted much of its time owing to checks suffered by the infantry and confusion in orders. The battalion's first task was to make the Cambrai road passable for horse traffic as far as possible with two companies and employ a third on a boarded track from the road to the division's left flank; the fourth was to be held in reserve. The road was finished to within 750 yards of the start-line that morning and these two companies had withdrawn to the Wancourt-Feuchy line, a mile

	Killed	Wounded	Missing
[1] Officers	4	7	—
Other ranks	11	131	—

in rear, by about 1.30 p.m. Thus three companies were standing by ready for orders; they had brought up transport; and the headquarters was with that of the 45th Brigade so that it could be communicated with immediately.

At 7 p.m. the battalion was informed that two companies would consolidate the front of the 46th Brigade, each working under a field company of the Royal Engineers. However, the order to move did not come till 12.30 a.m. on April 24th. One company started work at 3 a.m. and had to give up at 4 lest it should be caught in the open by dawn. The second failed to find the infantry battalion it was seeking. The delay in issuing the order may well have been inevitable owing to uncertainty about the position in front, but if that was so the companies ought not to have been sent forward at all. Later that day the other two companies did some good work on strong points. On the 25th the battalion dug a communication trench. On the night of the 26th it was ordered to assist consolidation after a local attack on Cavalry Farm. On arrival Major T. MacWhirter, in command of two companies, was informed that posts had been established out in front. He moved forward with a party in patrol formation, but almost at once came into contact with the enemy and was shot down. The other officer present withdrew the party. Counting battalion Lewis gunners who had supported the assault, the losses were 19, including Major MacWhirter wounded and missing.

Lieut.-Colonel Taylor's outspoken report is of interest because it attacks the custom of putting pioneers automatically under the direction of the engineers. He pointed out that on the night of the 23rd practically nothing was done by either. The nights, he said, were not long enough to allow any waste of time; companies should go up to the front line and wait while parties went forward to discover the situation; the senior officers should then decide what would be most useful and do it at once—otherwise it would be too late. He also pointed out that a trench well dug in darkness but rather out of the ideal alignment was far more useful than one hardly begun though ideally aligned. He added that his company commanders were experienced men and in practice little was gained by putting them under the orders of officers commanding field companies. The pioneer company commander's first job should be to establish touch with a senior infantry officer. The Royal Engineers might not have agreed with the argument, but it deserved attention because it was put forward by an experienced and efficient pioneer battalion commander.

The 51st Division's attack north of the Scarpe was carried out by the 154th Brigade on the right and the 153rd on the left. The final objective was the high ground on which stood two copses,

Hausa Wood and Delbar Wood ; Plouvain Station, 600 yards north-west of the village ; and on the left the height known as Greenland Hill. The 154th Brigade appeared to face the hardest task because it had to take the long, straggling village of Roeux and further north the château and its outbuildings, and the Chemical Works, all of which were within the second objective, on its way to the high ground across which the final objective ran.

The Corps Commander, Lieut.-General Sir Charles Fergusson, had some doubt as to whether this final objective were not too distant for a division which had had as hard a time in the battle as the 51st. He proposed that Roeux and the Chemical Works should be the final objective of April 23rd, but this change was not approved.

The 4th Gordon Highlanders was the left front battalion of the 154th Brigade, with the 7th Argyll and Sutherland Highlanders on its right. To describe its action in detail is scarcely possible because the confusion became so great and some sub-units were destroyed. It was indeed a day of tragedy for the battalion. According to its evidence, even the German front line was little damaged by artillery fire and the enemy got his machine guns into action directly the barrage lifted. The infantry of the 51st Division fought like tigers, but suffered terribly.

The leading companies were almost at once held up by flanking fire from south of the Scarpe and frontal fire from Roeux. The men would not give up, but continued to work their way forward in small parties. Their doggedness took them forward into the first objective, short of the Chemical Works, but not on the whole front. The other two companies, which advanced ten minutes later, passed through on the right, but were stopped on the left where their predecessors had failed. One platoon lost direction, veered right, and passed through Roeux, the objective of the 7th Argylls. Shot at from all sides, it made its way out across the open to the first objective. Another party, aided by a tank, entered the Chemical Works, but was shortly afterwards driven out. Two platoons of the right company were lost entirely, no one returning.

In the 153rd Brigade the 7th Gordon Highlanders attacked on the left in first line, the 7th Black Watch being on its right. The 6th Gordon Highlanders, detached from the 152nd Brigade, was in support to the Black Watch. The 7th Gordons had two companies in line which were to take the first and second objectives, one for the third, and one in reserve. The left company reached the first objective and killed a large number of the enemy who continued to resist. The right encountered heavy machine-gun fire and was pinned to the ground, but with the aid of the left company, which bombed to its right, the enemy was finally put to

10

flight. One body, mainly consisting of a single platoon, reached the second objective. The rest of the battalion was brought to a halt between the two objectives, capturing 76 prisoners in the open or in communication trenches.

Meanwhile on the 153rd Brigade's right the 7th Black Watch had failed to take even the first objective. The 6th Gordon Highlanders in its rear, which began its advance in artillery formation, therefore had to deploy before it was intended to. Carrying other troops with it and inclining slightly to its right, it passed through the Chemical Works and took up a position beyond. Then it was the turn of the 7th Gordons on its right to strike another blow. Taking advantage of the confusion into which the enemy had been thrown, Lieutenant Stitt led forward the survivors of two companies on the north bank of the Scarpe. The enemy gave way and were mown down as they retired towards Roeux. Another party from further north tried to cross Stitt's front but ran right into it and gave themselves up. He took 76 prisoners and reported that he was confident he had killed twice as many.

Stitt's companies now advanced to the second objective and reached it despite heavy fire. To consolidate it was out of the question with the force available, so he moved back through Roeux, fell on the most troublesome machine-gun post, and captured gun and team. By now the Germans had fallen back across the ridge. Lieutenant Stitt next went forward with his handful to keep the enemy under observation. At rare intervals Germans appeared on the ridge, but halted and lay flat when fired on. Finally he returned to the objective and waited some three hours for reinforcements which never appeared.

The Germans considered this sector critical. Their troops repeatedly tried to cross Greenland Hill, but were easy target to the artillery and were stopped on each occasion. Further north against Gavrelle, which had been captured by the 63rd Division, they did the same thing, with the same result. The German command was anxious that the British should not progress along the spurs which dominated its next line of defence. A local counter-attack did succeed in recovering the Chemical Works just after sunset. On April 24th there was a lull, apart from some artillery fire, the infantry on both sides being greatly depleted and exhausted to the last degree.

The 51st Division's front ran past the edge of Roeux Wood to Roeux Station, and thence east of the Roeux-Gavrelle road. It had been indeed a fierce and remorseless struggle, in which, though gains of ground had been relatively small, heavy loss had been inflicted on the enemy. Sir Charles Fergusson warmly praised the " splendid work " and the " fine fighting spirit " of the division.

The losses of the Gordon Highlanders make grim reading [1]. The 5th Battalion on this occasion provided only stretcher-bearing parties, and its losses, which are not recorded, are unlikely to have numbered more than about a dozen. The 325 losses suffered by the 4th Battalion must have represented over 50 per cent. of the number in action, and this in a day's battle in which the Army's casualties had not been exceptionally high. Among the officers wounded were those commanding the 4th and 6th Battalions, Lieut.-Colonel S. R. McClintock and Lieut.-Colonel J. Dawson.

The defensive was certainly holding its own. Five days after the battle, on the evening of April 27th, the Germans put in three battalions to recover ground lost north-east of Monchy, at the junction of the 3rd and 12th Divisions. When the 3rd was concerned it fell upon the 8th King's Own and B Company 1st Gordon Highlanders. It was not merely repulsed but routed, at a cost of 3 casualties to B Company.

The French offensive had meanwhile failed. Perhaps the word would not have been used about a battle in which 28,500 prisoners and 187 guns had been captured had it not been a moral defeat. Army and people had counted on a victory which would quickly decide the fate of the war. The disappointment amounted to a terrific blow. Nivelle was removed from his command and a series of mutinies rendered the French Army incapable of offensive action for a long time to come. Thus the British operations, which had been undertaken in support of Nivelle's—and would not otherwise have been undertaken at Arras—assumed a new aspect. The British Commander-in-Chief decided to turn to the plan which, as we have seen, had always been in his mind, that of the offensive of Flanders. However, while the French were still fighting hard he had prepared for one more major offensive at Arras, to be launched on May 3rd. As the French were due to attack again on the 4th he allowed this programme to stand.

The hard-tried and overworked 3rd Division took part in this last major attack of the Arras offensive. Major-General Deverell had kept the 8th and 9th Brigades as fresh as was possible by holding his front with the 76th. There is thus nothing to say about the 1st Gordon Highlanders beyond the fact that it had a spell in the front trenches under heavy shell fire. The attack achieved no marked success except on the front of the Canadian Corps.

[1]		Killed	Wounded	Missing
4th Gordons	Officers	6	10	—
	Other ranks	48	197	64
6th Gordons	Officers	1	11	—
	Other ranks	26	187	28
7th Gordons	Officers	6	4	1
	Other ranks		202 killed, wounded and missing	

The fighting did not die down all at once. Attack and counter-attack succeeded each other for some time, but they were local in type. One incident was the capture of the Chemical Works by the 4th Division, which also reached the centre of Roeux. On the night of May 12th the infantry of the 4th Division was relieved by the 152nd Brigade, which found the rest of the village abandoned and occupied it. On May 15th the enemy carried out a tremendous artillery preparation. Brig.-General H. P. Burn described it as the heaviest hostile bombardment he had experienced in two and a half years. He had placed his troops as far as possible away from buildings, but losses were still heavy and the fire foretold an effort to recover the lost ground. At night troops of the 17th Division were to be relieved north of the railway. Late in the evening the brigadier decided also to relieve his own two heavily-pounded front line battalions by the other two. Of these, the 6th Gordons were to relieve the 5th Seaforths on the right. This relief was delayed by gas shelling.

It was in progress when the Germans struck at 3.45 a.m. on May 16th. Posts east of Roeux were at once overrun, and a body which was at first taken for British got to the middle of the village before it was recognized by the Gordons. It was then dispersed with loss. The enemy thereupon abandoned his effort immediately north of the Scarpe. The 6th Gordon Highlanders had been caught in as awkward a situation as could well be imagined : its head beginning relief ; the rear company, heavily gassed so that some of the men were vomiting, having only just crossed the Scarpe from its camp on the south side. It had done well and played its part in a defence which had completely defeated the German attack.

Further north a company commander of the battalion, Captain Donald Clarke, counter-attacked with his own men and parties of the 5th and 6th Seaforths, drove out German infiltrators and reached the original front up to the southern side of the Chemical Works. He found the occupants of the front line posts in their places, firing on the enemy.

Next the 5th Gordon Highlanders, detached from the 153rd Brigade and put under command of the 152nd, arrived on the scene and was ordered to counter-attack to restore the situation at the Chemical Works and astride the railway. It was given no time to draw grenades or extra ammunition. Attacking with extraordinary gallantry and fresh by comparison with most of the infantry of the division, it regained all the ground lost as far north as the railway, including the Chemical Works, and shot down many Germans as they streamed back. At one moment it had recoiled in face of a fierce barrage but had simply shaken out, waited for another chance, and gone forward again as soon as the fire slackened. This again was a feat worthy of remembrance in the regimental annals.

The 5th Gordons had more work yet to do. North of the railway the British front line (Cupid Trench) remained in German hands. The Gordons were ordered to retake it in conjunction with a battalion of the 17th Division on their left. They had only a few minutes' notice, but they rushed Cupid Trench. Unhappily, the battalion of the 17th Division was too far away when the orders reached it and never got to the scene. This left the left flank of the Gordons open and they abandoned Cupid Trench. Except at this point the German offensive, carried out with energy by a fresh division, had utterly failed.

In a congratulatory message to the 51st Division Sir Charles Fergusson gave special praise to " General Burn and the 152nd Infantry Brigade, whose tenacity and pluck saved an awkward situation ". These words of course covered the 5th Gordons as well as the 6th. The losses of the 5th were very high, 11 officers and 234 other ranks ;[1] those of the 6th, 10 officers and 107 other ranks.

This might well be accounted the end of the Battles of Arras, but the official reckoning includes events of June 1917 and even later. After a pleasant month's rest in the generally beautiful weather of that spring and early summer, the 76th Brigade returned to the front with orders to take Hill 100, now known as Infantry Hill, east of Monchy-le-Preux, on June 14th.

The 1st Gordons attacked on the right. This battalion always moved as fast as it could, though sometimes forced by artillery programmes to go slower than it liked. It believed in getting clear of the German barrage line. This time there was neither British nor German barrage—simply a dash across the open to bring off a surprise, then a curtain of fire to cover the position when captured. The Germans were in fact completely surprised. The first objective was taken on time except for a pocket which was quickly cleared by grenadiers. The Gordons shared a haul of about 150 prisoners. Then the rest of the objective was secured. At 5.30 p.m. the Germans counter-attacked. Artillery and small arms fire broke them, though they got to within 45 yards of the posts.

A second counter-attack by a battalion in the early hours of the 16th regained two outposts on the hill, but the Gordons stuck to the main line. At their third attempt they killed every German

[1]

	Killed	Wounded	Missing
Officers	4	7	—
Other ranks	38	179	17

in one of the posts, but the enemy defiantly held the other. A third counter-attack was launched on June 18th when the 1st Gordons were about to be relieved. It was generally defeated and any ground taken by the enemy, except the post mentioned, was recovered. So the regiment said farewell to this battlefield with a success. It was costly enough, the losses mostly due to artillery fire.[1]

During these great battles a subsidiary attack was carried out by the Fifth Army further south at Bullecourt. Though accounted part of the Battles of Arras it is described separately and out of sequence because outside the main battlefield. The Fifth Army, on the right of the Third, did not possess the resources to give it more than limited aid. This was to take the form of breaching the Hindenburg Line at Bullecourt, near the right flank of the Third Army's attack, and if possible passing the 4th Cavalry Division through to join hands with the Cavalry Corps, which it was hoped would break through on the Third Army front some three miles to the north. The first attack on Bullecourt, in April, ended in failure. The offensive was renewed on May 3rd, the day of the last major effort of the Third Army. The first stage of ferocious fighting left Australian troops with a holding no more than 750 yards long in both trenches of the Hindenburg Line ; on the left Bullecourt remained untaken and two divisions, one Australian and one British, had been used up. The 7th Division, drawn in as early as the evening of May 3rd, had also suffered seriously.

The turn of the 2nd Gordon Highlanders came on May 7th. The objective was a limited one. Attacking from the south-east, the battalion was to secure only a triangle comprising the south-east corner of Bullecourt, but further east it was to take a thousand yards of the front trench of the Hindenburg Line. This would be still far short of establishing touch with the 2nd Australian Division in the holding described above. The Australians proposed to take the intervening 750 yards of trench by a grenade action on a grand scale, bombers and rifle grenadiers being covered by an artillery and mortar barrage.

Lieut.-Colonel P. W. Brown had under his command two companies of the 9th Devonshire, which were to mop up and garrison the first objective when secured—there had been too many cases of trench warfare of parties of determined Germans bobbing up after the assault had passed over them and breaking it by firing into its rear. These companies were to follow his own two leading companies, while the remaining two formed the third wave. The

[1]	Killed	Wounded	Missing
Officers	6	4	—
Other ranks	64	158	27

troops formed up on tapes at 3.15 a.m.   At 3.45 the advance began
behind a rolling barrage.   It was a bright night, with a full moon
now low in the heavens.

The 2nd Gordons had certainly recovered from their exertions
in the pursuit to the Hindenburg Line.   They went forward with
the utmost dash and determination.   Inevitably there was a lot
of German fire—this always had to be faced when operating on a
narrow front against which the enemy's artillery could switch
inward from either flank.   Yet the first objective was taken without
a hitch.   Nearly all the second objective then fell to the rear companies which passed through, but the terrific fire of the Germans
compelled the abandonment of a small proportion on the left
flank.   However, the job was done.   On the extreme right flank,
as the Australians fought their way along the front trench of the
Hindenburg Line, they saw a Highland officer leap on to the parapet.
This was Captain M. L. Gordon.   His action had doubtless been
taken in order to make sure that there was no clash between the
two partners as they came into touch.   Later on he was wounded
and missing.

This was one of the best executed operations of a furious and
at times ghastly battle, with a casualty list of a thousand a day for
a fortnight and a volume of fire which, in relation to the frontage,
can seldom have been surpassed.   The 2nd Gordons took 106
prisoners and 3 machine guns and claimed that they had counted
50 German dead.   Their own losses were 186.[1]   They were relieved at night and on May 8th were visited at Mory by the Fifth
Army Commander, General Sir Hubert Gough, and the V Corps
Commander, Lieut.-General Sir Edward Fanshawe, who congratulated and thanked them.   They had another short spell in
the captured trenches before the 7th Division was relieved.

Taking the Battles of Arras as a whole, we have seen that the
regiment took part in them on a scale never equalled before or
later.   It has been engaged in battles in which success was more
sweeping, but surely in none which do it greater credit.

[1]	Killed	Wounded	Missing
Officers	1	4	2
Other ranks	14	143	22

CHAPTER XIV

AFTER the Battles of Arras had come to an end, the British plan was to clear away the enemy from the Flemish coast. It was the one scheme in which success would turn the German flank instead of merely creating a salient. The capture of Ostend and Zeebrugge would be valuable and was urgently pressed by the Admiralty in view of immense shipping losses from submarines. The allies had agreed to continue the offensive so as not to allow the Germans to recover from their heavy losses. Just before Sir Douglas Haig was to strike his first blow he learnt from the new French Commander-in-Chief, General Pétain, as a military secret, the lamentable state into which most of the French Army had fallen. It made him think twice, because he now realized that, apart from the efforts of a force of picked divisions which was to serve under his orders in the coming battle, he would get little aid from the French. On the other hand, if the Germans found out about the mutinies, the war would end in sheer disaster.

Haig decided to strike the blow. It was the Messines offensive, beginning on June 7th, 1917, which put the British on to the ridge of that name, a spur of the main Ypres Ridge and covering the latter from the south so that no general advance would have been practicable without this preliminary operation. It was wholly successful, a clean-cut victory of a type rare in trench warfare.

The main offensive began on July 31st. Two of the divisions in which battalions of the Gordon Highlanders were serving were engaged on this first day, the 15th and 51st. The troops had been encouraged by the victory of the Messines Ridge and looked forward to this new trial of strength with confidence. The Germans had indeed been scared, but their relief over the fact that they had held Nivelle was more important still, and they had assembled reserves in considerable strength here.

The 15th Division advanced at 3.50 a.m. with its right flank on the Ypres-Roulers railway : 44th Brigade on the right and 46th on the left. The 8/10th Gordon Highlanders was the leading battalion on the right and attacked on a frontage of 350 yards with two companies, each with two platoons in line and two in support. The third company moved in similar formation in rear of the two foremost. The fourth company brought up the rear in artillery formation, and with it moved two machine guns and a Stokes mortar. A company of tanks was allotted to the 44th and 46th Brigades, which had the task of capturing the first and second objectives. On the front of the 8/10th Gordons the second was just over a mile distant from the start-line. It ran across what was called the Frezenberg Ridge, actually only a few feet above the plain. The 45th Brigade, with another company of tanks, was to take the third objective.

The Germans took four minutes to bring down their barrage, by which time the Gordons were clear. The morning was overcast, so that it was still dark, and in this flat and remorselessly bombarded country such landmarks as existed were at first unrecognizable. Apart from the usual machine-gun fire, there was hand-to-hand fighting short of the first objective—one officer, 2nd Lieutenant J. H. C. Grierson, afterwards himself killed, was seen to kill a German with a bayonet. Amid the stumps of a copse known as Wilde Wood the fighting was very sharp. Still, the first objective was secured by 4.25 without serious loss.

The experience was repeated in the advance to the second objective, except that this time the struggle was hotter still. The German system of defence in depth, worked out in the Arras fighting, was being exploited for the first time as a system laid down in advance and the main feature of the tactics. The Gordons met a number of machine-gun posts generally protected by ferro-concrete " pill-boxes ". However, they had practised rushing these in a long spell of rest after the Battles of Arras, and they made no mistake about it now. By 5.55 a.m. the second objective was in their hands.

At 10.18 a.m., after a long pause chiefly needed for the forward movement of artillery, the 45th Brigade passed through. After advancing some 500 yards it was brought to a halt in front of the Gordons, mainly because the 8th Division on the right had been unable to move beyond the second objective. Seeing that the 8th Division was stuck, the right support battalion of the 45th Brigade, the 11th A. and S. Highlanders, dug in on a line facing north-east. Prompt counter-attack was part of the German defence system mentioned above, and the enemy made several attempts to carry this out. On this part of the divisional front he had no success, and the Lewis-gun fire of the Gordons played a big part in breaking up his formations.

In the evening the heavens opened and the rain came down in sheets. For miles around officers, even if sheltered and comfortable, listened to the sound with leaden hearts. It did not require much military knowledge to realize how deadly were likely to be the results on soil spongy by nature and a surface on which the shell-holes were already almost lip-to-lip. In these unpleasant surroundings the Gordons relieved the Argylls at night, with a defensive flank on the Ypres-Roulers railway.

On August 1st heavy rain again fell. After a long period of tension the expected German counter-offensive was launched in strength astride the railway at 3 p.m. On the 15th Division's side it was held, but the left of the 8th Division, already some way in rear, gave ground. The 8/10th Gordons' right, now more in the air than ever, fell back 300 yards. The left maintained its position.

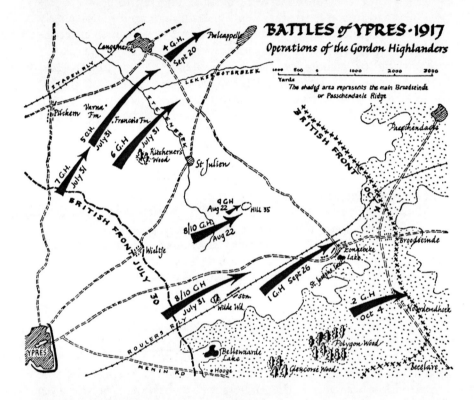

The adjutant, Lieutenant G. P. Geddes, collected every man he could lay his hands on to defend the ruins of Frezenberg station buildings. No runner could be sent back owing to the ferocity of the German machine-gun fire, so he dispatched two pigeons with s.o.s. calls to the artillery.

Despite this resistance and the fire which the left of the Gordons poured into their flank, the Germans pushed on towards the crest of the Frezenberg Ridge. Had they reached it they would have enjoyed wonderful targets because the most advanced British artillery was now east of yesterday's first objective. They never reached it.

A company of the 6th Camerons, sent to the aid of Geddes, now appeared. He concentrated his handful of Gordons and the two bodies together charged the German right flank. Another company joined in from the north-west. The Gordons' right went forward as the enemy flinched. Within a little over an hour of the German success the front had been restored. And it was done largely by the musketry fire in which the British had for the past two years become so weak. On the front of the Gordons the artillery was late in coming into action, but one of the pigeon messages got through, and when the guns did open fire they laid down such a tremendous barrage that the Germans could not withdraw. A number surrendered, some waving white sheets. Seventy-one prisoners were taken; many more who tried to surrender were killed.

Next day the 8/10th Gordons were relieved. It was a pathetically small battalion and completely worn out by three days of heavy strain in heavy mud and almost incessant rain. The losses in the attack had not been particularly high, but they had been more than doubled by the time the battalion withdrew and among the highest suffered by any battalion of the regiment in any offensive battle.[1] Among the wounded was the commanding officer, Lieut.-Colonel J. G. Thom. Lieutenant Geddes received the immediate award of the D.S.O.

The 9th Gordon Highlanders (P.) had worked throughout July on communications. On July 31st, the opening day of the battle, its main task was the clearance of two cross-country tracks, avoiding Ypres. Their first object was to enable the artillery to move forward. Later on these tracks were used by columns of pack-animals carrying food, water, ammunition, and stores. The Germans soon spotted them and shelled them with anything up to 8-in. howitzers. The sights to be seen on them were ugly.

On August 1st, after the weather had broken, the most urgent task became that of laying tracks of duck-boards, vast quantities of which had been prepared. It was these single-file tracks which alone enabled the Battles of Ypres to be fought. Over them every item that reached the front was carried in its last stages; along them every infantryman of the foremost battalions trudged up and down, kept out of the quagmire. Someone, however, had in the first instance to carry the boards up, walking through the quagmire. In this case every length of duckboard, as well as all other material, was carried by the pioneers themselves. They laid 2,620 yards in all. Their losses in four days were 61, but they had also a long sick-list.

The 51st Division front was a featureless waste hard to describe because there was on it virtually nothing with a geographical name,

[1]	Killed	Wounded	Missing
Officers	2	14	—
Other ranks	36	227	59

except that it was half way between Wieltje and Pilckem. It was divided by those of two other divisions from that of the 15th. Its third and final objective was the small but notorious Steenbeek, which was fordable before the rain. By now something was known of the enemy's use of fortified farms, though it could not be ascertained which hid " pill-boxes ". To guard against troops who had captured an objective being fired at a short range from such strong points, all farm buildings within 200 yards of each objective were to be assaulted under a barrage without a pause. The attack was carried out by the 152nd Brigade on the right and the 153rd on the left. Unlike the 15th Division, the 51st employed the two brigades which opened the attack to go right through to the final objective.

The 7th Gordon Highlanders led the attack on the right wing of the 153rd Brigade. The Gordons thought the hour a few minutes too early, but this was no one's fault and on a normal summer morning all would have been for the best. As it was, the four waves went forward without confusion. In front moved the barrage, a wall of fire. For once there was no badly calibrated gun firing short. The troops found they could keep within forty yards of the bursting shells, and no losses from them were reported. " Mon, the barrage was that fine ye could have lighted your pipe at it ! " an enthusiast declared later.

It was, however, not by a long way the mechanical operation which had become too familiar. The German posts distributed in depth between the main successive lines of defence were tackled with skill and in nearly every case put out of action by grenade attacks from the flanks, covered by Lewis-gun fire. Battalions under Major-General Harper's command were at this time among the best-trained on the Western Front, and the 7th Gordons were representative of them. The first objective was taken and its consolidation was well in hand when the battalions to take the second and third passed through.

In this case two battalions of the regiment were engaged : 6th Gordon Highlanders on the right of the 152nd Brigade, and 5th Battalion on the right of the 153rd. The task was now stiffer, and a number of reinforced concrete blockhouses, sometimes within the ruins of farm buildings, spurted death in all directions. One of these, Ascot Cottage, held up the 6th Gordons till someone hailed a tank which quickly decided the action. The battalion took its own section of the second objective and one of its platoons aided the 6th Seaforths to take theirs.

The 153rd Brigade met strong resistance in this phase and overcame it by the skill and courage of sections and even single men. One of these was 2nd-Lieutenant W. B. Maitland of the 5th

Gordons. The company which he commanded was held up by a
machine gun, and he went for it single-handed. Dodging and
jumping from one shell-hole to another, he got round to the flank
and ran into the emplacement. He shot down two men, clubbed
a third with the butt of his rifle, and took the gun. Lieutenant
Maitland, who was wounded soon afterwards, was awarded the
D.S.O.

Then came the advance to the final objective, the phase which
so often went wrong. It did not do so here. As they approached
the Steenbeek, however, the 6th Gordons came under deadly
machine-gun fire from beyond it. Private G. I. McIntosh, armed
with a revolver and a single grenade, waded across the stream under
fire, worked his way from shell-hole to shell-hole, killed two gunners
and wounded a third. He then picked up two light machine guns
and carried them back into the British lines. For this action of
conspicuous gallantry Private McIntosh was awarded the Victoria
Cross. The 6th Gordons took 134 prisoners. The 5th Gordons
took two little fortresses, François Farm and Varna Farm, using
Major-General Harper's " shell-hole " method of attack. In both
cases the enemy surrendered without waiting for the Highlanders
to come to close quarters, at François Farm 4 officers and 140 men.

To sum up, all objectives were taken by the 51st Division in an
attack in which three battalions of the Gordons took part. The
operation had been a complete success, though to meet the determined counter-attacks—all defeated—the front was withdrawn
across the Steenbeek. These three battalions had fought not only
with bravery and determination but also with a skill in minor
tactics altogether out of the common. They were all at the top
of their form. It was now that a German intelligence report
assessed the 51st Division as the most formidable in the British
Army. The losses of the 5th and 6th Gordons were heavy, but
the 7th Battalion, as often the case with troops concerned only
with the first objective, got off much more easily.[1] The remaining
battalion in the division, the 4th, did not move forward on the day
of the attack, but later on held as wet and uncomfortable a front
as could well be imagined on the bank of the Steenbeek.

A story told in the diary of the 6th Gordons may not be an
example of the brightest type of humour, but it stands for a

[1]

		Killed	Wounded	Missing
5th Gordons	Officers	1	7	—
	Other ranks	58	171	7
6th Gordons	Officers	9 killed and wounded		
	Other ranks	296 killed, wounded and missing		
7th Gordons	Officers	—	3	—
	Other ranks	7	70	13

fortitude which staggers the mind.   Marching back in the dark, and needless to say in rain, one man fell into a shell-hole full of water. " He immediately commenced to quack like a duck, and the remainder of the platoon, following his example, quacked their way contentedly back to camp."   It may be added that the camp awaiting them was abominable, the tents standing in mud often knee-deep.

The troops which took part in this attack had had a hard time, but they were in fact lucky by comparison with those who relieved them to take over the offensive.   When it was renewed on August 16th, after almost ceaseless rain for over a fortnight, it was a failure on this part of the front.   The 15th Division, returning to its former sector on the following day, found the position very much as it had left it.   The next attack was launched on the 22nd.

This time the 44th Brigade attacked on the left.   The leading battalions, 8th Seaforths and 7th Camerons, lost almost all officers and men of their front-line companies, which penetrated deeply into the German position but were reduced to shreds by fire from the blockhouses and finished off by counter-attacks.   Within a few minutes one company of the 8/10th Gordons, and later a second, were drawn into the fight.   The blockhouses continued to defy every effort.   Where progress was made much of it was abandoned.

Once long before, at Loos, the 9th Gordon Highlanders (P.) had been given a purely operational role.   The battalion itself was on this occasion ordered to dig a communication trench, but a detachment of six platoons under Captain R. Lumsden was placed under command of the 45th Brigade.   This was to hold a piece of commanding ground, Hill 35, near the left flank.   This feature had been taken on the first day of the offensive, but the Germans had regained it by a counter-attack and compelled the British to withdraw on both sides of it.   It was of great importance to two divisions.

Lieut.-Colonel T. G. Taylor accompanied his detachment, which had under command a Stokes gun of the 44th Trench Mortar Battery and four guns of the 44th Machine-gun Company.   He found that the enemy still held the crest and decided to dig in along the rearward slope.   Sharp losses were suffered in the process but they quickly decreased as the men found cover.   At about 8 a.m. troops of the 61st Division were seen retreating.   Captain Lumsden went across, stopped them, and induced them to dig in. He filled the gap between them and his own position with the mixture of troops generally to be found on a battlefield where things are going ill, using a few of his own as stiffening.   In the evening his machine guns and Lewis guns stopped a German counter-offensive on the crest of Hill 35.   It was not a satisfactory day, but the 9th Gordons had prevented it from being worse.   On this flank of the 15th Division and on the right of the 61st the infantry might, but for the effort of this detachment, have ended the day back on its start-line. The 8/10th Gordons, which had suffered 338 casualties three weeks earlier, now suffered 197, in all about 100 per cent. of the strength which it took into action.[1] The 15th Division returned to the now quiet Arras front.

The British Second Army now took over the principal role from the Fifth. General Sir Herbert Plumer decided to advance along the high ground in three short steps, with intervals long enough to enable guns and supplies to be moved forward. In these battles the Gordon Highlanders were engaged, either in the Second Army or in the supporting attacks of the Fifth on its left.

The first of the battles was fought on September 20th. Whereas the earlier fighting of the First World War had been confined to a very narrow zone and farmers were to be seen at work in the fields within a couple of miles of the enemy, the struggle had now taken on a broader aspect. The enemy used his long-range artillery to good effect. His aircraft bombed the camps behind Ypres and caused many casualties, particularly among horses in the transport lines. He used mustard-gas shell in vast quantities, and in wet, windless weather this would render ground, especially in hollows, dangerous for well over twenty-four hours.

Characteristically, Major-General Harper, commanding the 51st Division, decided to carry out his attack with a single brigade on a front which broadened to about 2,000 yards on the final objective. He was always inclined to attack in thinner formation than was customary, but now he had the additional incentive to doing so that the enemy's defence was largely governed by the amount of shelter in concrete blockhouses available. On the other hand, the enemy would use troops thickly in counter-attacks, so that the divisional commander had to be ready to support his leading troops quickly. Fortunately the ground was drier, though, of course, cut to pieces by fire. September was generally a fine month. The volume of artillery support was enormous. In the creeping barrage the no. 3 guns of each battery fired smoke shell. Special barrages, including 6-in. howitzers and 60-pdrs. were laid beyond it, dwelling on all known strong points and working up and down communication trenches. In the infantry a special body of troops was allotted to each blockhouse, first to take it, then to hold it.

The front faced the village of Poelcappelle, which, however, lay beyond the objective of this offensive, only some 1,200 yards

[1]		Killed	Wounded	Missing
8/10th Gordons	Officers	2	3	—
	Other ranks	22	157	13
9th Gordons	Officers	1	4	—
	Other ranks	16	54	1

deep. The zone was conveniently divided into a two-battalion frontage by a little stream, the Lekkerboterbeek, a tributary of the Steenbeek. The attack was launched at 5.40 a.m. on September 20th.

The leading battalions of the 154th Brigade secured their objectives, but only after heavy fighting. The experience of July 31st was repeated. Platoons or even sections of the Highlanders manoeuvred and fought for every strong point. They met with tenacious and even heroic resistance, but time and time again they prevailed. They lost heavily, however. By the time the 7th Argylls and 4th Gordon Highlanders went through to take the final objective, they had both already been involved in savage fighting for the remains of the German third line east of the Steenbeek and had suffered severely.

Three fortified farms in particular, Malta House, Delta House and Rose House, gave the Gordons great trouble. When the final objective was reached it was found that the six platoons upon it did not average much more than ten men apiece and three officers all told. The battalion also had to deal with a problem often faced by the 51st Division, an open flank. The division on the left was 1,000 yards in rear, and the Gordons had to cover half this distance with their own reserves. The first counter-attacks were made against the company allotted this duty, but both were small and were promptly wiped out. A tank which had progressed along the Poelcappelle road and had then broken down and been abandoned by the crew was put to the best possible use. A corporal kept its 6-pdr. in action ; its Lewis guns were used either from it or from trenches ; its reserve of ammunition was distributed ; and the company commander made it his headquarters.

Another counter-attack at 3 p.m. was stopped. At 5.30 however, the enemy advanced in great strength and so rapidly that the British barrage fell behind him. He was fought and held till the ammunition supply gave out. Then at last the front cracked and men streamed rearwards. For a time it looked as though all that had been won on the left flank was lost. However, officers—in some cases sent up to fill gaps—rallied the troops and led them back. The former front could not be re-established, but a satisfactory one was organized and held. Two days later a major German counter-offensive at this point was routed with heavy loss. The exact casualties of the 4th Gordons are not given but must have exceeded 200.

Six days later, on September 26th, the 3rd Division took part in the second thrust, known as the Battle of Polygon Wood. The 76th Brigade carried out the attack on the right, its left flank on the Ypres-Roulers railway. In its path lay the ruins of Zonnebeke.

The 8th King's Own and the 1st Gordons were the leading battalions, to take the first and second objectives, the second being
represented for the Gordons chiefly by a large group of buildings,
St. Joseph's Institute, on the south-western outskirts of the village.
In contrast to the popular picture of the battlefield, the ground
was at this time dry as powder, and shells threw up clouds of dust.

The advance began in thick mist, which made it difficult to
keep direction. Nevertheless the leading companies of the Gordons were on the first objective within about ten minutes, and the
other two on the second within twenty-five minutes. Yet though
it was all so smooth, it was neither an easy nor a cheaply won
success. Some of their officers thought the 1st Gordons had never
shown a sterner determination. The remaining two battalions
were also successful in taking the final objective.

Under the German system of defence, however, the test was
only half over when the objective was won. The counter-attacks
had still to be met. The enemy shelled the original front and his
own lost ground on the Zonnebeke Ridge very heavily, hour after
hour. The main counter-attack did not approach the British
front till 6.35 p.m. The British now knew of the system of defence
with previously allotted " counter-attack divisions " practised by
the enemy and had prepared long-range barrages and " area shoots "
on every route and at every point where fire was most likely to be
damaging. The artillery hit the German infantry so hard that it
took up to two hours to cover a single kilometre and arrived at
assaulting distance in a maimed state. It must be said that the
enemy came on with wonderful resolution. All but first-class
troops would have been stopped by the thick barrage which faced
them ; these came through here and there, but were then met by
steady musketry fire. The attack lost direction and petered out
by the lake in the park of Zonnebeke Château.

The 1st Gordons, though now in second line, took some part
in repulsing this counter-attack. Captain Alexander, Lieutenant
Campbell, and Lance-Corporal Baird did fine work in helping to
rally troops of the 8th Brigade and the 59th Division retiring on
the right. The enemy tried again on September 27th and again
failed. The Gordons had suffered severely, probably more from
the subsequent bombardment than in the attack itself.[1] The performance of the battalion had been without accident or flaw.

The third thrust, the Battle of Broodseinde Ridge, came on
October 4th, in the same part of the battlefield. The ridge which
was the objective of the 7th Division and the 1st Australian on

[1]	Killed	Wounded	Missing
Officers	2	7	1
Other ranks	37	203	10

its left was followed by the Becelare-Passchendaele road. The first objective was allotted to a single battalion, the 8th Devonshire. The 2nd Border Regiment and 2nd Gordon Highlanders were to take the final objective beyond the crest of the ridge, the biggest nut which they had to crack being the ruined hamlet of Noordemhoek. Next to the Gordons was the 4th Australian Battalion of the 1st Australian Brigade, which had bombed along the Hindenburg Line at Bullecourt to join hands with the Gordons. The brigade commander had made an appeal that they should fight beside his men today.

The Germans put down a barrage behind the leading battalion and partly on the support and reserve companies of the Gordons, an hour before the attack. These were at once closed up and were no longer troubled by it. The battalion moved off behind the 8th Devonshire and advanced 400 yards beyond the start line. The officers had great difficulty in restraining men from going on with the Devonshire, and it afterwards appeared that some had done so. At 8.10 a.m. the barrage moved on again, as the Gordons' war diary puts it, " driving everything before it ". There were unexpectedly large numbers of hostile troops in the area. Their presence—and the early German barrage—was accounted for when prisoners were examined and provided the information that a counter-offensive on their side had been fixed for an hour shortly after that at which the British had attacked. However, the reasoning of Major-General Harper that, in face of such fire-power as the British now possessed, numbers were useless without cover, proved applicable to the front of the 7th Division as it had to his own. The Germans were shaken and gave themselves up readily. Even the garrisons of the blockhouses came out with their hands up. The Gordons alone took 70.

Only when the battalion reached its final objective did it begin to suffer severely. The enemy's shelling was very heavy and almost continuous. At one time it looked as though no rations could be got up, but they arrived in the end. So thoroughly were the Germans beaten in this sector that no counter-attack was launched against the 7th Division. It took a tremendous pounding, however, and in all arms and services. As for the infantry, in most cases its loss was higher from the artillery bombardment than from the machine-gun fire which met the attack. The Gordons remained under furious fire until the night of October 7th, and by then their loss was very high.[1]

There is ample justification for talking of the " horrors " of

[1]	Killed	Wounded	Missing
Officers	3	9	—
Other ranks	50	236	26

the Battles of Ypres, in which men and even a few pack animals were drowned or smothered in the mud, and for criticizing its conduct. It must, however, be realized that these three deliberate advances had all been successful and had perturbed the enemy— the third, just recorded, was accounted one of the " black days " of the German Army. The weather of September had been favourable and the ground had dried remarkably. On the night of October 4th it broke for the second time, though it was a week before the really bad conditions returned. On the 12th Crown Prince Rupprecht wrote in his diary : " Rain, our best ally ! "

The Commander-in-Chief had given up the hope with which he had started of clearing the Flemish coast. A serious mishap in July, when the Germans had captured the Nieuport bridgehead north of the Yser, the delays and repulses due to the August downpour, and other causes, had made this impossible. He intended to halt for the winter on the main Ypres ridge. The Second Army had now secured this up to the Roulers railway, but his intention had been to secure it at Passchendaele and further north. Was he to halt now ? His army commanders, Plumer and Gough, were ready to go on, but would rather have closed down the offensive. He decided to go on. It may be that they were right and he was wrong, but his decision can be defended. The Australian official historian holds that it was the natural one to take after the victories of September. As, however, the weather remained very bad it involved a nightmare for the troops in the final stages.

Only one battalion of the regiment was involved in them, and it looks on the face of it rough luck that it should have been the 2nd, which was the most recently engaged. In fact, the 7th Division was given only ten days' rest and then brought back to take part in a subsidiary attack on the front further to the British right, astride the Menin Road. Its mission was to capture the ruins of the big village of Gheluvelt, scene of terrific fighting, in which the 7th Division had played a prominent part, in 1914. The troops found a tragic change, though they had been prepared for it by the rain which had fallen steadily on their rest billets. Movement off the duckboards was now virtually impossible. The Menin Road looked from a distance like a canal. No one entered the operation of October 26th with good hope of success, and at best it was only subsidiary to the main attack farther north.

The 20th Brigade attacked on the left, astride the Menin Road. The first objective of the division comprised the western corner of Gheluvelt and the ridge on either side of it ; the second ran round the eastern and southern outskirts. On the front of the 20th Brigade the second objective was allotted to the 2nd Gordon Highlanders and 8th Devonshire.

The story is as short as it is tragic.   The 91st Brigade on the 20th's right was completely held up, so that the latter came under enfilade as well as frontal fire.   Small bodies of brave men from this brigade actually entered Gheluvelt, but could not stay there. One battalion after another was cut to pieces by machine-gun and artillery fire.

The complete reversal of the division's fortunes in the last attack, that of October 4th, was due almost entirely to a single factor—mud.   First, the infantry could not keep anywhere near the barrage, though it moved at a crawl.   The result was that the pill-boxes, which had on the previous occasion been rendered virtually innocuous, dominated the battlefield.   In hardly any case was the infantry able to get to close quarters with them and their fire mowed it down as a scythe mows grass.   Secondly, such groups of infantry as did contrive to advance and escape this fire became helpless to defend itself.   Practically all its Lewis guns and the majority of its rifles were jammed or clogged by the mud.

The 2nd Gordons met the worst fate of any.   As they passed through the old front line their ranks were swept away by enfilade fire.   Some men followed the Devonshire into Gheluvelt.   Here and there other parties pushed on a short way.   Generally speaking, however, the battalion was stopped in its tracks.   The attack was a complete failure.   It was the mud that defeated the 20th Brigade.

What remained of the 2nd Gordons was withdrawn that night. Its losses were the heaviest of any unit in the division, though the 8th and 9th Devonshire and 2nd Border Regiment had more missing.[1]   The missing were in but a few cases reported as prisoners of war, so must have been for the most part killed.

So the efforts of the Gordon Highlanders in this great and appalling series of battles ended in disaster.   Yet, taking the offensive as a whole, the regimental record had been an extraordinarily good one.   The ratio of success to failure had been distinctly better than on the Somme in 1916.   The Gordon Highlanders can look back upon consistently fine conduct in some of the most adverse circumstances in which any prolonged offensive was ever conducted.   It remains only to add that early in November the village with the ill-omened name, Passchendaele, was taken.   Having gained virtually the winter line he wanted, Haig closed the offensive on November 10th.   Ten days later he launched the Cambrai offensive.

[1]	Killed	Wounded	Missing
Officers	4	3	5
Other ranks	16	232	86

CHAPTER XV

THE British had conducted three great offensives on the Western Front in 1916 and 1917. The Somme had had very limited strategic objectives and had developed into a battle of attrition. Arras had offered rather greater strategic possibilities, though none was attained but for the capture of Vimy Ridge. Ypres had been planned with the highest strategic aims in view : the capture of the high ground standing above the Flanders plain ; a seaborne landing ; exploitation in the direction of Ghent, only ten miles from the Dutch frontier, which would deprive the enemy of Ostend and Zeebrugge, narrow his submarine activity, and free a wide belt of Belgian territory. We have seen that the performance fell far short of success.

Cambrai held out less strategic promise than Ypres, but more than the Somme or Arras. It was hoped to breach the Hindenburg Line on a wide front by surprise, then to exploit northeastward to the city which gives the battle its name and northward to the marches of the Sensée. The first thrust would dangerously narrow the German communications with the coast. By reaching the Sensée at Oisy-le-Verger the British would be ten miles behind the German front at that latitude and would compel a precipitate retreat with great loss in material.

Cambrai was, however, particularly significant for its tactics. It marked a long step forward in the methods of armour and artillery. Little has been said in this narrative of tanks because the battalions of the Gordon Highlanders had rarely seen them, and never more than one or two. Now for the first time they were to be used as those who had designed them had hoped. They could, it had been proved by experiment, roll out even such dense wire as that of the Hindenburg Line, thus avoiding the long and laborious process of wire-cutting by gun and mortar. This was the first and most important step towards surprise.

A second concerned artillery methods. Hitherto, apart from the wire-cutting and preliminary bombardment, the enemy had always been put on the alert by the registration of the extra artillery moved in to support an offensive. Now the new batteries were to remain silent until zero. When they opened fire it would be by the map and without registration, " predicted " fire as it came to be called long afterwards. But with unregistered fire it was hopeless to expect a rolling barrage of the extreme accuracy recently attained or one to which the infantry could keep so close with safety. There would be no question of lighting one's pipe at the barrage as the Highlander had declared would have been possible at Ypres. Here, however, the tanks came in again. With numbers of them advancing ahead of or in line with the infantry, there

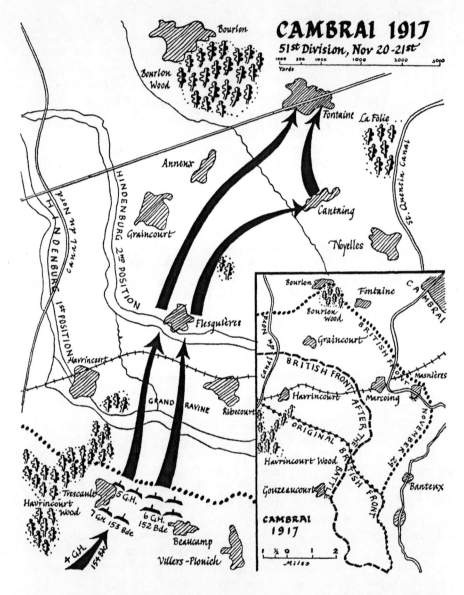

was no need of such extreme precision or for the infantry to keep quite so close to the barrage. In any case barrages were now in great depth, and the artillery present before the reinforcements came in, which of course had registered, could be used to fire the rearward part of the barrage.

The country, rolling chalk downland, rather like Salisbury Plain, but somewhat less poor and bleak, was ideal for manoeuvre and for tanks. The one serious obstacle was the Canal de Saint-Quentin, which wound its way in a general southerly direction from Cambrai.

The 51st Division had some rest and a spell on a front which was almost equally restful by now, south of the Arras battlefield. The training was very thorough and on this occasion devoted to open warfare. The area was part of that devastated by the enemy in his retreat to the Hindenburg Line, so that such training aids as ranges could be provided. Use was also made, however, of a training area where attacks were practised with tanks. The 7th Gordon Highlanders give some details of an exercise which embodied an attack on a reserve German defence system, in which tanks replaced the artillery barrage and the battalion followed 100 to 150 yards in their rear in artillery formation. On November 13th the division celebrated the anniversary of Beaumont-Hamel with a holiday, and that night the sergeants of the 7th Gordons entertained the officers. On November 17th the battalion began its move to the front of the coming offensive.

The 51st Division was attacking from the spur named after the village of Trescault in a northerly direction. In its path the ground sloped gently down to a valley known as the Grand Ravine, at right angles to the line of advance. Thence there was a rather sharper rise to more high ground on which stood the village of Flesquières, round which ran the double-trenched Hindenburg support system. Thereafter the ground fell away to the north in slight undulations, but rose once more in a very prominent and striking knoll, its summit three and a half miles north of Flesquières. It was densely covered with trees and named Bourlon Wood after the village on the northern slope. Bourlon Wood, the better part of a square mile in extent, commanded the northern half of the battlefield, indeed three-fourths of it except in the hollows.

The number of tanks allotted to the divisional front was enormous by comparison with anything hitherto experienced : a battalion of thirty-six to each of the leading brigades, the 152nd on the right and 153rd on the left. Twelve " rovers " were to move 150 yards ahead of the foremost infantry, with the job of flattening the wire. The second wave of thirty-six tanks was to deal with the German trenches up to and including the first objective, which was in the main the Hindenburg front system. The third wave of twenty-four tanks was to form up in the Grand Ravine an hour and a half after zero, with the objective of the Hindenburg support system and the Flesquières Ridge. In the 152nd Brigade the leading battalions were the 8th A. and S. Highlanders and 5th Seaforth, followed by the 6th Gordon Highlanders and 6th Seaforth ; in the 153rd Brigade the 6th Black Watch and 5th Gordon Highlanders led, followed by the 7th Gordon Highlanders and 7th Black Watch. The leading battalions were to capture the first objective. The other four had as successive objectives, first, the Flesquières Ridge, and then a section of the sunken Marcoing-Graincourt road.

The attack was launched at 6.30 a.m. on November 20th. What followed was a wonderful experience for the infantry. Hitherto it had been glad enough to see a single tank turn up at a critical moment and reduce a strong point. Now the tanks swept forward in tremendous strength and cracked open the shell of the German defence. The programme was not without a flaw because a number of tanks got ditched. They could easily get over a narrow trench, but to cross those of the Hindenburg Line they carried on their backs huge fascines, with a device which tipped these forward into the trench. But, big as these fascines or faggots were, they only just sufficed, and they did not do so if the tank approached the trench aslant. In the main, however, the tanks did all, and more than all, that had been hoped of them, which included the demoralization of the defence. Where the worst tank hold-up occurred, at the Hindenburg front system, the infantry showed that it did not rely on them entirely and pushed on boldly and cleverly.

The 5th Gordon Highlanders had a great day. It took the front Hindenburg trench without difficulty, but found itself for the time being bereft of aid from armour. On its right a platoon made its way up a sunken road in which it penetrated the wire, entered the second trench, and began to work its way along this. On the left a platoon waited for the tanks of the second phase which cleared a way through the wire. About 400 prisoners were sent back by the battalion. Its own losses were 6 men killed, 4 officers and 52 men wounded. When the brigade staff asked if it were fit for more Lieut.-Colonel McTaggart had no hesitation in answering yes.

At 7.50 a.m. the four battalions of the 152nd and 153rd Brigades went forward in artillery formation to pass through and take the Hindenburg support system and push on to the Marcoing-Graincourt road. The 6th and 7th Gordons were in line, but each on the right of its brigade, so that they were separated by the 6th Seaforths. The leading wave of the 6th Gordons deployed on the Bapaume-Cambrai railway line. Then the battalion had a perfect view of one of the most dramatic episodes of the war, which has been discussed, adorned, misrepresented, and taken

as a text again and again, so that people who were not born when
it occurred have often heard of it.

As the six tanks moving in front of the battalion reached the
wire in a straggling line, one after the other was knocked out by a
77 mm. battery firing at a range of about 500 yards. It was pretty
cool shooting, and other tanks coming up later were treated in the
same way.

The officers could see the tank tragedy clearly, but they were
unsure about how far they had got before the killing. At first it
looked as though they were through the wire, and if so there must
be lanes. The battalion, therefore, went on. Alas! the tanks
had not got through, with the consequence that the enemy, secure
behind it, got several machine guns into action. In less time than
it takes to tell the story some sixty men were hit. The main body
of the battalion was then withdrawn to cover. One platoon
doubled forward and managed to enter the trench, but found it
so shallow that fire from Flesquières rendered movement along it
impossible.

The famous 51st Division machinery was not working at its
best that day. The 7th Gordons got into the second trench of the
support system but was driven back to the front trench. Even
there it was in a fairly good position to attack and Lieut.-Colonel
A. de L. Long prepared to do so. He was told to hold his hand
because a " set piece " with artillery and tanks was being arranged.
His own evening patrols thought Flesquières was now held only
by a handful of men, snipers for the most part, but they could not
be sure. The obvious remedy, if the place could not be cleared
by the troops on its outskirts, was to thrust in behind it through
the front of one of the flanking divisions which had pushed on.
Darkness prevented this from being done. It is one of the great
disadvantages of an offensive so near the shortest day. This factor
also affected the cavalry which had been milling round trying to
find a way through.

Thus the 51st Division found itself in a situation as unwelcome
as it was unfamiliar. It had often enough had to cover one flank
or both because it had outdistanced other troops. Now it was
hanging back in an extraordinary way. The division on its left
was in Graincourt, a mile and a half to the north. That on the
right was almost equally far ahead. The 51st lay in a sack. The
confusion continued after dark. Several tanks entered the village.
The enemy lay low ; the tanks came out as two platoons of infantry
moved in ; the enemy then fired on those platoons, and they in
turn withdrew.

Whatever the German strength in Flesquières and the trenches
round it, the village was abandoned during the night. At 2.45 a.m.

on November 21st a patrol of the 7th Gordons passed through and reached the second objective. A company was sent forward on its heels and other battalions also closed up. The situation was thus restored, but the delay had handicapped the British in their race for Bourlon Wood with the reinforcements which the Germans at once set in motion. It is only fair to say that the delay might have been longer but for the active patrolling of the 153rd Brigade, especially the 7th Gordons. During the advance to the second objective the 6th Gordons took four guns and howitzers of various calibres and the 7th Gordons eight.

The advance to the final objective, the Marcoing-Graincourt road, was now carried out with little difficulty and at very slight cost. Patrols towards Cantaing, which was protected by a good trench system, found the place strongly held. The 154th Brigade was ordered to break through these trenches, known as the Cantaing line, and capture Fontaine-Notre-Dame, east of Bourlon Wood.

At 6.20 that morning the 4th Gordon Highlanders and 7th Argyll and Sutherland Highlanders of this brigade had moved forward in column of route from the old British front line in which they had spent the night. Again there were signs of the sort of mental paralysis which the hold-up seems to have brought about. The battalion halted an hour before it received word that the way through Flesquières was clear. Then it moved on and made touch with the troops of the 152nd Brigade, from whom it learnt that Cantaing was holding out. At 10.30 the Gordons went through to the attack.

At first they were held up by machine guns and wire and another delay occurred, the front remaining motionless till about noon. At that hour half a dozen tanks appeared and broke into Cantaing. The Gordons went in at top speed behind them. The greater part of the village was quickly taken with many prisoners, but a pocket of Germans put up a splendid resistance, which was not overcome until 3 p.m. The haul of prisoners amounted to nearly 300, while the casualties were exactly 100.

The Argylls were unable to advance on Fontaine simultaneously with the Gordons because of fire from Anneux on their left. When, however, the 62nd Division took this village, the battalion moved on. Fontaine was secured without resistance from within, but under fire from Bourlon Wood. A few civilians were found in the village.

Whether or not Fontaine could be held depended to a large extent upon whether or not Bourlon Wood could be taken. It was not taken on this day, and on November 22nd, after the 4th Gordons had been relieved, the enemy recovered Fontaine after very fierce fighting. Late that night the 152nd Brigade was ordered to

retake it on the morrow, in concert with the capture of Bourlon
Wood by the 40th Division. The fact that the wood was being
attacked simultaneously with the village secured the left flank of
the brigade. The right flank, however, lay completely open and
its defence was to be built up yard by yard as the advance progressed by two other battalions. This measure was an adequate
precaution against a counter-attack, but it did not prevent the
right battalion from being subjected to enfilade fire.

The right battalion was the 6th Gordon Highlanders. Realizing
this fire was likely, the commanding officer, Lieut.-Colonel the
Hon. W. Fraser, asked for a smoke barrage to be laid between
La Folie Wood and Fontaine, but the batteries which had advanced
to support the attack had not brought up ammunition of this
nature. Twelve tanks were allotted to the attack.

The tanks moved off first, at 10.10 a.m. twenty minutes before
the infantry, so that they should enter the village from the flanks
simultaneously with it. Fontaine itself was the objective of the
6th Gordons, and they were to be joined on the high ground north
of it by the 6th Seaforths, which would first of all have captured
the ground lying between Fontaine and Bourlon Wood.

What followed was what Lieut.-Colonel Fraser had feared.
The battalion was raked by fire from La Folie Wood. Frontal
fire met it from a number of houses in Fontaine and it was finally
brought to a halt. The tanks were not by any means as dominant
as in the surprise of the first day. Some were put out of action
by direct hits. The tank crews were ready to accept their luck in
this respect, but they were made very cautious by a new method of
defence. The Germans were beginning to make fairly large issues
of an effective armour-piercing bullet, which at short range drilled
holes in the tanks and kept velocity enough to kill inside them.

The Germans fared no better when they counter-attacked from
the east and north-east over open, rolling ground. The blast of
fire which met them was so fierce that their venture never really
got started. In the afternoon another bid was made to take
Fontaine, this time by the 5th Seaforths, from the south-east corner of Bourlon Wood, held by the 40th Division. One hundred
men of the 6th Gordons and two companies of the 8th Argylls were
to support this operation on the flank as soon as it developed. In
fact, it never did develop. Any chance of its success was ruined
by the fact that the 40th Division gave way before a counter-
attack in Bourlon Wood. The terrific German barrage supporting
this knocked out several tanks, and without them there seemed
no prospect of taking a stoutly built village which had not been
subjected to heavy bombardment. The enterprise was, therefore,
called off.

Lieut.-Colonel Fraser's comment was that insufficient time for reconnaissance had been given, that at this stage there was insufficient shell, especially smoke. He also considered that the original attack should have been made from Bourlon Wood as soon as enough of it had been cleared, with only a small holding attack from the south. The battalion marched back to Flesquières, which it reached about 3 a.m. on November 24th. The men were very tired. They were also sad at heart. Their losses had been heavy, though far less so than in some other battles.[1] The root cause of their depression lay elsewhere. It was disappointment that things had not gone better on the 22nd and 23rd. The youngest soldier among them had not only been thrilled by the early success of the Battle of Cambrai but had felt that this marked a new era and that open warfare was once again on the horizon. Hence disappointment was in some ways sharper than if one of the trench-to-trench attacks had been held up by the enemy before it had made any progress.

The great German counter-offensive can be mentioned only briefly because the regiment was not concerned in it. It was a major operation, improvised in haste and carried out with troops rushed to the battlefield. As such it must be accounted a brilliant feat. On the southern flank it was a great success, the Germans actually breaking through the original British front and penetrating far beyond it. On the northern flank, however, though some ground was recovered, the attack was generally held and the British gunners had one of the days of their lives tackling wave after wave of German infantry swarming southward over the open country between Bourlon Wood and the Canal du Nord. Ludendorff had hoped to destroy all the British divisions in the Cambrai salient, but, far from accomplishing this, he had to bring the counter-offensive to an end by the third day.

On the British side hard-tried divisions had to be relieved as speedily as possible. On the very day of the counter-offensive the 51st Division was ordered to return to the scene, and that evening its leading battalions were in trains, their transport marching. By December 2nd the 51st Division had relieved the 56th on the British left flank, partly on ground won in the battle, partly on the original front. The British Commander-in-Chief decided to reduce the salient in which his forces stood and on the 3rd ordered

---

[1] The 6th Gordon Highlanders does not give its losses in its two engagements separately, but lumps together all those suffered in the month of November 1917. They are as follows :

	Killed	Wounded	Missing
Officers	3	8	—
Other ranks	22	166	—

a withdrawal to a good line, including Flesquières and a section of the Hindenburg line. Little time was given for demolitions, but the 5th Gordons report that they made the abandoned front as uncomfortable as possible. In particular, communication trenches were filled in. The division remained in this sector.

It need hardly be said that the Battle of Cambrai was a landmark. It pointed the way to the final stages of the First World War and indeed more clearly still to the tactics of the second. It was the great dress rehearsal of the armoured fighting vehicle. It had also some strictly contemporary significance which was on the whole disquieting. The British infantry had adapted itself to fighting with armour and was likely to be extremely successful on the offensive in conjunction with it. It was, however, already apparent that Cambrai was likely to be the last major British offensive for a considerable time. The collapse of Russia, the Bolshevik Government's demand for an armistice (October 21st, 1917) and the cessation of hostilities on the Eastern Front (December 2nd) were followed by the meeting of delegates of the belligerents at Brest Litovsk to negotiate terms of peace (December 22nd). The Germans did not need to await the signature of a dictated peace treaty to begin sending divisions to France as fast as trains would carry them. By March 21st 44 divisions had arrived in the west. On the other hand, eleven British and French divisions went to Italy between the beginning of November and mid-December in consequence of the Italy disaster at Caporetto. The success of German strategy is illustrated by the fact that, as the allied divisions moved to the aid of the Italians, the seven German divisions which had aided the Austrians to win at Caporetto and drive the Italians back to the Piave were moving, or getting ready to move, to France. A great German offensive in the west in 1918 therefore appeared almost certain.

Despite the fact that the defensive had been in the ascendant since the autumn of 1914, this was a prospect which could not be regarded without some misgiving. The young and gallant British infantry had shown weak places when facing the Cambrai counter-offensive. If the Germans struck at all it would be with tremendous force. Should we be able to stand the shock ? Few Britons besides the Commander-in-Chief knew the straits to which the French Army had been reduced, but he must have felt still more anxious about its powers of resistance.

The account of the battle of Cambrai is concerned only with the doings of the four Territorial battalions of the Gordon Highlanders, 4th, 5th, 6th, and 7th. It is fitting that this chapter should close with a tribute to them and their division, the 51st, in the year 1917. In the great offensives of Ypres, Arras, and

Cambrai, practically every objective set had been taken. There had been some confusion on Vimy Ridge and again at Flesquières, but the achievement had been nevertheless remarkable. The diaries of these battalions are not all equally well kept and in some cases are written by one individual for a short period only, but in every case they bear witness to the growth of tactical skill, despite losses. In a year in which many disappointments were encountered the record of the Territorials of the Gordon Highlanders is matter for honest pride.

CHAPTER XVI

FOR most of the B.E.F. the early part of the year 1918 was quiet and uneventful. In two respects, however, both unpleasant, the Germans were aggressive. Night bombing from the air, a feature of the Battles of Ypres, though not a very important one, increased considerably during the winter. In some sectors it became so heavy and frequent that troops could no longer be assembled for entertainment and both concert parties and cinema shows had to be abandoned. This was the case with the 51st Division, which remained on the Cambrai battlefield. Rather later the enemy staged a number of artillery bombardments with mustard gas, British losses being serious in some instances.

The British worked on their defences as the likelihood of a German offensive changed to certainty. They had adopted, in part borrowed from the Germans, a system of defence in depth. This comprised a " forward zone ", which included a front and an intermediate system, and a " battle zone ", perhaps two miles, or rather more, in rear. Both the intermediate system of the forward zone and the " battle zone " contained redoubts wired and sited for all-round defence. Their object was to allow time for reserves to reach the scene, but their effect was to tie down and immobilize too large a proportion of the infantry.

This now numbered only nine battalions per division. Despite the protests of the Army Council, the War Cabinet had insisted on the reduction and on that of pioneer battalions to three companies. The battalions rendered redundant were to be used for drafting and were for the most part temporarily formed into " entrenching battalions " ; sometimes two weak battalions made up one entrenching battalion. In a few cases battalions of proven merit were transferred to other divisions.

This was the fate that overtook the 5th Gordon Highlanders, which was ordered to join the 61st Division. It was a sad moment. The 5th Battalion had always belonged to the Highland Division. It had not even been temporarily separated from it like the 4th and 6th, which had come out in advance of the division. On January 31st, 1918, the 5th Battalion was inspected by Major-General Harper, who expressed his deep regret at its departure and said that he would always look upon it as a detachment of his division. The battalion gave him three rousing cheers before marching off the parade ground. On February 2nd, when it left the divisional area, the 6th and 7th Black Watch and the 7th Gordon Highlanders lined the route with bands playing and cheered it as it passed. It joined the 183rd Brigade of the 61st Division on a front not long taken over from the French, a short way north of Saint-Quentin.

Major-General Harper was unaware when he bade the 5th Gordons farewell that he himself was within a few weeks also to leave the 51st Division, with which he had become so deeply identified. He was promoted to the command of a corps in March and succeeded by Major-General G. T. C. Carter-Campbell. "Uncle" Harper should not be forgotten by the Gordon Highlanders. Four of the regiment's battalions, its total active Territorial representation, served under his orders for a long period, two and a half years in the case of two of them, and their high state of efficiency, the credit in which they were everywhere held, owed a good deal to his leadership.

The 7th Division was one of those sent to Italy. The 2nd Gordon Highlanders began the long journey on November 19th, 1917. It travelled in two halves, by different routes : the left half, which entrained first, by Chambéry, Turin, Novara, and Mantua ; the right half by Avignon, Marseille, Nice, Piacenza, and Mantua. They did not unite again until November 29th. The journey had been tedious, but it was a novelty to the men, who also, so the right half's diary avers, took an interest in the scenery. They were warmly welcomed, but the Italians looked " depressed ", as well they might at the moment. The 7th Division was, to begin with, held in reserve in the region of Treviso, south of the new front on the Piave.

" Being Christmas Day ", records the Gordons' diary of December 25th, and it being uncertain whether or not the division would be in the line on December 31st, the men had their festival dinners on the earlier date. This function went off well, but later on three men " had trouble with the Italians ". The diary adds : " The Italians were entirely to blame." It may have been so. Officers and sergeants were able to bring the New Year in in Highland fashion. The career of the 2nd Gordon Highlanders in Italy must be set down later.

At the opening of the German March offensive the distribution of the battalions was as follows, from right to left : 5th Gordons, in the 61st Division, north of Saint-Quentin ; 4th, 6th and 7th Gordons, in the 51st Division, on the Bapaume-Cambrai road ; 1st Gordons, in the 3rd Division, south-east of Arras, left wing at Guémappe ; 8/10th and 9th Gordons, in the 15th Division, east-south-east of Arras, with centre at Monchy. The 15th Division was thus next door to the 3rd to the north, and at one moment of the battle the 1st and 8/10th Battalions fought side by side. All the battalions in France were involved in the German offensive.

By March 10th the British G.H.Q. intelligence had decided that the attack was imminent and that it would extend from the Scarpe (Arras) to the Omignon (Saint-Quentin). Actually, it was to extend a few miles further south, to the Oise, and an improvised attack was launched north of the Scarpe a week after the first stroke on March 21st.

On the 61st Division front the 5th Gordon Highlanders was disposed in depth in the forward zone, with battalion headquarters and one company in a redoubt named after the village of Fresnoy-le-Petit. The night of March 20th was foggy, and at 4.30 a.m. on the 21st visibility was limited to a few yards. At 4.40, with a tremendous crash what was perhaps the greatest artillery and mortar bombardment began. Yet the fire on the Gordons is reported to have been only gradually worked up. The density of falling shells of all calibres was, however, tremendous, and the fire was most scientifically applied. This was the front of the German army commanded by General von Hutier, the victor at Riga over the Russians and an artist in quick penetration, who had brought with him the famous gunner, Colonel Bruchmüller, aptly nick-named " Durchbruch Müller " (Break-through Miller). In the forward zone some battalions had a majority of their men killed, wounded, buried by the heavy trench-mortar bombs, or at best dazed before the infantry attack. As for infantry, it must in fairness be pointed out that the 61st Division stood on a front attacked in far greater strength than the other three divisions in which battalions of the Gordon Highlanders were serving. The Germans massed forty-three divisions against the twelve of Gough's Fifth Army and nineteen divisions against the fourteen of Byng's Third Army.

There is little to be said of the fate of the 5th Gordons except that they were overrun and thereafter existed only as a handful of survivors of the shock, in addition to what was known as " Echelon B ", the party, strong in officers and n.c.o.s, kept back at the transport lines, transport men and cooks, and such officers and men as rejoined from leave. At 12.30 p.m., the 183rd Brigade headquarters received a message from the commanding officer, Lieut.-Colonel M. F. McTaggart, that his redoubt was surrounded and that he feared he would be unable to hold out for long. Soon afterwards, about 1.30 p.m., the defence was swamped by an overwhelming tide. The number of survivors who managed to get back to brigade headquarters was not more than thirty.

One incident on the front of the 61st Division will live in the annals of the Gordon Highlanders as long as the regiment itself, though it concerned none of the battalions serving on the Western Front. Lieutenant A. E. Ker, 3rd Gordon Highlanders, was attached to the 61st Machine Gun Battalion. With a single Vickers gun, he and his sergeant, with some help from wounded men of the detachment, held up a strong force of the enemy until his ammunition was exhausted. The Germans then worked round to his rear and attacked with bomb and bayonet. Lieutenant Ker and the sergeant actually drove off several attacks with no other weapons than their revolvers. Then, in one hand-to-hand encounter, they captured a German rifle and some ammunition. The party was exhausted by lack of food as well as by the strain of the fight, and both officer and sergeant were suffering from the effects of mustard gas. Nevertheless, they held out for three hours, till rushed by large numbers. They had played a leading part in holding up over 500 of the enemy. Lieutenant Ker was awarded the Victoria Cross, one of the four gained by the Gordon Highlanders in the First World War.

The 61st Division held its battle zone, and left it on March 22nd only when ordered back to the " army line ". Again it was ordered back, in consequence of German progress elsewhere, this time to the line of the Somme, and the handful of the 5th Gordons was posted at the bridge at Voyennes. On the 24th, being now sixty strong, it took part in a counter-attack against German troops who had crossed the Somme at Bethencourt, fighting under the orders of the regimental sergeant-major because no officers remained. This effort met with success at first, but the force engaged was too weak to have any chance of altering the situation for more than a matter of minutes.

On March 26th, the 183rd Brigade was formed into a composite battalion. To this the 5th Gordons, with the survivors of March 21st and the 2nd Echelon now united, contributed one company. On the 27th this battalion was in reserve behind the junction of the British and the French forces which had taken over the southern half of the battle front. Next day it was put into the first wave of a counter-attack on Lamotte, thirteen miles east of Amiens on the Roman road running through Villers-Bretonneux. Exhausted though the troops were, they advanced a mile and a half over flat country and got within 200 yards of the objective. There, however, the counter-attack broke down. The force was withdrawn to Marcelcave, and the Gordons company was not again engaged.

The division was relieved, but perforce kept fairly near the front. The 5th Gordons managed to do a little training, but their fighting strength increased very slowly. The blow they had been dealt was deadly. Every officer with the fighting part of the battalion, a total of 24, had been killed, wounded, or captured. Among the captured was the commanding officer, Lieut.-Colonel McTaggart. Few officers not belonging to the regiment commanded any of its battalions on active service. Lieut.-Colonel McTaggart was a cavalryman, 5th Royal Irish Lancers. He had commanded the battalion capably for the better part of three years, with a break of a couple of months due to a wound. The losses of the rank and file numbered 560, of whom 446 were missing. It must be borne in mind that by 1918 the number of men employed by the brigade or division on various guard and administrative duties had become considerable, so that this figure represents virtually the whole fighting strength.

The 51st Division, astride the Bapaume-Cambrai road, had the 154th Brigade on the right, the 152nd in the centre, and the 153rd on the left. The division formed part of the IV Corps, now commanded by the former divisional commander, Lieut.-General Sir Montague Harper. Here the Germans did not make a full-dress assault along the whole front but, after a tremendous bombardment which crushed its defenders, forced their way up the Louverval valley in the centre of the division. The right of the 154th Brigade, held by the 4th Gordon Highlanders, was not engaged on March 21st.

The 6th Gordon Highlanders, on the right of the 152nd Brigade, had a desperate day. The enemy's thrust along the Louverval valley turned the battalion's left flank, and soon Germans, headed by men with flame-throwers, pressed along the trenches and in the open from Boursies, driving all before them, as these weapons so often did. The Gordons made them pay a heavy price, but could not hold them. A hastily organized counter-attack failed. The battalion then formed a defensive flank south of Doignies, in the battle zone.

On the 153rd Brigade front the front battalions, 7th and 6th Black Watch, suffered a disaster. The enemy made another break-through on the front of the division on the left up the valley next to that of Louverval. He then fought his way behind their forward zone garrisons (two and a half companies each) and swallowed them up. Finally—an example of brilliant leadership—he attacked across the spur dividing the two valleys and linked his two holdings together. By about noon he had taken Louverval.

The 7th Gordon Highlanders was in brigade reserve at Beugny, a demolished village over six miles from the German front line but plastered by high-velocity guns from soon after 5 a.m. At 7.54 the battalion was ordered to send two and a half companies to the rear trench of the battle zone. This position was taken up with hardly any loss, despite very heavy shelling, and was subsequently reinforced till the whole battalion was upon it, or just in rear of it. The trench was a good one and the wire was intact. The enemy's scouts showed themselves only 300 yards in front, but no serious attempt was made to force this line of defence in the Gordons' sector and no further progress was made against the 51st Division.

During the night the front was reorganized and strengthened by the 57th Brigade (19th Division), which had been put at Major-General Carter-Campbell's disposal, coming in on the left of the 154th, south-west of Doignies. The 152nd Brigade continued the line to the Bapaume-Cambrai road. The 153rd Brigade, now consisting of the 7th Gordons and small remnants of the two Black Watch battalions, continued to hold the rear trench of the battle zone—known as the Beaumetz-Morchies line.

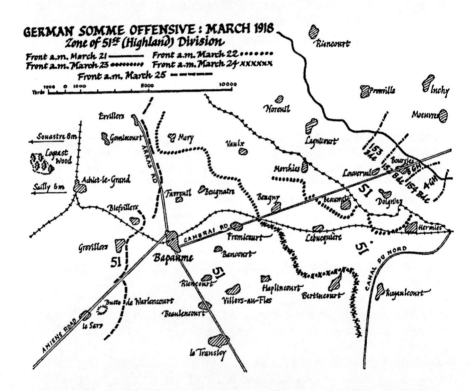

It has been mentioned that the 4th Gordon Highlanders had not been attacked on March 21st. The reason was that it stood on the northern flank of the so-called " Flesquières salient "— representing the remaining gains of the Battle of Cambrai—which the Germans were drenching with gas shell but did not intend to attack with infantry. At 1.30 a.m. on March 22nd the battalion, hopelessly isolated where it stood, was ordered back to the battle zone north of the village of Hermies. Even now it was further advanced than any other troops of the division, and the only battalion in the foremost trench of the battle zone.

Hardly had it taken up its new front than a tremendous German bombardment began. Fortunately, it was directed mainly on Hermies, which was not occupied either by the Gordons or the troops of the division on their right. At 10 a.m. the German infantry advanced in strength. The right of the Gordons began to give way, but was rallied and kept under control. The enemy kept up the pressure and about 1.30 p.m. widened a gap on the Gordons' right, but this was not a very serious matter.

The Germans strove to make progress all through the day, but the 51st Division did not yield another foot of ground before 5 p.m. One German attack ended in disaster. The fire of the German heavy howitzers fell short, whereupon some 200 of the enemy ran forward and gave themselves up to the 153rd Brigade. We know from a German narrative that those who ran back were burning with rage and were with difficulty restrained from attacking the gunners. The 7th Gordons records that six attacks in all were beaten off.

There had, however, been a breach in the 6th Division's front on the right, which resulted in the 7th Gordon Highlanders being outflanked and forced southward as far as the Bapaume-Cambrai road. The fighting here was very hot. Lieut.-Colonel A. de L. Long turned out all available men of battalion headquarters to thicken the defence. Again the enemy was checked, after suffering very heavy loss from both artillery and machine-gun fire. The brigade diary notes that he seemed to have " lost his zest ", but that, on the other hand, the defence at this point had been fought to a finish. A flank was established between the Bapaume-Cambrai road and Beaumetz and held until after dark.

During the night of March 22nd the remnant of the 153rd Brigade, together with the 6th Gordons of the 152nd, was withdrawn to Fremicourt, two and a quarter miles east of Bapaume. The 7th Gordons at this time numbered 8 officers and about 100 other ranks. The 6th had not lost quite so heavily. Major-General Carter-Campbell had received orders to withdraw the remainder of the infantry to Bancourt, south-west of Fremicourt, at nightfall on March 23rd. As, however, he had also been warned that a further withdrawal of the whole corps front was probable and feared that it might be forced to fall back earlier than its commander intended, he made preparations to get his troops out in daylight. No battalion of the Gordons was engaged in this day's fighting, the 6th and 7th being at Fremicourt as stated, and the 4th being held in reserve to the 154th Brigade near Lebucquière, whence it was later in the day moved to Bancourt. The other two battalions of the 154th Brigade, after fighting all day, did not rejoin the 51st Division until the small hours of March 24th.

Hitherto the ground yielded by the Third Army had been trifling in comparison with that lost by the Fifth. The Germans had been foiled in their aim of pinching out the Flesquières salient and the troops holding it had been withdrawn. By remaining in it too long, however, they had lost touch with the left flank of the Fifth Army on their right. The Germans soon found the gap, in the morning 5,000 yards wide, and quickly increased it. This was the main reason why March 24th was so bad a day for the Third Army, though the Germans made a big contribution to the success which they achieved by attacking as well as outflanking it.

Once more the 51st Division found itself in the front line, and after its right had been enfiladed itself received orders to withdraw. The 6th Gordons were heavily involved in this movement. Their adventures are hard to unravel, but what can be made of them is enough to illustrate the extraordinary confusion which was beginning to prevail. Brigades were attached to divisions other than their own ; battalions passed from one brigade to another. Communications forward of brigade headquarters, sometimes of divisional, could generally be kept going only by messenger or the personal visits of commanders and staff officers, with the result that orders constantly arrived too late to be acted on or did not arrive at all. Troops were ordered to hold " at all costs " positions already lost or the holding of which involved them in almost certain destruction. In these circumstances brigadiers and battalion commanders did what seemed best, and it is to their credit and that of their troops that, if they did not stop the enemy, they continued to cause him heavy loss.

The very weak 6th Gordons began the day attached to the 56th Brigade of the 19th Division and under command of one of its battalions. In the general withdrawal in consequence of the enemy's progress on the right it reached Riencourt, where the G.O.C. 154th Brigade laid hands upon it and placed it in reserve to his brigade. Next it was deployed astride the Bapaume-Péronne road to cover the withdrawal of troops of the 17th Division. These soon made their appearance, but, to the dismay of the handful of troops through whom they were to pass, they were making no effort to help themselves by fighting a rear-guard action. Almost immediately after they had passed through the men of the Gordons began to follow them. The company on the road itself, however, kept the enemy out of Le Transloy. The Germans were actually marching in fours, a sign that they were not greatly troubling themselves about the defence. The 4th Gordons in their turn covered the withdrawal of the 6th.

In the course of the afternoon and evening the infantry of the 51st Division was withdrawn to a position over two miles south-west of Bapaume and 2,000 yards in rear of the 19th Division but extending further south. By next morning the three brigades were disposed as they had been on March 21st : 154th on right, 152nd in centre, 153rd on left. The right flank was near the Butte de Warlencourt. They were back now in the heart of the Somme battlefield of 1916.

March 24th had indeed been a day of disaster. Hitherto the right of the Third Army had been giving ground by the hundred yards. Here it had lost six miles—and more further south. The abandonment of Bapaume was a serious matter because it was an important road centre. Nor, in view of the state of the troops, did the future prospects look good. For the first time they were becoming depressed. Still influenced by the traditions of trench warfare, all they could understand, they, poor souls, had got it into their heads that they were retiring upon an immensely strong line on which they would find a line of fresh divisions. Now they were beginning to realize that there were no such divisions and no such line.

The 4th Gordons was in the centre of the 154th Brigade, which had all three battalions in line ; the 6th Gordons on the right of the 152nd Brigade ; and the 7th Gordons in reserve to the 153rd Brigade. The morning of March 25th was quiet so far as the division was concerned. Then the Germans, simultaneously forcing a way through on the right and driving back the 19th Division by frontal attack, came up against the Highlanders' front. His frontal advance was held up. The 7th Gordons, moved up into the brigade firing line, had in their possession a single Vickers machine gun, without a tripod. The moment the troops of the 19th Division in front had vanished this was brought into action with tremendous effect. The Germans, thinking that the British were all on the run and not expecting to find a support position, 2,000 yards in rear of those whom they had dispersed, were caught in thick closed-up waves and shot down in great numbers. Then, as happened over and over again in this stage of the fighting, the communication system gave out. Artillery support there was none because the artillery had been blocked on the road by runaways.

The pressure on the right flank of the division where the 4th Gordons were engaged was even more deadly because it came from the flank as well as the front. The Gordons, on ground a little higher than that over which the enemy was advancing, maintained their position until 1.30 p.m., when they began to give way. Rallied every now and then, they made something of a rear-guard action in the direction of Miraumont. Finally they were withdrawn to Sailly-au-Bois behind the newly arrived 62nd Division.

The 6th Gordons on the right of the 152nd Brigade in the

centre of the line were holding their front steadily when the commanding officer, Lieut.-Colonel Thom, learnt from officers of the
154th Brigade on his right that the front was turned and that they
would have to draw back. He ordered one of his companies to
keep touch with them, but they moved too fast and far for that to
be possible. The other two companies in the line hung on for
another quarter of an hour. He did his best to form a new front
on the high ground east of Irles, but—always candid in his reports
—states that no other troops would stand and that he could not
make his own men do so alone.

In the retreat of the 153rd Brigade on the left after the fine
initial defence the 7th Gordons cannot be distinguished from
other troops. At this stage there were no longer battalions, or
even remnants of them, but groups of men who were controlled as
well as might be by any officer available. In the case of this
brigade the commander, Brig.-General A. T. Beckwith, who had
ridden up and prolonged the resistance at Loupart Wood, stayed
with the troops and exercised a strong influence over them. He
spread out his staff and actually led men who were withdrawing
through Pys back to the ridge east of it, where they continued the
defence. His troops were, however, considerably scattered by
nightfall. Like Lieut.-Colonel Thom he reported that the troops
of other divisions had set a bad example ; he saw no signs of panic,
but sensed an atmosphere of apathy and a desire to get back *somewhere*, presumably behind fresh troops.

There were fresh troops in front now, though unhappily there
was a wide gap in the corps front. On March 26th the 51st
Division completed concentration at Sailly and then moved back
towards Souastre. The intention was to withdraw it from the
front as soon as possible to be filled up by drafts and reorganized.
The further advance of the enemy caused it to be deployed once
more, south-east of the village. This time a considerable force of
artillery was available. The Germans were brought to a halt and
made no more progress that day.

At Souastre the men of the 51st Division were witnesses of an
unedifying spectacle. The return of some mounted patrols sent
out to ascertain the enemy's movements gave rise to the rumour
that German cavalry was advancing. A few agricultural machines
being moved to safety behind Ford tractors were mistaken for
German armoured cars. One of the rare cases of a panic, the only
serious one in these battles, now broke out. Stragglers, transport,
and troops, mostly non-combatant, and civilians fled along the roads
running northward and westward from Hebuterne. The Germans
were reported to have entered the village. Troops far from the
scene were ordered to dig in. However, the alarm did not last

long. The fighting units sent out mounted officers who discovered that the Germans had not in fact broken through. The incident was afterwards spoken of as " the Pys to Pas point-to-point " but the jocular title was used rather wryly.

Far from being disastrous, March 26th was actually a good day on the front of the IV Corps. Now the 51st Division could really be withdrawn. As regards its infantry, it was a mere shell, but the Royal Artillery and Royal Engineers—who were often employed as infantry—had also suffered heavy loss. The returns of casualties made by the three Gordons' battalions vary widely, that of the 7th Battalion being nearly twice as large as that of the 6th. The round number, for the rank and file, given by the 4th Battalion, without differentiation of the form of the casualties, is clearly only an estimate. Stragglers notoriously find it more difficult to rejoin their units in a retreat than in an advance, and men may have rejoined after the dates of these returns.[1] Among the wounded was Lieut.-Colonel A. de L. Long, commanding the 7th Battalion. He was succeeded by Major W. H. Newson, who was appointed temporarily to the command but actually remained in that position until mid-April, throughout the battalion's engagement in the Battle of the Lys.

The division was moved northward and came under command of the First Army. Near Frévent the 6th Gordons met the car in which King George V was visiting his sore-tried forces. Greeted with a volley of cheering, he stopped and spoke to some officers and n.c.o.s. In the new area drafts came in fairly fast and the strength of the battalions rose, though not to establishment. A large proportion of the reinforcements were very young. Some training was undertaken, but as will appear, there was little time before the next German blow fell, this time in Flanders.

The story of these three battalions in the German offensive of March, 1918, has been told downrightly, with no concealment of occasional weaknesses. Historians who write of the troops of their own side or of the units or formations which are their subjects as consistently heroic are not only deforming history but helping to create a dangerously false impression which may in future recoil

---

[1]

		Killed	Wounded	Missing
4th Gordons			Officers 19, Other ranks 400.	
6th Gordons	Officers	2	11	3
	Other ranks	41	159	24
7th Gordons	Officers	1	5	12
	Other ranks	36	178	482

The return of the 7th Battalion includes under the heading of wounded " wounded, at duty " and " gassed " ; that under missing includes those known to be wounded and missing.

upon the Army itself. The one group whom they never deceive is that of soldiers who have themselves served in a hard fought war with phases of adversity. These men know the truth. They have had experience of three facts : that all troops are not in practice of equal military value, even if they have trained and fought side by side ; that individual men vary even more and that the more their numbers are reduced in battle the greater is the extent to which they are deprived of their best men, including private soldiers ; and that heavy losses, extreme strain and fatigue, and the depression caused by continual retreat must tell.

When this much has been said, it has to be qualified in the light of the German reports and comments on the battle. These exhibit continual disappointment. The enemy got behind his timetable. He failed to take Amiens. We shall see that he failed to take Arras—and he was to have exploited victory at Arras to beyond Saint Pol.

Taken as a whole, the British defence was dogged. Only on rare occasions did the German troops have the impression that they were sweeping all before them and almost always when that impression spread it was snuffed out by some stiff stand which took a heavy toll of the attackers. The 51st Division, which had shown so much bite when on the offensive, proved itself above the average on the defensive. The record of the Territorial battalions of the Gordon Highlanders in this fierce trial is an honourable one.

CHAPTER XVII

AT the beginning of the battle on March 21st, 1918, the 51st division was, as has been narrated, standing astride the Bapaume-Cambrai road. On that day the 3rd Division had its left flank on another great and still more famous highway, the Arras-Cambrai road. Where the front line crossed these two roads they were just on ten miles apart. North of the 3rd Division and between the Arras-Cambrai road and the Scarpe was the 15th Division. On the left of the 3rd Division's sector the 1st Gordon Highlanders was in support in the battle zone about Guémappe. On the right flank of the 15th Division the 8/10th Gordon Highlanders was in the front system. Headquarters, with one company, of the 9th Gordon Highlanders (P.) was in Arras and the two remaining companies were engaged in wiring the battle zone. It has already been mentioned that, when the establishment of brigades was cut down to three battalions, pioneer battalions had been reduced to three companies. The records of the battalions of the regiment in the 3rd and 15th Divisions can be given together day by day in the account of the battle in this area because they were so close together.

In view of the extension of the British front, the withdrawal of a battalion from each infantry brigade made life much harder. When the 1st Gordons entered the line on the Arras front on January 26th, 1918 they could look forward to the prospect of four days out of sixteen in billets on the outskirts of the town, amid the luxuries of cinemas and *café-au-lait*. The disbandment of their old friends the 10th Royal Welch Fusiliers killed this hope. The brigade remained on a two-battalion front, so that the routine became : eight days in front line, four days in reserve, then another eight in front line. The battalion never got a night's rest until finally relieved after the battle because when in front line it always had to work and when in reserve either worked or carried. Even on relief nights, after eight days in, the men would dump their packs in the reserve position they were to occupy and then file down to the supply dump at the head of the light railway, load up and carry various stores to the front position, returning to the reserve position in time for stand-to. The strain was increased by the fact that during the eight-day spell in the line the battalion had three companies up close behind the wire and only one in the slightly more comfortable situation of close support. That they lasted out so well was proof of their good spirit as well as of their physical fitness. The 15th Division also had all three brigades in line, but held its front for a shorter period than the 3rd and had available more camps in proximity to rearward positions of defence.

The front held by these two divisions was outside the scope of the original German attack. Arras was indeed to be attacked and

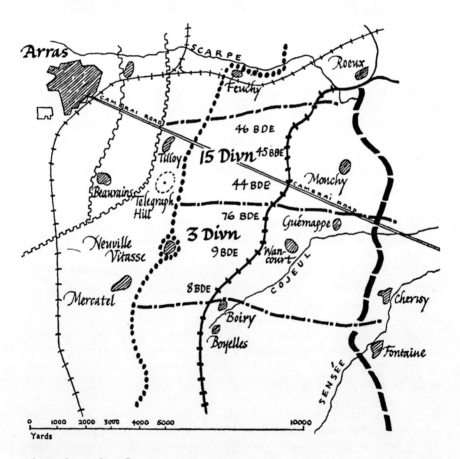

taken, but the German plan was to do this in an entirely new offensive. The enemy did, however, extend his preliminary bombardment for some distance north of the limit of his infantry assault for the purpose of deception, so that it involved both divisions. The shelling was extremely heavy by normal standards, but less so than on the real front of attack. It was expected and did not cause great loss. The casualties of the 8/10th Gordons were about thirty.[1]

South of the 3rd Division the Germans gained a great success about Bullecourt on this first day, penetrating to a depth of two and a half miles. Against the 3rd Division they carried out a number of raids, one of which broke in on the right, as part of their plan of deception, but the front was intact until after 3.30 p.m. Then the German " position " division facing the 3rd Division carried out an improvised attack to exploit the success won further south. It was an extraordinarily bold and enterprising action, which few but German troops would have undertaken. It gained a slender footing only on the front of the right brigade, the 9th, but this marked the beginning of some serious trouble for the 3rd Division. The 1st Gordons on the left were in no way affected on this day and the front of the 15th Division was virtually undisturbed after the morning bombardment.

March 22nd witnessed only a trifling change in the front of the 3rd Division, the 9th Brigade being bent back a little further. For the 76th Brigade on the left the day was quieter than the 21st. To the south, however, German progress continued all too fast. In the afternoon the army commander, Sir Julian Byng, decided that, to maintain a continuous front, he would have to withdraw the 3rd Division to its battle zone during the night. Later on orders to the same effect were sent to the 15th Division. For the 3rd Division the difficulty was on the right flank, where it was in close contact with the enemy, but this was overcome because the Germans were apparently too weary to interfere. The 76th Brigade had no trouble and the move was completed in the early hours of March 23rd. The 15th Division faced an insoluble problem : how to retain Monchy-le-Preux and at the same time withdraw its right far enough to join hands with the 3rd Division. The corps commander, Sir Charles Fergusson, fought hard for the retention of Monchy, whence observers could spot every German gun firing as far east as Cambrai. He had finally to give way because this would have added 5,000 yards to the front of the 15th Division. For the men of that division the withdrawal was melancholy. It had fought here in the Battle of Arras less than a year ago and was abandoning strong defences on which it had worked hard without having defended them against the enemy. The 8/10th Gordons, leaving one company in the original front line as

---

[1] The Diary of the 1st Gordons for the period in which the battalion was engaged is missing, so that where it is concerned the account has to be drawn chiefly from that of the 76th Brigade. It is difficult to follow the doings of the battalion.

a rear guard, withdrew to a camp south-east of Arras behind the army line, which it was to hold in case of need.

Against the 3rd Division the enemy began the day of March 23rd with a three-hours' bombardment of the trenches evacuated under orders during the night. In the 76th Brigade the 8th King's Own were now on the right and the 1st Gordon Highlanders on the left. One attack was launched against it during the day, but not in great strength by the standard of the offensive. This took place at noon and affected both battalions. It was generally repulsed, except that a body of Germans reached some half-dug trenches on the front of the right company of the Gordons. They were evicted, though at considerable cost.[1] In the 44th Brigade of the 15th Division the 8/10th Gordons company which had been left in the old front line fought a rear-guard action back to the new position without incurring many casualties. Both divisions worked to improve their present defences, which were generally rather sketchy.

On the 24th the brunt of the attack on the 3rd Division was borne by the 8th Brigade, now on its right. This brigade beat off one attack after another and punished the Germans severely. On the front of the 76th an attack was pressed as far as the wire of the 1st Gordons, where it was stopped with serious loss. It extended to the right of the 44th Brigade, but here it was stopped 300 yards away. It did not affect the 8/10th Gordons, who were now given the duty of holding a switch line on the Neuville-Vitasse ridge, at which the enemy's attack on the 8th Brigade seemed to be aimed. The 9th Gordons had now all been withdrawn to Arras and were working by night on this retrenchment.

There was relative quietude throughout the 25th and 26th. On the 27th a party of the enemy bombed its way along a communication trench, but were killed or driven out by the 8th King's Own of the 76th Brigade. Everyone by now expected a big attack on the Arras front.

It must be realized that all this while hard and often very unfavourable fighting had been going on on the front of the corps next to the south and the rest of that of the Third Army. It must also be borne in mind that the attacks hitherto directed against the 3rd and 15th Divisions had been secondary, efforts to aid the main attack further south. These two divisions merited high praise for their bearing and conduct, but they had at no time been taxed

---

[1] This incident is reported by an officer of the regiment, Lieutenant Lockhart, who wrote an account of his experiences while in hospital recovering from a wound received on the 28th. His record is valuable in view of the absence of the battalion diary, though of course he sets down only what he saw. It has been used for the following days.

as fully as those facing the main offensive.   Clearly, if the Germans meant to do the real thing at Arras the test would be very different.

They did mean to do the real thing.   Ludendorff had not gained all the success he had hoped for in " Michael ", the code name for the attack from the Oise to Croisilles, but he had now ordered the new phase, " Mars ", to be begun.[1]   This was to cover not only the front of the two divisions south of the Scarpe but also that of two more north of it.   The frontage of " Mars " had been strongly reinforced.   Ludendorff believed that if he broke the Arras defences he would give a new impetus to the whole operation.

The blow fell on March 28th.   At 3 a.m. an intense bombardment burst out.   At an early stage it was reported to the headquarters of the 44th Brigade that the field artillery in rear was being neutralized by the counter-battery fire.   At one time the deep curtain of fire on the forward trenches crept forward, then returned to its original objective, where it slackened for a little and was next renewed in full force.   In front the shelling was devastating.   The 7th Cameron Highlanders, holding the whole extent of the 44th Brigade's front, had its leading companies almost annihilated, only twelve men being left in one of them.

If all the reports are correct, there was a curious variation in the timing of the attacks.   That on the right of the 3rd Division began at 5.30 a.m.; the 76th Brigade was attacked at 6.45 ; the 44th Brigade of the 15th Division, next further north at 6.

The German infantry, which had made use of the darkness to work its way to close quarters, assaulted with determination.   The British artillery, however, gave it a hot reception, and to begin with its only success was on the right of the 44th Brigade.   Here it obtained a footing in the trenches left defenceless by the losses of the 7th Camerons.   Elsewhere the line held, and as wave after wave of Germans appeared through the smoke, they made good targets and were shot down in large numbers.

The enemy was not held for long, however.   About 7.30 a.m. the right of the 76th Brigade was swept away.   The other two brigades had already begun to withdraw gradually to the rear line of the battle zone, but part of the 76th Brigade came back in some confusion.[2]   However, by 8.30 the new front was established. Against the 44th Brigade the Germans thrust with equal force. The remnant of the 7th Camerons were driven back to the Neuville-Vitasse Switch line, where it joined hands with the two leading companies of the 8/10th Gordons.   Far from owning themselves

[1] The British used code names for operations little in the First World War.   The Germans used them freely.

[2] Lieutenant Lockhart, previously quoted, speaks of " a dark mass of men, at first thought to be the Boche ".

to be beaten, the officer commanding the Camerons (about 156 all ranks by this time) and Captain J. B. Wood, commanding the two companies of the Gordons, determined to counter-attack. However, owing to a break-down of communications, it took a very long time to arrange for supporting artillery fire, and before this could be done the enemy was seen to have made dangerous progress on the front of the 45th Brigade, along the Cambrai road.

There was now no point in counter-attacking. Indeed, the enemy began a series of attacks on the new position. Each time his infantry called for a bombardment with fireworks and renewed the assault when the guns lifted their fire. An observer said that the attacks were " an example of perfect infiltration, and the way in which light signals met with response from the German artillery was an object lesson ". Our men were dealing with good troops.

Some time after 1 p.m. a further withdrawal on the part of the 3rd Division set in. It is believed to have been caused by misunderstanding of the new principles of defence in depth, foreign to previous British ideas. It appeared to the troops that the line to which they had already withdrawn was now to be regarded as an outpost zone and that the army line had therefore become the line of resistance. The retirement in fact did not greatly matter because Major-General Deverell had already decided to withdraw to the army line as soon as darkness had fallen.

More or less at the same time the 15th Division withdrew to it. The Germans pressed the retiring troops nearly all the way, so that the movement developed into a trying rear-guard action. The 8/10th Gordons had a particularly difficult time because both their flanks were in the air, the right because of the earlier withdrawal of the 76th Brigade, the left because of the enemy's continued progress along the Cambrai road. The battalion fell back by companies, getting fine support from the guns of the 15th Machine Gun Battalion and prevented the Germans from closing with it.

The troops were back now on the last continuous line of the Arras defences, except for the old trenches of 1917. In their rear all units that could be assembled had been put into the best defensive positions that could be found. The 9th Gordons had moved thrice, ending up as dusk fell on Telegraph Hill, where two scratch companies of divisional details came under Lieut.-Colonel Taylor's orders. The battalion did not come to close quarters with the enemy during the day, but it suffered 57 casualties from his fire.

A splendid British triumph took the curious form of an anti-climax. The Germans had fought very well. They had, at the junction of the 3rd and 15th Divisions, advanced about a mile and a half, but against troops who had never been broken and who now

stood facing them in well-dug and heavily wired trenches. For
seven hours or more they had been under constant artillery fire
and, whenever they had shown themselves, that of machine guns
and rifles. Their attack did not so much break down as first
slacken then peter out. No large bodies approached the new
position closely, and the small ones were easily dealt with. By
5 p.m. the attack on the 3rd and 15th Divisions had ceased. North
of the river the fighting went on longer, but took a very similar
course. About 6 p.m. the 15th Division actually advanced its
front east of the army line. The British, of course, made all possible preparations to meet a renewed attack on the morrow, but
none came. " Mars " had failed.

From the regiment's point of view it is a sad pity that the records
of the 1st Battalion are missing and that so little light can be thrown
on its action from other sources.[1] Nor can the battalion's casualties be given. Those of the 8/10th exceeded 300.[2]

In terms of what the German command had aimed at and
required for success on this new front the events of March 28th
amounted to a heavy defeat. " ' Mars ', to which so much blood
was offered, was unable to break open the British Arras salient and
give a fresh aspect to the great battle on the northern wing ",
writes a German commentator. The very fact that Ludendorff
closed down " Mars " at the end of a single day is proof that he
regarded it as a failure pure and simple, and one which he could
not hope to remedy. All he could now do was to continue for the
time being the exploitation of his victory further south, where the
front was still fluid, and meanwhile start moving northward the
mass of his heavy and medium batteries, his " battering train ",
in preparation for a new offensive in Flanders. There could still
be no question in his mind of doing anything but attack. It
would not be worth while to conserve his forces and then be overwhelmed by the vast numbers of Americans who would soon be
available. If he could not win a decisive victory now he was
doomed to utter defeat, probably before the year was out. It was
all or nothing.

The British realized equally quickly that they had won a defensive victory of the first importance. Brig.-General E. Hilliam,
commanding the 44th Brigade, praised his battalions warmly. But

[1] Lieutenant Lockhart speaks of an unsuccessful counter-attack made by the 1st
Battalion during the retirement from the Neuville-Vitasse Switch to the army line,
with no artillery support and no time to draw grenades. Other evidence of this is
not to be found.

[2]

	Killed	Wounded	Missing
Officers	1	5	—
Other ranks	25	193	79

13

for their steady resistance, he wrote, the 15th Division might have been destroyed and would at best have been compelled to retreat. " The divisional commander today, in expressing his thanks for the work of the 44th Brigade, in all sincerity told me that your work had saved Arras." It was a tribute to be proud of because from Arras to Vimy Ridge ran a hinge which the Germans managed to bend slightly but never succeeded in forcing.

The achievement of the 3rd Division, in which the 1st Gordon Highlanders had played so determined and gallant a part, was equally great in more adverse circumstances. The 3rd prevented the right flank of the 15th from being turned, but its own right was turned by the success of the Germans to the south and it stood in deadly peril of being rolled up and losing virtually all its infantry and probably the greater part of its artillery. If any division in that great battle can be said to have held a key position, it was the 3rd. In all its long and honourable service none of its achievements had been more vital. Its resistance broke the offensive.

The area of this brief but critical struggle at once became quiet. On March 30th the 76th Brigade was relieved by Canadian troops. After a sleep behind the line the 1st Gordons moved to Warluzel, a distance of eighteen miles. The men marched very well, no mean feat after fifty-seven days in trenches and seven days' fighting. The 3rd Division then moved north to the coal-fields, where the 1st Gordons had good billets and carried out training. One of their drafts, numbering 57, was mostly composed of boys of nineteen, but the adjutant noted that they were keen and should make good soldiers. It will appear how short a time they had.

The 15th Division, on the other hand, remained holding the front taken up on March 28th. For just on a month the 8/10th Gordons never got further from the trenches than the Grande Place in Arras. Then, however, the 15th Division was withdrawn into army reserve.

The main German offensive closed on April 5th. In view of the hardening of allied resistance, which he could no longer overcome, Ludendorff abandoned the attack on Amiens, which would have been a greater prize than even Arras and the loss of which would have maimed the communications between the allies. A very brief calm followed.

CHAPTER XVIII

THE German supreme command had had an offensive in Flanders in mind since before the end of 1917. It was to be known as " St. George " and to be a " second act " to " Michael ". How disappointed the command was as early as March 24th with what at the time appeared to be the overwhelming success of " Michael " was proved when it was then found necessary to modify the northern offensive. The code name was modified also, becoming " Georgette ". Its immediate strategic objective was Hazebrouck, a town of only 12,000 inhabitants but a railway centre for Dunkirk, Calais, Boulogne, and Amiens, highly valuable to the movement of British military traffic. The front north of the La Bassée Canal was a dangerous one. Various forms of exploitation were to follow the capture of Hazebrouck—after it the next objective might be the Flanders heights, then Calais.

The Germans struck on April 9th, the earliest date by which their battering train from the Somme could be made ready, on a narrow front, their right south of Armentières, their left on the La Bassée Canal. In the centre of this zone of attack the British had inadvisedly, even admitting their difficulties, left a Portuguese division, widely extended, despite the fact that these troops were known to be weary, depressed, and without interest in a war which had no appeal to them and which their Government had entered for political reasons. The division was actually to have been relieved that night. After a heavy bombardment the German assault captured or scattered to the winds these unhappy strangers in a strange land. This was not just the case of a division being reduced to rags, as had happened to some British divisions in March. By 11 a.m. practically the whole Portuguese division, field artillery included, had vanished from the battlefield.

That was bad enough, but it might have been worse. On the Portuguese right was one of the best Territorial divisions in France, the 55th, which had not been in action since Cambrai and had thoroughly organized its defences. It held firm, though in view of the yawning void on its left it had to throw back a flank to the canalized Lawe. North of the Portuguese sector the attack on the 40th Division, exhausted and shaken by fighting in March, had graver results. To block the gap itself there were immediately available only the 1st King Edward's Horse and the XI Corps Cyclists. They got into the gap, despite heavy mist, with praiseworthy speed, and displayed great gallantry. Their resistance led the advancing Germans to suppose that the force in front of them was far greater than was in fact the case.

Something has already been said of the terrain in the early part of this narrative. It was that over which the 1st Gordon Highlanders had advanced in October 1914, when it crossed the Lawe at Fosse. South of the chain of heights running across the Flanders plain from Wytschaete to Cassel the ground is flat as a table. The

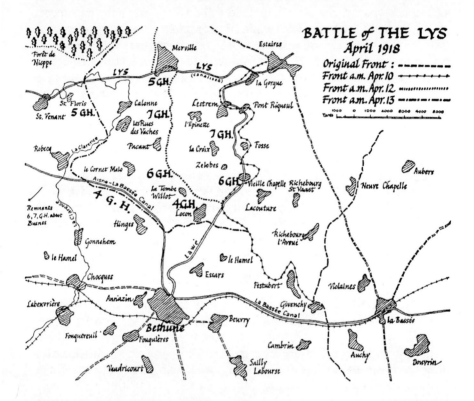

main features are the Lys, which gives the battle its name, running through Estaires and north-east through Armentières; its tributary the Lawe, entering it west of Estaires; and on the northern bank of the Lys, between Merville and Hazebrouck, the Forêt de Nieppe, seven miles long and virtually impenetrable except by the rides. The drainage ditches dividing the fields are often too wide to be jumped and too deep for wading. The high level of the sub-surface water made defensive tactics very different from those of the previous German offensive. Instead of seeking a site suitable for digging in, the platoon or machine-gun detachment in retreat looked for a hedgerow or even the slight shelter afforded by the ridge-and-furrow pattern into which many even of the grass fields had been shaped for the purpose of drainage. The difficulty of moving large bodies of troops across such country had caused it to be regarded as favouring defence, but fine weather had made it less so in April 1918 than usual at this time of year.

The 51st Division was in XI Corps reserve about Busnes, eleven miles west of the original front line at Neuve Chapelle. The German attack and the summons which followed caught it in the midst of reorganization, and in some cases very young reinforcements had been only a couple of days with their units. First the 152nd Brigade was ordered forward to relieve the mounted troops. Some delay occurred owing to the buses provided being sent to the wrong place and to long-range fire on the roads, and it was getting on for noon when the 6th Gordons debussed at Zelobes a little west of the Lawe. Then at 9.40 a.m. the 154th Brigade was ordered up to Locon, south of the front of the 152nd, and to come under command of the 55th Division. As the situation in all its ugliness became clearer the call came for the 153rd Brigade to move up to the Lawe on the left of the 152nd. The 7th Gordon Highlanders received its orders at 1.10 p.m., but its billets were so scattered that it was unable to march before 2.30. On the completion of these moves the three brigades would be in line, 154th on the right under the orders of the 55th Division, 152nd in the centre, and 153rd on the left.

The leading battalion of the 154th Brigade, the 6th Seaforths, crossed the Lawe with orders to make good Lacouture, about three-quarters of a mile to the east. The enemy, however, was first into the village, and in strength. The Seaforths fell back fighting, recrossed the Lawe by a footbridge, and took up a position on the left bank, their left flank on Vieille Chapelle. The 4th Gordons were held in reserve. As, however, the third battalion of the brigade had been put directly under command of a brigade of the 55th Division, the 6th Gordons of the 152nd Brigade were also placed in reserve behind the junction of the two brigades. At 4.20 p.m. they were ordered to put a company into Vieille Chapelle for the defence of a little bridgehead over the canalized river. D Company (Captain J. R. Christie) was sent.

The 7th Gordon Highlanders of the 153rd Brigade had the most frustrating day. Its fighting strength was 19 officers and 625 men, but it had few n.c.o.s of standing or experience and the larger part of the men had joined only within the last few days. Among the stores issued to it were only five shovels. Major W. H. Newson [1] was ordered to ride ahead to Pacaut, four miles by road from the position to be taken up. Here he met the brigade commander, Brig.-General A. T. Beckwith, who told him that the

_____
[1] Temporarily in command since Lieut.-Colonel Long had been gassed.

battalion would hold the right of the brigade front ; such points beyond the canal as could be maintained would be, but the canal was to be the main line of defence. Greatly delayed by fugitives, both Portuguese troops and civilians, the battalion did not come up until 5.20 p.m. and the troops fell out for a very brief rest while company commanders got their orders for the approach march. As they neared the canal the Gordons were told that the enemy was over it at one lock, and the 8th Durham Light Infantry of the 50th Division, which had relieved part of the 40th Division on the left, called for aid in a counter-attack. One company and a half was allotted to the task about 6.30 p.m., but before this force had reached the scene it grew too dark to move across country in their unreconnoitred area. In point of fact the Durhams reported at 9.45 p.m. that there were now no Germans west of the canal here and that the lock was not held by either side. At the day's end the front ran along the Lawe from opposite Locon to the confluence with the Lys at La Gorgue and thence through Estaires and for some distance further along the latter river. The 51st and 50th Divisions had accomplished what the official historian describes as " almost a miracle " in holding back victorious troops after being rushed up to stop their advance in the gap left by the Portuguese. It so happened, however, that none of the three battalions of the Gordons had been heavily engaged so far.

On April 10th the enemy renewed his attacks on the front already active. He also extended them north of Armentières against the Messines Ridge and as far as the Ypres-Comines Canal, this doubling the frontage of his operation. The day opened gloomily, with low clouds and mist which hung about for a long time and reassembled early in the afternoon.

On the right the 55th Division once more repelled all attacks, but called on the 154th Brigade to extend its right a little. At 5.30 a.m. this brigade returned to the command of its own division. The 4th Gordon Highlanders remained in reserve.

At the junction between the 154th and 152nd Brigades the enemy kept on dribbling troops up to the footbridge and ended by getting a body across and occupying two farms on the west bank. The 6th Gordon Highlanders was ordered, soon after 2 p.m., to drive him out of this bridgehead. The young troops of the company employed went forward gallantly. They took the first farm buildings, but were raked by fire from the second and suffered heavy loss. The company then fell back to the first farm and there beat off another hostile attack. This fine action brought the German advance here to an end for several hours. At 10.45 p.m. Lieut.-Colonel A. A. Duff was informed that the enemy was across the Lawe in strength further north and moving down upon

him along the west bank. He disposed his remaining two companies to face northward, but the troops were rather nervous in
the open and in darkness, so that he and another battalion commander had some trouble in preventing them from drifting away.
Once he had them in hand—and they were quite ready to obey
when taken hold of by strong and experienced leadership—the
flank held its ground. During the remainder of the night no
change occurred.

Meanwhile the Germans had been launching determined attacks on Vieille Chapelle, a key point in the defence of the river
line, with two bridges. Captain Christie's company of the 6th
Gordons and a party of King Edward's Horse put up a very stout
fight. The Lewis guns of the Highlanders and the Hotchkiss of
the cavalry took a fearful toll of the enemy. The pressure, however, was so heavy that the defenders were gradually forced back
into the village, where they made a last stand. Finally they were
hemmed in. They made an attempt to break out, but when they
found this impossible fought on. The end came on April 11th
when some twenty men, several of them wounded, surrendered.
The 6th Gordons had assuredly made their full contribution to
the defence of the Lawe.

How the battalion came to be attacked in flank west of the
Lawe must now be explained. On the morning of April 10th the
7th Gordons of the 153rd Brigade had taken over the defence of
Fosse, on the east side of the canal, rather under a mile north of
Vieille Chapelle. The men of King Edward's Horse had held a
bridgehead here with great courage on the 9th. Its defence was
now to be shared with the Gordons by the 5th Seaforth, but as only
20 men of that battalion could be collected the post was under-
manned. That morning the enemy forced a passage of the canal
on the front of the 50th Division at Pont Riqueul, on the north side
of the big loop at Lestrem. The left company commander of the
7th Gordons made the best defensive flank he could contrive with
one of his own platoons and such stragglers as he could lay his
hands on. He was reinforced, but there was little to spare for him
because the remainder of the battalion was engaged with the enemy
advancing from the east. Eventually the party in Fosse were
driven out, fighting every inch of the way and narrowly escaping
being cornered, and, despite two flank-guard actions, the rest of
the battalion was rolled up by the advance from the north. During
the night or early on the morning of April 11th, the 152nd and
153rd Brigades scraped together a front at varying distance from
the Lawe, but it was not one on which reliance could be placed.
The 154th Brigade, on the other hand, was still on the canal, with
a defensive left flank.

The historian finds it hard to make clear the details of the struggle along the Lawe. He is, however, in possesion of such records as have been left by the brigades and battalions, whereas they in many cases knew only what was happening to themselves and in that of the brigade headquarters news came through slowly. We must try to imagine the unavoidable confusion in the darkness, the difficulty of bringing artillery fire to bear on the enemy because of doubt regarding the position of friendly troops, the intermingling of units of different brigades and, on the left flank, of those of the 153rd Brigade and the 50th Division on its left, and how hard it was for battalion commanders to control raw battalions with a shortage of experienced officers and an even graver lack of competent n.c.o.s. At the same time we must bear in mind that the enemy was also handicapped. He found enormous difficulty in advancing his artillery and ammunition wagons. It was this factor, as well as a stout defence, which made the progress of the Lys offensive slower than that of the Somme. Had the Germans not had the good fortune to find the Portuguese division on an unusually wide front, the offensive might have been a relative failure. Even as things were it was not coming up to expectations.

April 11th was a black day for the 51st Division. During its course the fire of the defenders grew weaker and weaker and it became more and more difficult to organize a front as officer after officer of the scanty complement became a casualty. Throughout the morning the troops of the 152nd and 153rd Brigades were at one point or another, and sometimes at several, always moving rearwards. The division had so far accomplished wonders, but now it was getting near the end of its physical and spiritual resources.

At the beginning of the day the 154th Brigade was in the best shape of the three. At 4 a.m. the 4th Gordons sent forward two platoons to try to recover a footbridge over the canal a little north of its flank which had been abandoned by other troops, but the enemy's fire was too hot. However, the front, though exposed by the withdrawal of the other brigades, was for the time being firm. The 4th Gordons had two companies forming a flank facing north, and another in close support. Soon, however, attacks of increasing violence were directed against it. About 1 p.m. the right company of the flank-guard was driven back a couple of hundred yards. In face of one assault after another in greatly superior strength, a little more ground was yielded in the region of Locon, but in general the front held. Shortly before dark the brigade staff noted that the 4th Gordons were firm and confident. They had, however, been fiercely battered and had suffered very heavy losses.

Two more divisions which were to relieve parts of the 51st were moving up on this day, and it chanced that they were two in which battalions of the regiment were embodied. On the right the 3rd Division (less the 9th Brigade and artillery, already under command of the 55th and helping to hold its front) moved up from south-west of Bethune. At 1 p.m. the 1st Gordon Highlanders was carried by bus to the neighbourhood of Hinges, but it was never seriously engaged in the course of this battle. At night an order was sent to the 8th Brigade to relieve the 154th, but the motor cyclist carrying the message to the 8th fell into a shell-hole, so that the 4th Gordons had seen no signs of a relieving battalion by 5.30 a.m. on April 12th. An hour later the 154th Brigade heard that the enemy had broken the front of the 152nd and 153rd Brigades.

It was true. During the 11th these brigades, or what remained of them, were driven back to a line in front of Pacaut, over two miles west of the Lawe, and the place where the 7th Gordons had halted on their way up on April 9th. Fortunately, the second division containing a battalion of the Gordons, the 61st, arrived in the nick of time, and the first two battalions to reach the scene took up a position behind the junction of the 152nd and 153rd Brigades, so that if forced back again they could rally and as far as possible reorganize. As usual during the German offensives, the British administrative services stood the strain well. The 5th Gordon Highlanders, detraining at Steenbecque, was carried by buses to Saint-Floris, marched thence to Merville, and at once took up a position south of the town. That night, its diary records there were " many conflicting rumours ". There always are in a great retreat under pressure.

The pressure was in this case very strong but not quite as fierce as in the March offensive. The great problem was to stop the habit of drifting away which beset the gallant youths who made up the majority of the infantry when they became physically worn out. (We have seen how they could fight before this stage was reached.) The commander of the XI Corps in which the 51st Division was now serving, Lieut.-General Sir John Du Cane, said on this day to a gunner officer : " The situation on my corps front would be quite O.K. if only I could induce anyone to stand still instead of retiring."

A corps commander may seem too remote from the sufferings of the rank and file to be a reliable authority. The commanding officer of a battalion brigaded with the 4th Gordons, the 7th A. and S. Highlanders, comes into another category because he lived with the troops and fought in their midst. He wrote first of the skill with which the Germans trickled forward to close quarters and the destructive fire of their light machine guns before they assaulted. He was astonished by the way they maintained their supply of small-arms ammunition ; we found it hard to keep the Lewis guns in action, but they had more light machine guns and fired without stint. He went on to say that a continuous defensive was harmful to morale and recommended that when the enemy secured an objective such as a farm house he should if possible be attacked that night. It was, he said, urgently necessary to stop the habit of withdrawing when the Germans got to within three hundred yards. Often, however, senior commands were as much to blame as the battalions. The troops were ordered to hold " at all costs " and then ordered to withdraw because a flank had been turned. The men then came to look upon " at all costs " as meaning until the enemy was within three hundred yards or a flank was threatened. This is frankness which should be embodied in military history, though it is too often left out.

And yet the defence never ceased to resist and take toll of the enemy. If there was temporary yielding at one point there was stout and effective defence somewhere close at hand. The Germans never got the impression that they were having their own way. Gaps were closed up in front of them and galling fire, slackened for a while, reopened. If individual units, reduced to shadows of their former selves, faded, British will to fight on never did. That was the crucial fact. And that was the reason why the German Lys offensive, starting with such an easy success, was to be classed by the Germans themselves as a *Misserfolg* (failure).

They began the day on April 12th with something far from a *Misserfolg*, a big success in fact. On the previous evening they had been held up by the fire of the remnants of the 152nd and 153rd Brigades and the artillery supporting them, which had actually caused them to yield some ground. Before daylight on the 12th the leading companies crawled forward and got quite close to the British front without attracting attention.[1] At 5 a.m. the assault was launched. It surprised the defence and broke clean through. All we know from the British side of the fate of the Gordons' battalions is that the 7th Battalion was not on the front of assault, that it first formed a defensive flank, and then as the light increased saw that the enemy had penetrated nearly two thousand yards to the village of Le Cornet Malo, the headquarters of both brigades. The battalion then withdrew through Calonne. In Le Cornet Malo the commander of the 152nd Brigade, Brig.-General J. K. Dick-Cunyngham, was captured.

---

[1] In the official history, " France and Belgium, 1918 ; March-April, Continuation of the German Offensive ", is given an account of this attack from the German side, written by the then Director (in 1936) of the German Historical Section of the Army.

Lieut.-Colonel L. M. Dyson, an officer of the divisional artillery who had taken over command of the 153rd when Brig.-General Beckwith went sick, had a very close shave, quitting his command post when the enemy was within two or three hundred yards of it.

We left the 4th Gordon Highlanders of the 154th Brigade awaiting relief by troops of the 8th Brigade, 3rd Division, in the early hours of April 12th. Brig.-General K. G. Buchanan, commanding the 154th, did not receive a report of the completion of the relief until 7.55 a.m., long after he had heard of the overrunning of the other two brigades. At 9.15, by which time the 4th Gordons were assembling south of the La Bassée Canal, he was alarmed to see stragglers falling back over it. One company of the Gordons fought a rear-guard action north of the canal while the remainder manned the southern bank from a little east of Hinges to the neighbourhood of Robecq. The enemy hardly tried to cross the canal and never did so.

North of the gap made at Pacaut, the 5th Gordon Highlanders of the 61st Division held the front west of Merville with the pioneer battalion of the division. Another battalion of the 183rd Brigade was in reserve and the third was still on the march from its detraining station. The Gordons, constantly enfiladed from the gap on the right, withdrew first to a support position, but were finally forced over the Lys Canal. Throughout their retirement they were under machine-gun fire which caused huge losses. Meanwhile a fresh front was congealing as reinforcements reached the scene of action and the slender remnant of the 51st Division could be assembled at Busnes, the centre of the area from which it had marched to battle on April 9th.

From south of Hinges to north of Merville, a distance of six miles, the enemy had made a deep breach in the front. South of Bailleul he had carved another. Both had been patched up, and after the first few hours his efforts to exploit his success had not been strong. But the Messines Ridge further north was gone and at Ypres preparations were being made to abandon Poelcappelle and Passchendaele, won at the cost of so much blood and suffering in 1917.

There is little more to tell of the 51st Division in the Battle of the Lys. The 152nd and 153rd Brigades were formed temporarily into a battalion each. The 154th, which was a little stronger, was brought up to the Robecq defences, but it was shortly withdrawn.

The 61st Division put up a fine defence in the days that followed, particularly when it is recalled that this division had suffered vast losses in March. On April 13th, when the 5th Gordons were in brigade reserve, good shooting by the artillery kept the Germans in check. Next day the brigade was subjected to four attacks. They were all beaten off, except that the last secured one post by the river—and that was retaken at night. These attacks were all met by the 8th A. and S. Highlanders and there is no evidence that the 5th Gordons took a part in repelling them.[1] This was the day on which General Foch astonished Lord Milner and Sir Douglas Haig by concluding their conference at Abbeville with the remark: "La bataille d'Hazebrouck est finie." He proved to be right, though some minor attacks occurred after April 14th, in one of which the 61st Division was engaged.

Though "la bataille d'Hazebrouck" was over, this was far from being the case with the whole offensive, the Battle of the Lys, which had another fifteen days to run. There were, however, only trifling changes on the southern half of the battlefield during that period. It was on the front of the Second Army, including the large French detachment now interpolated in it, north of Bailleul, that the fighting continued with extreme violence. Here the main object of the enemy was to secure the chain of the Flanders heights. The high command believed that if this could be done the whole British and Belgian front to the sea would have to be abandoned. The Germans gained one more signal success when they captured Mount Kemmel from the French on April 25th, but they suffered a bloody repulse on the slopes of the next hill, the Scherpenberg, on April 29th. That evening Ludendorff resolved to bring the battle to an end. Realizing that more than half the French Army now stood north of Amiens, he decided that the next step must be to deal it a heavy blow on the Aisne.

Yet the German object remained as before: to destroy the British Army. The Aisne offensive was undertaken only for the purpose of mangling the French sufficiently to prevent their coming to the aid of the British for the third time. It was, in fact, to be a gigantic diversion. By the middle of June the offensive in the north was to be resumed under the title of "New George". That was to be the *coup de grâce*.

The force of the Lys offensive in April 1918 was less than that of the Somme offensive of March. On the other hand, the British were in one sense less capable of holding it because so large a proportion of their troops were depleted in strength and worn

---

[1] It hardly needs to be said that the battalion records covering the two great German offensives are sketchy—we have seen that those of the 1st Gordons in the March affair are missing altogether. It ought to be mentioned that the excellent short history of the Gordon Highlanders by the Rev. P. D. Thomson goes astray at one point in its account of the Lys. He speaks of "the four Gordon Territorial battalions" with the 51st Division, not realizing that the 5th had been transferred to the 61st Division. He does not mention either the 5th Battalion or the 61st Division and describes the 51st Division as being "driven through the 62nd Division at Pacaut". The 62nd Division in fact took no part in the Battle of the Lys.

out, though their fortifications were better. It has been pointed out that a large proportion of the drafts received by divisions such as the 51st and 61st, which had been through the mill on the Somme, consisted of youths aged eighteen and a half or nineteen. It must be added that, despite the great number of reinforcements received, few battalions were brought up to establishment between the two battles. The losses suffered in the Battle of the Lys represent therefore a considerably higher proportion of the total strength of battalions than appears on the surface. A good deal has been said about the difficulty of keeping these raw young troops in hand after their first magnificent ardour had worn off. In heavy and prolonged fighting an undue proportion of recruits of any age must be a disadvantage, but more so if they are below the age of twenty.

There was nothing wrong with these lads. That generation was almost certainly tougher and more self-reliant than its successors of today, even if less well educated. Those who survived and learnt their job were to prove themselves good soldiers in the days to come, good soldiers because they could do more than make a splendid start. In many cases when troops were reported to be abandoning the struggle the truth proved to be that all their officers had become casualties and that they themselves were merely lost and ready to do what they were told when someone arrived with orders and a sense of direction. The soldier in war is called on not only for high but also for sustained effort. All in all, the British did very well in their adversity. Their valour prevented the Lys offensive from becoming the great strategic success which had at times seemed probable. The Gordon Highlanders had played a notable part in bringing about this result.

In few phases of the war are the losses of the Gordons so ill reported as in the Battle of the Lys. Those of the 4th Battalion are given in the round figure of 200 and those of the 5th not at all. Those of the 6th are given as 12 officers and 346 other ranks, which must have been among the highest suffered. The losses of the 7th, 282, are detailed.[1] Among the losses of the 6th Gordons was Captain Donald G. Clarke, D.S.O., M.C. His death was deeply regretted. He was one of " the originals " and his courage and leadership, allied with good looks and happy disposition, had made him a hero throughout the battalion.

The main contribution of the 1st Gordons had been reinforcement of the front during the battle. It held the La Bassée Canal near Hinges, with bridgehead beyond, to begin with, constantly on

[1]	Killed	Wounded	Missing
Officers	—	4	1
Other ranks	17	114	146

the alert. It was warned to expect an attack on April 18th, but none took place. On April 30th, when in reserve, two companies were shelled out of their quarters, hangars near Lannoy—too attractive a target for artillery, it may be thought—with 21 casualties.

On May 4th B Company with one platoon of D attacked the enemy's defences in an orchard, before dawn at 2.30 a.m. The artillery support was strong and the hostile fire was trifling in volume. All went to programme, and by 3 a.m. the objective was secured with 42 prisoners and three light machine guns. Three officers of the Gordons were wounded, one remaining at duty, 3 other ranks killed and 8 wounded. After the attack the enemy laid a thick barrage on the canal, but the battalion itself was in brigade reserve and the attacking force appears to have suffered no further loss. Nor was there a counter-attack.

On the night of May 19th, when it was again in reserve, its working parties came in for an exceptionally damaging gas bombardment, which must have caught a great number of men before they could adjust their respirators. That night an officer and 11 other ranks were gassed and 7 others wounded, but on the following day 120 cases reported to the medical officers. The vast majority must have been slight because the victims would not otherwise have been able to go about for so long, but it was an unpleasant experience.

No other martial event of moment remains to be recorded of the Gordons' battalions before five of them became involved in the next German offensive. There is, however, a domestic event, partly happy, partly sad : the transfer of the 5th Battalion to a Scottish division and the amalgamation of the 5th and 8/10th. The heavy Scottish losses and the shortage of Scottish recruits was the cause of the amalgamation. The 8/10th had a high reputation, but it was the junior battalion on active service, apart from the 9th, a pioneer battalion, and it therefore had to lose its identity.

The whole of the infantry of the 183rd Brigade (the " Scottish Brigade " of the 61st Division) was transferred to the 15th, all being Territorial battalions going to a New Army division. The 5th Gordons reached Maroeil, the old Arras front so familiar to the regiment, on June 2nd. The amalgamation was completed on the 8th, the new battalion taking the title of 5th Gordon Highlanders. It was allotted to the 44th Brigade, in which the 8/10th had served. Lieut.-Colonel G. A. Smith, senior to Lieut.-Colonel Lord Dudley Gordon, who had commanded the 8/10th, retained his command on amalgamation. His first headquarters was north of the famous Railway Triangle which the 8/10th had helped to take in the Battle of Arras.

CHAPTER XIX

THE Germans brought off one of the great surprises of the war when they launched their assault on the Chemin des Dames, north-west of Reims, on May 27th, 1918. The French and some tired British divisions sent to hold this supposedly quiet front were broken to pieces or hustled back, and when the enemy stopped the operation on June 3rd he had reached the Marne at Château-Thierry. He claimed 45,000 prisoners. This was, however, essentially a diversionary offensive, and in any case the attackers had outrun their transport. On June 9th came a renewed attack, on the northern flank of the salient—actually between the two salients created by the May offensive and that of March. The offensive of June 9th, the Battle of the Matz, was, however, on a smaller scale and was brought to a halt by a French counterstroke—something new and a good sign. Another good sign was that American divisions had been engaged in both battles and fought splendidly.

Yet another feature lightening the darkness of this depressing and anxious period was the success gained by both allies in a number of minor actions. One of the smaller of these concerned the 1st Gordon Highlanders. The 3rd Division was still in its old position and the object of the attack was to obtain greater depth on the east side of the La Bassée Canal. It was a night attack carried out on June 14th—the anniversary of the never-forgotten affair at Infantry Hill—by the 9th and 76th Brigades on a two-mile front, with no preliminary bombardment but strong artillery support. In the 76th Brigade the 2nd Suffolks were on the right and the 1st Gordons on the left. The two battalion commanders—Lieut.-Colonel R. A. Wolfe-Murray, commanding the Gordons—set up a combined headquarters in a fortified house on the eastern slope of Hinges Hill. They must have had an anxious night, for in the darkness news came in only in doubtful scraps from walking wounded or prisoners of war. At 11.45 p.m. the two leading companies of the Gordons advanced under a barrage moving at the rate of one hundred yards in five minutes. At 4 a.m. on June 15th it was learnt that the flanks were on their objectives, some four hundred and fifty yards deep, but that there was trouble with machine guns holding up the centre and both company commanders, Captains J. M. Wilson and E. F. Horne, had been killed. However, about 5.30, in broad daylight, platoons of the support companies rushed the machine guns. The whole objective was then secured. The division took 175 prisoners.

Despite the magnitude of the success won by the Germans in their Champagne offensive, they felt that they had not attracted southward a high enough proportion of the allied reserve. They therefore decided that the time was not yet ripe to reopen the Flanders offensive which, it will be recalled, was to be decisive and to destroy the British Army. Instead they struck once again in the same region as before. This new offensive, begun on July 15th, started in two sections : one to force the passage of the Marne where the river had already been reached, and the other east of Reims, to advance to the Marne and join hands with the former. The first gained a dangerous measure of success. The second was contained by defence in depth, the finest stand yet made by the French. This time there was no question of surprise. The French knew what was coming. Foch demanded British aid and Haig at once sent the XXII Corps (Lieut.-General Sir Alexander Godley) with the 51st and 62nd Divisions. These were followed by two more divisions, the 15th and 34th. Thus, though only four British divisions took part in the Second Battle of the Marne, five battalions of the Gordons, 4th, 6th, and 7th, in the 51st Division, 5th and 9th in the 15th, were engaged in it. No other British regiment was represented by so many.

The 51st Division began its move south on July 14th, the day before the enemy attacked. Major-General Carter-Campbell was probably informed of its destination, but battalion commanders were given no hint of it. For the sake of space the experiences of the journey will be represented by those of one battalion, the 6th. It was in the train all day on July 15th, but the troops got a wash and some even a bathe during a halt of forty minutes at Gisors. On the 16th it detrained at Romilly-sur-Seine. The day was very hot, but a shady bivouac was available. For the moment the battalion was completely out of touch with its brigade. Next day French transport carried it to Mesnil-sur-Oger, south of the Marne. C Company which had travelled separately, rejoined. On the 18th there was a break-down in administration and no rations arrived, so that the troops were reduced—in theory at least—to the emergency ration. On the 19th the battalion, with the rest of the division, had an arduous march across the Marne at Epernay in great heat and amid clouds of dust, and moved up to the east side of the salient.

On the previous day, July 18th, the French Sixth and Tenth Armies on the west side had launched a major counter-offensive, with astounding success, the most heartening event of the year 1918 to date. The two rearward divisions of the XXII Corps, the 15th and 34th, had been diverted to this flank, but not in time to take part in the first phase of the counter-offensive. The

XXII Corps with the leading divisions reached the scene on the east flank in time for the first French advance on this side, on June 20th. The part played by the Gordon Highlanders in the 51st Division will, therefore, be described first.

The Italian troops in the Marfaux sector, who were to have been relieved by the British, were battered and shaky. It was therefore decided that the troops of the XXII Corps should pass straight through them and the French division on their left, without a formal relief. The French orders were issued late on June 19th, so that there was little or no time for reconnaissance. Moreover, the country was of a type new to the troops. What were called woods or even forests up in Flanders were copses to these, and the first part of the advance involved passing through a big one, the Bois de Courton. All that was known of the victory gained on the west of the salient and the fact that on the southern side the Germans had abandoned their bridgehead south of the Marne was communicated to the troops and inspired them to the strongest effort.

Each of the front brigades of the 51st Division, 154th on the right and 153rd on the left, advanced with its three battalions in column. The right boundary of the 154th and of the division was the river Ardre, beyond which the 62nd Division was attacking; the left a line through the villages of Nappes and Espilly. The advance of the leading battalion, the 4th Seaforths, began at 8 a.m., and that of the 4th Gordons at 8.40. It was soon realized, if any one was in ignorance of the fact, that it was a very different matter to attack German troops by surprise, as had been done on the other side of the salient two days earlier, and to do so when they were thoroughly ready, as was now the case. The troops lost direction amid the trees, and it is almost impossible to reconstruct the action from the scanty records of the 4th Gordons, or those of the brigade. The battalion was counter-attacked and driven back, its commanding officer, Lieut.-Colonel Bickmore, being wounded and captured.

In the 153rd Brigade the 6th Black Watch attacked in first line. To begin with resistance was slight. Many prisoners were taken and the 7th Gordons, though in support, found exhausted men asleep. The wood was exceptionally dense, and the battalions became to some extent intermixed. However, the Gordons reached the western edge without undue loss, but were there met by a storm of fire. Finding that the 154th Brigade was in rear, Lieut.-Colonel Menzies formed two of his companies into a defensive flank. A party, apparently of all the battalions, reached the outskirts of Les Haies, but with both flanks in air—for the French on the left were also well behind—could not remain there. In brief, all that was accomplished by the 51st Division, despite great gallantry, was an advance of about a mile from the start-line, involving the capture only of the enemy's outpost zone, without any

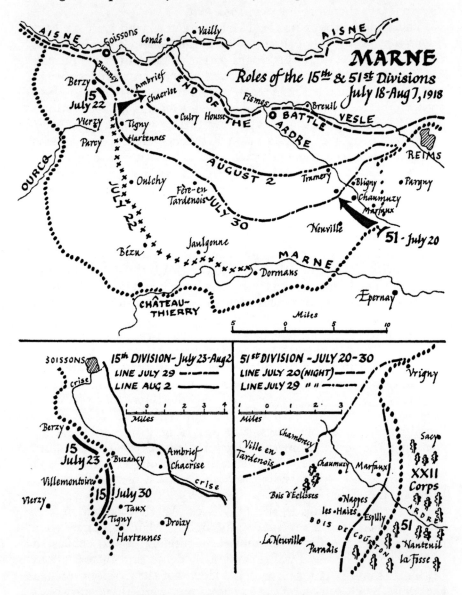

permanent penetration of his main zone of resistance. The 62nd Division's advance had been even shallower. The attack had without doubt been necessary: even if it had gained no ground it would have been worth while in order to ensure that the enemy did not withdraw divisions from this flank in order to reinforce the other. Both divisions had, however, lost heavily, and the results were disappointing. At one time a mile of ground gained had been considered a success, but now, with the development of defence in depth on the one hand and improved offensive tactics on the other, this was no longer so.

For July 21st the 62nd and 51st Divisions were ordered, before trying to advance along the Ardre valley, to secure the wooded ridges flanking it, the buttresses of the famous Montagne de Reims. On the south bank of the river Major-General Carter-Campbell set his troops three objectives : the western edge of the Bois de Courton, the middle of the next wood to the north-west, the Bois d'Eclisses, and a road just beyond that wood. The attack was entrusted to the 152nd Brigade, which had been in reserve on the previous day. It was again to be made on a front of one battalion, the 6th Gordon Highlanders, up to the first objective, the flanks being protected by the 153rd Brigade. The operation was thus a limited one to get hold of an extremely difficult stretch of ground before continuing the offensive on a full scale. The orders of the commander of the Fifth Army, General Berthelot, called for something different, "a blow which may be decisive ", but the French troops south of the 51st Division neither attempted nor achieved more than it did.

Almost all who have taken part in forest fighting, or even practised it on manoeuvres, are agreed that it is the most difficult type and calls most insistently for training and experience. When the trees are deciduous the difficulties are, of course, greatest in summer. French forestry is normally good, but after four years of war these woods had been neglected and were choked by undergrowth through which it was often hard to force a way even when there was no human opposition. The troops felt lost in them. They were given no time for deliberate reconnaissance—the one relatively easy feature of woodland warfare—so never knew when they would be assailed by heavy fire at close quarters from an invisible position. They constantly lost direction. Compass bearings were useful at times, but not always, since their point or line of departure was often incorrectly fixed. The Germans had similar problems to face, but they did not affect the defence as much as the attack. In the course of this day it was, however, made obvious that the staffs knew little about the situation, since several officers on horseback were shot down at short range in the rides. The Highland troops were bewildered by the sudden chatter of light machine guns from unexpected directions.

The start was marked by a calamity due to the haste with which the attack was mounted. Fire was encountered a long way east of the line on which the 6th Gordons had been ordered to form up. The enemy was in strength, and there was no time to apprise the artillery—some of which was French and Italian—of the situation. The battalion had to begin its advance seven hundred yards behind the barrage, with the consequence that no benefit was derived from it. The troops went forward with determination, but both the Gordons and the French on their left were held up after advancing 500 yards. The right flank got to within two hundred yards of the north-west corner of the wood. In the end the line was withdrawn to within between two and three hundred yards of that from which the attack had started, that is, well short of the start-line laid down in the orders. This was a sad and costly disappointment.

The operations of July 22nd, where the 51st Division was concerned, were limited to the advance of a single battalion, the 7th Black Watch, on the south-western fringe of the wood in aid of a French attack on the village of Paradis. The attack failed in face of machine-gun and musketry fire as hot as ever.

It was indeed hard going. But, if the troops were getting weary, they had not lost heart. July 23rd proved a better day. On this occasion the 186th Brigade of the 62nd Division, commanded by Brig.-General J. L. G. Burnett of the Gordon Highlanders, made a fine advance which included the capture of Marfaux, on the north bank of the Ardre. That of the 51st Division was carried out by the 152nd Brigade with three battalions in line, the 6th Gordons being allotted the left wing; but owing to some confusion only three companies of the battalion were available, the fourth not having been relieved in its previous position. On the right the Bois d'Aulnay, a small wood north of the Bois de Courton, was captured and the final objective was reached and held. On the left the 6th Gordons had another mishap at the start. A barrage of French 75's fell short and caused many casualties. It was a severe trial for any unit after what had happened on July 21st, but the Gordons once more put in a brave effort. They reached a sunken road three hundred yards short of Espilly. They were, however, unable to cross the slope above the village in face of murderous fire. After they had been brought to a halt their lost company arrived and was put in on the left. Apart from the impossibility of taking Espilly, the battalion shared in what was a fully successful limited offensive.

Mention has already been made of the abandonment by the Germans of their bridgehead south of the Marne. They had now begun a planned and deliberate withdrawal from the southern part of their salient on a much greater scale. To enable this to be carried out it was urgently necessary to hang on at the elbows of the salient. Here, far from withdrawing, they had reinforced their front. The two British divisions had been attacking near the eastern elbow, and this was the explanation of the ferocious resistance they had met. It will appear later that the 34th and 15th Divisions were at the western elbow and therefore had similar experiences.

Little can be said about the next three days except that the 4th Gordons of the 154th Brigade gained a little ground on July 24th and 25th by short rushes. A fresh general advance was ordered on the 27th. As the French had taken over part of the front of the 62nd Division, its 187th Brigade was transferred to the 51st and placed under Major-General Carter-Campbell's command. The advance was made with three brigades in line : 152nd Brigade with right flank on the Ardre, 5th Seaforths leading; the 187th in the centre ; the 153rd on the left, 7th Gordons and 6th Black Watch in line.

The objective was again only a limited one, but the blow was struck in the air. " Jerry " had gone. The troops had to put up with a good deal of shell fire, but they hardly saw a German soldier and met practically no small-arms fire. In the 152nd Brigade the 6th Gordons reached Chaumuzy, which was then being shelled with fine impartiality by French and German guns. At 12.40 p.m. Brig.-General R. Laing issued orders that the advance should be continued through the village, the 6th Gordons now moving on the left. This was done without any greater opposition being met. A line was established running from the Ardre to about three hundred yards west of Chaumuzy. The weather throughout the offensive had been hot but with occasional heavy showers. Now came the turn for one of these. The 6th Gordons, for the second successive night, lay out in the wet.

The 7th Gordons in the 153rd Brigade also reached its objective, passing through Les Haies to do so. It may be remembered that a few men had reached the outskirts of this village on July 20th, the first day of the offensive. The orders the battalion then received were cautious because this country was ideal for a trap. First it was bidden to establish itself on the ridge between the Bois de Courton and the Bois d'Eclisses ; then it was told to reconnoitre the latter wood and, when it was reported clear, to push on and occupy an old French trench beyond it. This was accomplished in the course of the night. The 152nd Brigade on the right was so exhausted that it did not come into line till the morning of the 28th. As the Germans fell back the front was of course rapidly diminishing in length. In consequence the 187th Brigade had been withdrawn.

On July 28th, a report being received that the French on the left of the 51st Division had captured the village of Chambrecy, the

153rd Brigade was ordered to advance once more in touch with them. In the process, as the front continued to retract, the 152nd Brigade would be squeezed out. The 7th Gordons and 6th Black Watch went forward at 4.30 p.m. Unhappily, if the French had ever been in Chambrecy, they were not there now. The two battalions were raked by machine-gun fire from the place and suffered heavy loss. However, the Black Watch were not to be deterred. They took Chambrecy, though it was in the French sector. The Gordons too struggled on to the slopes of the Montagne de Bligny, but when the 4th Battalion of the 154th Brigade came up to relieve them that night the two commanding officers decided that it would be better to hold a line rather in rear, in the old French trenches.

The 51st Division did not move on July 29th. On the 30th the enemy counter-attacked the Montagne de Bligny, held by the 154th Brigade, now the only brigade of the division in line. This counter-attack, which was routed, did not involve the 4th Gordons. Next day the division was relieved by the French and began its move back to the British front as soon as possible.

The two British divisions had advanced four miles in constant fighting, with many rebuffs. Between them they had taken 1,169 prisoners from seven different divisions. This was not a large haul, but it was harder to take men than to kill them in these woods, and the troops said they had never before seen so many German dead. Their own losses had naturally been very high, since they had been engaged day after day. Those of the 6th Gordons are given as 344 for the whole month of July, which would include a few in Flanders up to July 10th ; those of the 7th were 272. The nearest figure which can be given for the casualties of the 4th is about the same as that of the 7th.[1] Of the " missing " in the division a number were picked up by French ambulances and taken by hospital train to the south of France, so that it was some time before they were reported as wounded instead of missing, and it is almost certain that this occurred in the case of some men of the Gordon Highlanders.

The reinforcements received during the battle were only one-fifth of the casualties, so that all battalions were very weak when they left the area. They were also very weary after almost incessant fighting and a great deal of marching. Yet they came away with the sense that they had taken part in a victory. As they boarded their trains many of the Highlanders were observed

[1]

		Killed	Wounded	Missing
6th Gordons	Officers	3	10	—
	Other ranks	42	266	23
7th Gordons	Officers	4	8	—
	Other ranks	25	197	38

by indulgent eyes to have prepared themselves for the journey with a tin of bully beef carried in one hand and a bottle of the wine of this region, champagne, in the other.

We now turn to the western side of the salient made by the enemy in his great offensive launched in May.   Here it was that the main blow was dealt ;   the operations on the eastern side, while necessary and effective, were secondary.   The massed French artillery opened fire at 4.35 a.m. on July 18.   General Degoutte's Sixth Army on the right and General Mangin's Tenth on the left then attacked.   The huge French array, which included three American divisions, had been in great part hidden in woodlands, and the surprise was complete and devastating.   Two days earlier the movement of artillery and mortars to Flanders for the offensive against the British had begun, and on the very morning of the 18th Ludendorff had gone from his headquarters at Avesnes to Mons, headquarters of Crown Prince Rupprecht's Army Group, to make the final arrangements.   The news arrived while the conference was sitting.   The reactions of the men round the table can be imagined.   The Flanders offensive was postponed.   It was in fact never to be launched.

In the first rush a number of divisions covered four miles by noon.   Then there was a pause, but after the field artillery had been moved up, with astonishing speed by comparison with former experience, progress was resumed.   This was continued next day, though now the advance was faced by countless machine guns.   By the 20th, the day on which the Fifth Army, including the 51st Division, joined in, Mangin alone had taken 15,000 prisoners and 400 guns.   On the 21st he was stuck.   The German retirement from the Marne having begun, the divisions at the western elbow hung on like limpets west and south of Soissons, so that the next stage became as difficult and costly as that already described on the eastern side of the salient.   The British 15th and 34th Divisions came into the fighting at an unpleasant moment for themselves.

The four divisions sent to the aid of the French had been divided and the single corps headquarters had, as has been shown, accompanied the 51st and 62nd to Champagne.   The 15th and 34th therefore came under the command of French corps.   Owing to differences in method such an arrangement was apt to lead to misunderstanding and delay, but in the case of the 15th Division there seem to have been no unhappy results, except that its orders to relieve the American 1st Division on the night of July 22nd and to attack at 5 a.m. next day did not arrive until after dark.   Even this may not have been the fault of the French XX Corps, and in any event such things were not unheard of in our own forces.   The division had a very hard time of it in this battle, but it was fortunate in its corps commander, General Berdoulat, and indeed in all its dealings with the French, the air as well as the land forces.

The first attack of the 15th Division was carried out by the 46th and 45th Brigades on a front facing Buzancy on the right and bounded on the left by the Crise stream. The 5th Gordon Highlanders in the 44th Brigade was in reserve. The 9th Gordon Highlanders (P.) was also held in divisional reserve, at Missy-au-Bois. This was open warfare; there was no entrenchment except for occasional temporary rifle-pits, and from first to last the battalion had no pioneer work to do.

The attack was met by withering fire at short range and at the same time enfiladed by heavy artillery from the region of Soissons. The ground gained was very narrow, and some of it was abandoned at night as too exposed. The advance, indeed, was not sufficient to be shown on any but a large scale map. The division had marched in with a high heart and had met with a grim disappointment.

No infantry action took place on July 24th and 25th, but the German artillery was extremely active. The woodlands and the narrow valleys characteristic of the country were deluged with mustard gas—the 9th Gordons report that thousands of these "yellow cross" shells came over in the space of two hours. On the night of the 25th the 44th Brigade relieved the 46th on the division's right wing, the 5th Gordons on the right in touch with French troops of the 87th Division. On the following day, however, General Berdoulat ordered the division to extend slightly farther south. Its relief of the French made the Gordons the left battalion of the brigade front and brought the division in face of the château and village of Buzancy, the combination of the two making a very formidable objective.

On the morning of the 27th the French 87th Division took the village of Villemontoire. General Berdoulat thereupon ordered Major-General H. L. Reed, commanding the 15th Division, to capture the château and village next day. The unusual hour of 12.30 p.m. was chosen in order to effect surprise if possible and to make sure of good aircraft observation. Several barrages were put down on the 27th and on the morning of the attack, in the hope of accustoming the enemy to such action by the artillery without any move on the part of the infantry. The main objective was allotted to the 8th Seaforths. That of the Gordons was hardly less difficult, and its capture and retention depended on the success of the Seaforths.

The Château de Buzancy lay to the north-west of the village. It was a large, solid building set a little west of the centre in a small wooded park, hardly what would be called a park in Britain but about sixteen acres in extent, surrounded by high and stout stone walls. The western wall was close to the front line. The northern, some four hundred yards long, formed the right boundary of the 5th Gordons. The left boundary followed an east-and-west road which skirted a narrow wood. The intervening ground over which the battalion was to attack was an open ridge, partly covered with high standing corn. The breadth of the battalion's frontage was nearly seven hundred yards, and the objective at its deepest eleven hundred, on a ridge.

The Gordons advanced with two companies in line. For a few minutes there was no check. Then a strong point on the edge of a cornfield on the battalion's left centre held up the advance. This was taken with the grenade and progress was resumed. The right flank ran into trouble from a machine gun firing from an embrasure cut in the park wall. Lieutenant F. W. Lovie brought up his platoon from the support company, worked round the post, and rushed it. He himself was wounded and his platoon suffered severely, but he had cleared the way for the advance to continue. Thenceforth all went well and the objective was reached at 1.20 p.m., fifty minutes after the launch of the attack. Meanwhile the château had been captured. The village was secured after fierce hand-to-hand and house-to-house fighting, in which the Seaforths received invaluable aid from a French flame-thrower detachment.

Unhappily the French 87th Division, which had been in line since July 22nd and was now depleted and fatigued, had not taken a strong point or cleared the woods south and south-west of Buzancy, so that the right flank of the 15th Division lay open. Against the flank guard the Germans quickly advanced, making particularly good use of a sunken road leading into the village from the south. About 4.30 p.m. the Gordons made a withdrawal, which had to be continued to the original line when the Germans recovered the château and raked them in flank with fire. The French made arrangements to renew the attack with another regiment, but called it off when it was found that the 44th Brigade had already withdrawn. The German account, from regimental histories, pays homage to the bravery with which Buzancy and the château were defended.

The Highland Brigade had fulfilled its difficult task, though the Seaforths, with their right exposed, had not been able to go on to the final objective as the Gordons had. The fruits of the victory had been lost through no fault on its part.

On July 29th the British 34th Division attacked further south, but the 51st was not called upon.[1] On that night and the following

---

[1] The two British divisions never fought side by side or in the same corps, but their flanks were at most two and a half miles apart and at one time less.

the 51st Division virtually changed places with the French 87th Division, so that its left was just south of Buzancy. General Berdoulat's object in making this redistribution, curious at first sight, was that the 51st was still fit to attack, but was not to be launched against the fortress of Buzancy ; whereas the 87th was not fit, but could not be relieved for lack of another fit division. The 44th Brigade had passed into reserve. Now, however, not for the first time, the pioneers were given an infantry role. The 9th Gordons were put under command of the 45th Brigade and relieved a French battalion in a bombardment, counting themselves lucky to escape with only 10 casualties.

A fresh attack was launched on August 1st. All that need be said of it is that a very slender measure of success was gained. Neither battalion of the Gordons was involved. The 9th had been informed that it would take part, and it is said that the men were genuinely disappointed when they heard that this would not be the case. The historian can only set down this statement as he finds it, but he can say with certainty that the morale of these pioneers was always very high. The 5th Gordons were to have had a role in covering the right flank, but the advance was not deep enough to make this necessary. They nevertheless came in for considerable loss.

That night the 44th was again brought up. It relieved the 46th Brigade in the right sector. The 5th Gordons took over on the right. The 9th Gordons relieved a battalion of the 45th Brigade and consolidated such ground as had been won in the morning. The division had given all it had to give and was approaching the point of exhaustion. Major-General Reed was informed that it would be relieved during the nights of August 2nd and 3rd.

At 8.30 a.m. on the 2nd the news reached him that the Germans were in retreat opposite the French 12th Division on his right. He at once issued orders that under cover of strong patrols every effort should be made to keep contact with the enemy.

For a few minutes the troops hesitated, as had happened in 1917 when the Germans disengaged in their retreat to the Hindenburg Line. Brig.-General N. A. Thomson, commanding the 44th Brigade, wrote : " It was certainly a dramatic moment when orders for the advance reached my brigade. In the front line the men formed up in groups on the parapet of their trenches, seemingly dazed at these, to them, new conditions of warfare. Fortunately, a few older hands remembered their early training at Aldershot and Salisbury Plain. . . . Never on any field day or in action have I seen men press forward in such eagerness when once the game was realized. . . . The brigade pushed boldly across the

Crise to the line Ambrief-Chacrise . . . and the Seaforths and Gordons dug in, in full view of the enemy, in open fields."

The leading company of the 9th Gordons reached Ambrief, nearly three miles from their morning position, at 4 p.m. Long-range shelling was pretty heavy and 22 casualties were suffered during the advance. The 5th Gordons moved up between Ambrief and Chacrise. The enemy was some miles distant ; in fact French cavalry was operating in front of the division. The final stroke dealt by the Germans, was, however, still to be felt. They had deluged woods and valleys with mustard gas. This does not appear to have had much effect on either battalion of the regiment that day, but both were hard hit that night. The 5th had 68 and the 9th 67 men of their support companies gassed in caves. The men did not notice the smell of the gas on entering. Fortunately, the effects were very slight, and even of those sent to hospital the majority were back at duty within a fortnight.

This fact makes the losses suffered by the 5th Gordons, huge though they were, appear even more terrible than was actually the case. For the months of July and August, 1918, which must include a certain number on the Arras front before they left it for the Soissonnais and after they had returned to it, the gross loss is given as 434.[1] There is, however, a note that the numbers had been over estimated by 27. Among the killed was the commanding officer, Lieut.-Colonel G. A. Smith. He was extremely popular and had been a life-long Volunteer.

No formal relief of the 51st Division was carried out. The French 17th Division, which had only just arrived on the battle-field, simply moved through it to continue the advance. The Germans withdrew behind the Aisne and its tributary the Vesle. There they stood firm, and Foch, who received the Baton of a Marshal of France on August 6th, did not intend to continue the offensive. He had other plans in view.

The Second Battle of the Marne was more than a fine, though less than an overwhelming, victory. It was also a land-mark in Anglo-French relations. Each ally had complained of the other in the previous German offensives ; in particular the loss of Kemmel Hill by the French had not raised the British soldier's opinion of the troops of his ally. In this respect the Marne fighting did a great deal of good. The two Scottish divisions had been thrown into the battle on either side of the salient at the most difficult stages and on fronts which the enemy made the greatest efforts to

[1]

	Killed	Wounded (or gassed)	Missing
Officers	3	15	—
Other ranks	54	325	37

hold to the last in order to make a safe retreat over the Vesle and the Aisne. They had won no decisive successes. They had, how-ever, won warm admiration from French commanders and troops for their bravery, willingness and fortitude. For their part they witnessed how great an effort the French could make. They con-tributed to the spreading of the reality of this victory in the ranks of the British. They were treated with friendship and received many French decorations for gallantry. On July 30th General Berthelot issued the following Order of the Day :

At the moment when the British XXII Corps is under orders to leave the Fifth Army, the General commanding the Army wishes to express to it all the gratitude and all the admiration due to the great deeds accomplished by it.

It had hardly arrived when, taking it as an honour to participate in the victorious counter-offensive which had halted the furious onrush of the enemy to the Marne and was beginning to drive him back in disorder towards the north, the XXII Corps hastened its movements, reduced to a minimum the length of its reconnaissances, and hurled itself with ardour into the struggle.

Keeping up its efforts without respite, harassing and pressing the enemy, after ten successive days of hard fighting it secured for itself the valley of the Ardre, deeply imbrued with its blood.

Thanks to the heroic courage and the proverbial tenacity of these sons of Great Britain the continuous and repeated efforts of this brave Corps were not made in vain.

21 officers, more than 1,300 men, 140 machine guns, 40 guns, were captured from the enemy, four of whose divisions were battered and driven back successively ; the upper valley of the Ardre and the heights dominating it from the north and south were regained. Such is the record of the British participation in the effort of the Fifth Army.

Soldiers of the Highlands, under the command of General Carter-Camp-bell, commanding the 51st Division ; sons of Yorkshire under the command of General Braithwaite, commanding the 62nd Division ; New Zealand and Australian Cavalry—all of you, officers and men of the XXII Corps, so brilliantly commanded by General Sir. A. Godley, have added a glorious page to your history.

Marfaux, Chaumuzy, Montagne de Bligny—these miraculous names can be written in letters of gold in the annals of your regiments.

Your French friends will recall with emotion your brilliant courage and perfect comradeship in battle.

General commanding the Fifth Army
Berthelot.

General Mangin, commanding the Tenth Army, also issued an Order of the Day, addressed to the 15th and 34th Divisions which had fought under his command :

Officers, non-commissioned officers, and men of the British 15th and 34th Division,

You entered the battle at its fiercest moment.   The enemy, already once vanquished, again brought against us his best divisions, considerably out-numbering our own.   You continued to advance step by step in spite of his desperate resistance, and you held the ground won in spite of his violent counter-attacks.

Then, during the whole day of August 1, side by side with your French comrades, you stormed the ridge dominating the whole country between the Aisne and the Ourcq which the defenders had received orders to hold to the last.   Having failed to retake the ridge with his last reserves, the enemy had to beat a retreat, pursued and harassed for twelve kilometres.

All of you, English and Scottish, young soldiers and veterans of Flanders and Palestine, have shown the magnificent qualities of your race : courage and imperturbable tenacity.   You have won the admiration of your comrades in arms.   Your country will be proud of you, for to your chiefs and to you is due a large share of the victory we have gained over the barbarous enemies of the free.

I am happy to have fought at your head, and I thank you.

Mangin.[1]

One other notable tribute must be mentioned.   General Gas-soins, commanding the French 17th Division which had passed through the 15th in the pursuit to the Vesle, first established his headquarters in Buzancy.   There he saw evidence of the fight put up by the Highland Brigade, which deeply impressed him.   He erected a small stone monument on the highest ground and on the spot where the body of the soldier who had advanced the farthest had been found.   This was probably a man of the 5th Gordon Highlanders.   On one face of this memorial was a tablet or medal-lion, on which were inscribed thistles and roses.   Beneath were the words :

Ici fleurira toujours le glorieux chardon d'Ecosse parmi les roses de France.

La 17 D.I. Française—La 15 D.I. Ecossaise

[1] General Berthelot's order is translated by the present writer ; for that of General Mangin the translation is taken from the history of the 15th (Scottish) Division.

The allusion by General Mangin to Palestine has no reference to the 15th Division. The 34th Division, temporarily reduced to cadre after crushing losses, had been reconstituted with battalions from that theatre of war.

CHAPTER XX

THE GREAT COUNTER-OFFENSIVE

SINCE Marshal Foch had been entrusted with the co-ordinating role of Commander-in-Chief and the strategic direction of the operations of the allies, he had been inspired by the hope of returning to the offensive. The failure of the Germans in the Second Battle of the Marne gave him the opportunity. In consultation with Field-Marshal Sir Douglas Haig, he decided first to disengage Amiens and the Paris-Amiens railway and to drive back the enemy between the Avre and the Somme. This offensive was entrusted to the British Fourth and French First Armies, the latter being placed under Haig's orders.

The attack was launched on August 8th, 1918, " the black day of the German Army ". It resulted in a great victory. The front was advanced some twelve miles and nearly 20,000 prisoners were taken. By August 12th the offensive was virtually closed down and the Canadian Corps, which had taken a vital part in it, was relieved by the French and transferred to the Arras front to put its weight into a fresh blow. Among the British divisions relieved by the Canadians was the 15th. After ten days of rest and reorganization including the absorption of 3,000 reinforcements, it had spent only from ten days to a fortnight holding a front north of Neuville-Vitasse. It now moved a short way north to the Loos sector. The 9th Gordons, who as pioneers had in their ranks more old-timers than other battalions, found themselves on ground familiar to, and hated by, many officers and men. There stood as of old the Hohenzollern, in a sector which some men had declared to be the most undesirable on the Western Front. The Loos front was, however, very quiet now. The tide of war was to flow past it, but not again through it.

The 1st Gordon Highlanders in the 3rd Division at last said goodbye to the La Bassée Canal. After ten days of training and sports in early August it moved south by train to Sus-St. Leger and marched to Berles-au-Bois, eight miles south-west of Arras and on the northern flank of the great salient left by the German offensive of March. It went almost straight into action with the minimum time for preparation, though it was, it is true, at the tail of the division. It did not reach Berles until the early hours of August 20th, where it lay out in an orchard. That did it no harm in fine August weather, but the attack was launched at 4.50 a.m. next day.

August 21st was, in fact, the beginning of the second phase of the offensive which had opened so well on the 8th. On that day

the British Third Army struck in the direction of Bapaume.
Nothing sensational was to be attempted on this first day. The
object was in part to obtain a good position for an assault on the
Hindenburg Line, in part to reach Bapaume at a bound and as far
as possible prevent the destruction of the road and railway communications which passed through it. At z+90 minutes (6.25 a.m.)
the 3rd Division and the armour supporting it were to pass through
the troops of the 2nd Division and reach the Arras-Albert railway.
The 3rd Division was disposed with the 9th Brigade on the right,
the 8th on the left, and the 76th in support, the 1st Gordons
being in the second line of the 76th. If all went to plan the
battalion would not be engaged that day.

All did not go to plan, though in general the attack was sucess-
ful. The Gordons began their advance in column of route in
dense mist. After a mile had been covered and Quenoy Farm
had been reached the battalion shook out into artillery formation.
By 11 a.m., when a hot sun dispersed the mist, it had reached the
valley west of Courcelles-le-Comte. As the railway line had not
been reached and no call had been made upon it, it then moved a
little north to the shelter of a hollow road to await developments.

In the evening two companies were sent forward to co-operate
with the 63rd (R.N.) Division in an attack on the embankment
just north of Achiet-le-Grand ; but at 7 p.m. they learnt that this
had been tried and had failed. Perhaps rather quixotically, at
the request of the Anson Battalion, the Gordons then tried without
artillery support, but were held up and suffered very heavily.
The commanding officer, Lieut.-Colonel R. A. Wolfe-Murray, was
wounded leading the attack.

August 22nd was spent in moving up artillery and other preparations for the next step. Major N. G. Pearson assumed temporary command of the 1st Gordons. In the evening the battalion
moved up to cover the right of an attack on Gomiecourt, six
hundred yards east of the railway, next morning.

The 23rd was a highly successful day for the Third Army,
which advanced from two to four thousand yards on an eleven-mile
front and captured over 5,000 prisoners. The 1st Gordons had no
heavy fighting but did their job effectively and saved the assaulting
battalions many casualties. They dug in for the night south-east
of Gomiecourt. The 2nd Division had now passed through the
3rd, but the Gordons had to lie low throughout August 24th
because they remained under direct observation. The battalion
was withdrawn that night.

The Germans were still putting up a fairly strong resistance,
and where the advance hit a particularly good division the fighting
was almost as stiff as had ever been the case. Yet generally speaking

the enemy had lost a large measure of the endurance and determination which he had so persistently displayed.   Ground down
by the allies in 1916 and 1917, he had by his immense efforts

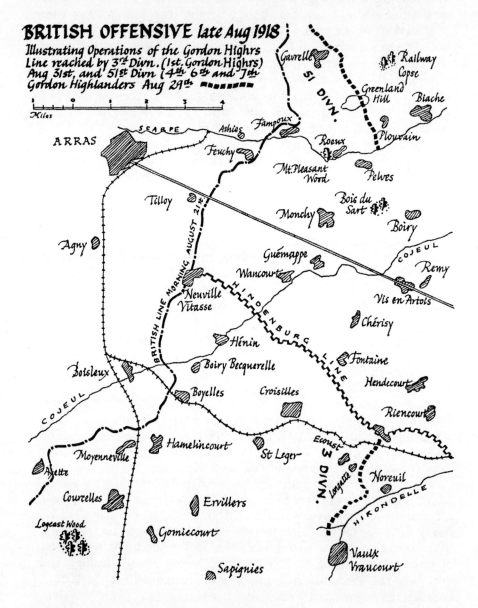

BRITISH OFFENSIVE late Aug 1918

Illustrating Operations of the Gordon Highrs
Line reached by 3rd Divn. (1st Gordon Highrs)
Aug 31st, and 51st Divn (4th 6th and 7th
Gordon Highlanders Aug 29th ▰▰▰▰▰▰▰

between March and early July 1918 himself brought about a grave
decay in the fighting spirit of his troops.   On the other hand, the
British had maintained theirs to a greater extent than any of the
belligerent forces but the Americans, who were only just beginning

to be engaged in strength.   The British infantry was not what it
had been, and it was estimated that 50 per cent. of the battalions
which attacked in the Third Army on August 21st were " boys " ;
but they possessed a fine resolution in attack, if less steadiness in
defence than of old.   Moreover, men's hearts had been borne up
by the victories of the summer.   There had been a certain depression as the Germans struck one deadly blow after another, threaten-
ing to separate the allies, to secure the Channel Ports, to reach Paris,
and it seemed impossible to wrest the initiative from them.   This
was now a thing of the past.   Spirits were high.

August 26th was an important day.   The right of the First
Army joined in the battle north of Arras.   It was first to advance
to and break through the Drocourt-Quéant Switch, which ran
northward nine miles east of Arras as a continuation of the Hindenburg Line, and then to turn south-eastward behind the Hindenburg
Line, on which the Third Army was closing and which it would
shortly attack.

The Third Army made little progress on the 26th, the Germans
using to good effect the old trenches of the Somme battlefield.
The 1st Gordons were not engaged.   They moved a couple of
miles north from Gomiecourt to Hamelincourt.

On pulling out of the Marne counter-offensive the 51st Division had returned to the familiar Arras front.   Once again, notes
the diary of the 6th Gordon Highlanders glumly, a promised rest
had been denied.   It found nothing to grumble about, however,
in the position, support battalion to the 152nd Brigade, first allotted to it.   Its right flank was on the Scarpe close to Athies.
" If left in peace ", writes an unusually informative war diary
keeper, " amenities of this place are considerable.   The railway
embankment, 70 feet high, affords complete protection to tiers
or terraces of comfortable huts.   Also a clean-flowing river and
several lakes for bathing and even boating.   The embankment
gives cover to a large area in which free movement by day goes on."

Too good to last nowadays !   Two days after this passage had
been written, on August 21st, the 6th Gordons took part in a
small operation.   The Seaforths had just captured a sunken road
running due north from the eastern end of Fampoux.   Now the
Gordons attacked the trenches beyond this with two companies.
The advance began at 1.30 a.m. by the light of a full moon and
the objective was secured after a sharp fight.   Three prisoners and
three machine guns were taken.   The losses were 2 killed and 27
wounded, and the diary asserts that of these 29 casualties 26 were
caused by the British artillery.   There was no German reaction,
as would in all probability have been the case in earlier days.   The
enemy, however, as so often in 1918, used mustard gas shell in

15

abundance and the Gordons suffered a number of casualties from this cause on the 23rd. Mustard gas was always deadly in the muggy heat then prevailing.

August 26th was, as already stated, the day of a major offensive by the First Army's right wing. South of the Scarpe the Canadian Corps was to take Monchy-le-Preux, a famous and much disputed point of vantage. The 6th Gordons were to co-operate by covering its left flank. This task, the brigade commander, Brig.-General W. H. E. Seagrave,[1] understood to be only temporary, having been told that a fresh division would shortly relieve the 51st, still tired after its gruelling days in the Battle of the Marne and not yet fully brought up to strength. In fact the 51st carried out a highly important attack.

From the north side of the Scarpe the 6th Gordons watched the Canadians walking majestically behind a colossal barrage straight over Monchy. The Gordons themselves advanced at 10 a.m. Apparently in order to avoid risk to the Canadians their right moved without a barrage. Their first objective lay just beyond Mount Pleasant Wood, near Roeux Château—the very ground over which the 51st Division had advanced in the Battle of Arras in 1917. They did not quite reach the second, but did reach a line running north from Roeux. An acrimonious discussion now took place with brigade headquarters, which believed the report of the 153rd Brigade that it had reached the summit of Greenland Hill. Lieut.-Colonel J. G. Thom believed his eyes, which told him that this was not so. He therefore resisted all demands that he should try to push on further, with the risk of being " pocketed " by the Plouvain lakes ahead and exposed to fire from the high ground on his left.

He was right about the situation. The 153rd Brigade had, however, begun a fine and memorable advance. The 7th Gordons moved in support to the other two battalions of the brigade. When the battalion passed through it was held up rather short of the summit of Greenland Hill by very hot fire. The attack was renewed on August 27th, when the 6th Gordons reached their second objective and the 7th crossed the summit of Greenland Hill. A counter-attack then drove them back to the trenches taken on the previous day.

Yet the summit was to fall to the Gordon Highlanders, though the 7th Battalion had not been able to hold it. The 154th Brigade on the left now extended its flank southward in order to cover this objective. On August 29th the 4th Gordons carried the hill and established outposts well down its eastern side. Ninety prisoners were taken at relatively small cost. The loss was, however,

[1] Successor to Brig.-General Laing.

increased by a big bombardment later in the day so that, counting men gassed, it reached a total of 109. Those of the 7th Battalion had been almost the same, 104.

Meanwhile a few miles to the south the 3rd Division had been preparing for a further advance. On August 30th the 76th Brigade attacked Ecoust and Longatte—outposts of the Hindenburg Line which had been stubbornly defended in 1917. Both villages were allotted to the 2nd Suffolks, the 1st Gordons being ordered to establish a defensive right flank. The attack failed after initial success and the brigade was then relieved by the 9th, its freshest battalion, the 1st Gordons, remaining where it was. A renewed attack on the 31st secured all objectives after hard and fluctuating fighting. The battalion had to mourn the death of its excellent adjutant, Captain H. S. Gammell. All through the advance he had refused to let his hard office work absorb all his time and had at each step conducted reconnaissances himself. On September 5th the Gordons marched back to rest between Moyenville and Ayette. Here, on the 5th, Lieut.-Colonel the Hon. W. Fraser assumed command. Though there were trenches in plenty, many of them had fallen in and there had been to a large extent a phase of open warfare. From now on the conditions were to be such as may be called at least " semi-open warfare ", considerable advances against limited opposition, halts in front of fortified positions, pursuit after German withdrawals, followed by further " full-dress " attacks.

The success of the British attack on August 26th had brought about a German retirement towards, though not quite up to, the Hindenburg Line. This retreat affected also the north, where on the night of August 29th the enemy began a deep and deliberate withdrawal in which he finally abandoned the hard-won ground captured by him in the Battle of the Lys in April. The movement rearward did not, however, extend as far as the position of the 15th Division at Loos, which lay south of the salient. There all remained quiet at this time and indeed throughout September. The division thus had time to benefit—for the last time in military history until the ill-fated Maginot Line appeared—from one of the latest developments of trench, or more properly siege, warfare. This was a wonderful tunnel system which the 15th Division found on returning to its old battlefield. The following passage describes a tunnel from the Hulluch-Vermelles road to fortified " localities ".

The passage was about 4 feet wide, varying in height from 5½ to 7 feet and, cut out of the solid rock, needed few supports. Down the centre ran an 18-inch tramway for the purpose of carrying rations, water, ammunition, &c., to the front system. At various points other passages branched off, each leading to a post or strong point, or to large dug-outs, from which could be heard voices of men talking, officers calling orderlies, &c., the garrison of that locality.   Farther up one passed an officers' mess, signal and dressing stations, a cook-house, and the headquarters of the battalion.   The whole of this glorified rabbit-warren was lit by electricity, and was a marvel of construction.   Undoubtedly these tunnels saved many lives, and moreover greatly lessened the fatigue caused by long journeys up miles of traversed communication trenches, often knee-deep in mud or water.

Close to the exit nearest to the enemy was a large block of cement on wheels, so arranged that it could be rolled out to close the passage if required. Just past this the tunnel branched off in five directions, each leading to posts in the " battle zone ".

Such underground communications and quarters undoubtedly constituted a great boon, from the point of view of both comfort and safety. They must not be regarded, however, as comparing with similar work constructed in the conditions of peace. The historian does not claim to have known these tunnels in the Loos sector, but he did know others. Though they were ventilated, the atmosphere was sickly, as was the effect of living in them for long periods. Water was apt to trickle down the walls and even flow into slight depressions, so that pumping had to be resorted to. This is not to decry their value but is inserted in case it should be imagined that the infantryman's existence was easier than was the case.

The year 1918 was marked by a widespread disease, for long diagnosed, or left undiagnosed, by British medical officers as p.u.o. (pyrexia of uncertain—or as some said unknown—origin). The records of the Gordon Highlanders are in general surprisingly lacking in information about its incidence, though the regiment must have suffered like all other troops. In the 15th Division, then containing two battalions of the Gordons, the maximum number affected at any one time amounted to 1,700, well over 10 per cent.[1] A layman asserts, with all due caution, that p.u.o. was identical with what was afterwards called " Spanish 'flu ", which later on ravaged a great part of the world and was responsible for deaths by the hundred thousand.

This scourge was clearly a product of the war ; for in the most beautiful summer weather it attacked its victims on a scale unknown in normal influenza epidemics. The summer type was, however, less vicious than that which followed in the winter and accounted for the bulk of the mortality, and the patients in the well-fed British Army generally recovered within four or five days. The Germans, whose victuals had greatly deteriorated as a result of the allied blockade, suffered far more severely. Some divisions were temporarily immobilized.   " Flanders fever ", as the Germans

[1] Hospital admissions averaged over 15 per cent. in the allied armies.

called it, became an affair of major strategic importance. On July 11th, just before the enemy launched his Champagne offensive, Prince Rupprecht of Bavaria, the northern army group commander, noted in his diary that the offensive against the British in Flanders which was to have followed might have to be postponed on account of the epidemic. As we have seen, it was not merely postponed but cancelled, for other reasons.

The first phase of the allied counter-offensive had, as stated, begun on August 8th. The second had followed on August 21st and spread north to the British First Army east of Arras on August 26th. This phase may be said to have come to an end by the last day of August, though such a reckoning is for convenience only and the phases cannot actually be as precisely limited as this sketch would imply. It seems, however, safe to say that the third phase was opened on September 2nd by the breaching of the Drocourt-Quéant Switch (to the Germans the Wotan Position) by the Canadian Corps. This had an immediate effect. The Germans did not wait to have their Hindenburg Line rolled up from the north as Haig had intended to do. That very afternoon Ludendorff ordered a further withdrawal to begin that very night. Whereas the last had involved the abandonment of the ground gained in the Battle of the Lys, this involved the evacuation of the great salient won in March. It also meant the loss of a good deal of material, since only the most valuable could be moved back. And Germany was now running desperately short of material of many kinds.

East of the region in which the 76th Brigade and the 1st Gordons had last been engaged, the Germans had not attempted to hold the Hindenburg Line, the northern end of which had been rendered useless by the breach of the Drocourt-Quéant Switch. They had decided to make their next stand on the Canal du Nord, a pretty formidable obstacle and in particular an excellent tank-trap. The Gordons did not take part in the pursuit. They missed nothing. The retreating enemy never presented a serious opening. We have since seen retreats conducted deliberately and successfully in defiance of armour far more powerful and mobile and of aircraft of far higher performance than those of 1918.

From the ruins of Moyenneville and Ayette the 1st Gordons marched back on September 6th into unscarred country and to good billets at Gaudiempré. It is significant of the change in circumstances and tactics that on the 9th, after practising rapid loading, the troops were exercised in artillery formation, and that in the evening the new commanding officer, Lieut.-Colonel Fraser, lectured officers and n.c.o.s on attack formations in general. By September 12th the battalion had returned to the devastated area, but now to good huts, the legacy of the Germans, in Sapignies. Here it received a draft of 114 rank and file, all under nineteen. Next it moved east again, some seven miles to a sunken road between Beaumetz-lez-Cambrai and Morchies. The moment of the greatest offensive of all was approaching, involving on this part of the front the breaching of the Hindenburg Line and, from Havrincourt northward, of the Canal du Nord.

The 51st Division also had a quiet time in September; for it in fact, the pause lasted rather longer. The 4th Gordons have nothing to record but a spell in line, some unpleasantly heavy shelling, rest and training in rear. One very minor but exciting and gallant episode breaks the quietude of the 6th Battalion's records. The German retreat north of the Scarpe had not been deep, but as a result of the breaching of the Drocourt-Quéant Switch the outposts were now well east of Plouvain. On September 10th Lieutenant T. D. Thomson with 2 men went out to patrol between the Scarpe and the marshes. Near Biache-Saint Vaast he encountered a party of from a dozen to 15 Germans, who tried to cut him off. Lieutenant Thomson killed at least 3, wounded others, cleared the way for his return, and brought in his 2 men, both wounded. Their wounds were actually trifling, but he himself was punctured like a dartboard. He had five bullet wounds with grenade splinters for good measure. He was indeed a very fortunate as well as a stout officer.

All three battalions had a spell out of the line, pleasant at this time of the year. But there were no longer to be three. Yet again shortage of recruits called for an amalgamation. This was the third among the battalions of the Gordon Highlanders on active service. The first had been the amalgamation of the 8th and 10th, which became the 8/10th. Then there had been what amounted to a swallowing of the 8/10th by the 5th rather than an amalgamation, though it was officially described as the latter. Now the 6th and 7th were amalgamated.[1]

The event took place at midnight on October 5th at Frévent-Capelle. In this instance the junior battalion, the 7th, survived as little more than a name because the 6th was at the time almost up to establishment. The 6th took from the 7th only 3 officers and 107 other ranks. Four officers and 143 other ranks were transferred to the 4th Battalion, which was weaker. The rest, officers and men in numbers not specified, went to the base. The new battalion was to be known as the 6/7th and to be commanded by Lieut.-Colonel J. G. Thom of the former 6th.

It is perhaps sentimentality to look back with regret at the disappearance of a fine battalion at this stage of the war. Before

[1] See pp. 77 and 206.

very long all the New Army battalions were to disappear altogether and those of the Territorial Army were to revert to their peace-time pattern. Yet at the time officers and men of the 7th Gordon Highlanders were saddened.

For one thing, though hopes were higher than ever, few, from highest to lowest, realized how short a time there was to go—actually only five weeks from the date of the amalgamation of the 6th and 7th Gordons—or how nearly the war was already won. The planners were still absorbed in preparing for the final campaign of 1919, when vast armoured forces would be available to sweep the enemy away. In fact, the German Army was already in a situation in which it could no longer carry on.

CHAPTER XXI

THE 2ND GORDONS IN ITALY

THE arrival of the 7th Division, including the 2nd Gordon Highlanders, in Italy has already been described. The Italian disaster at Caporetto which caused the despatch to Italy of a large Anglo-French force of eleven divisions (five British and six French) has also been mentioned. A few words more about the background may be useful before we turn to the fortunes of the Gordons.

The Austro-German offensive had come to a halt on the Piave, but this was rather because the armies of the central powers had ceased to press on than the effect of Italian resistance. The Italians were nervous and disorganized. The campaign had cost them well over 300,000 casualties, of whom the fantastic number of 265,000 were prisoners of war, and 3,000 guns. Talk was circulating about a renewal of the enemy's offensive and of the Italian retreat. The arrival of the Anglo-French forces had, therefore, an immense moral value. Without it there can be no telling what would have happened—or perhaps there can.

Both British and French sent as commanders-in-chief officers of the highest seniority, reliability, and prestige, in view of the moral effect of the presence of such personalities rather than the size of their commands. They were Generals Sir Herbert Plumer and Fayolle. To look forward, the whole situation changed by the beginning of the year 1918, for the better in Italy and for the worse in France. On the one hand the German divisions which had played a notable part in the victory of Caporetto returned to France and the Italians gradually reorganized ; on the other the shadow of a German offensive on a tremendous scale—already described in these pages—loomed over the Western Front. In these circumstances the western allies felt compelled to withdraw part of their forces from Italy. Two of the British five, and four or the French six divisions were brought back to France either before or after the launching of the German offensive there on March 21st, 1918. We shall see that the 7th Division also received orders to return which were cancelled at the last moment. General Plumer left on March 10th, handing over command of all British troops in Italy to Lieut.-General Lord Cavan, commanding the XIV Corps, and this corps headquarters was expanded to a British G.H.Q. in April.

The 2nd Gordons did not at first experience even such activity as was to be met with on the Piave, and that was not a great deal. To begin with the 7th Division was held in reserve. Then, after the division had closed up to the Piave and taken over the right of the Montello front on January 18th, the Gordons remained with the 20th Brigade in divisional reserve. Not until January 26th, two months after their arrival in Italy, did the Gordons enter the front line.

The battalion found itself in a curious position. The Montello itself was an oval hill, seven miles long and standing in isolation above the plain and the river bed. It afforded good observation, but the steep unmetalled tracks traversing it from north to south were hard on transport animals. The defences consisted of outposts on the foreshore, here along a sort of esplanade. The two left posts were on an island reached by a pontoon bridge. The line of resistance was on the cliff, sixty to two hundred and fifty feet in height, but the British had not had time to complete the fortifications. The Italians had not absorbed the recent doctrine of defence in depth, and though their arrangements were not very different from what the British would have made in such country earlier in the war they now looked archaic. There was another line further to the rear.

The Piave was rather a torrent than a river, very fast-flowing, with patches of shingle which often changed their shape. It was impassable in a military sense except by bridges, and all the existing ones had been destroyed. The river was nearly a mile wide above the Montello, but there narrowed to some two hundred and seventy-five yards. Below the Montello the banks of shingle or sand which divided the river into channels became in some cases islands. These afforded the best hopes of a crossing should an offensive ever come within the bounds of possibility. At present they were, on the contrary, a threat. However, the Austrians were placid in the extreme. The Gordons could not have found a quieter front.

At the beginning of February the 2nd Gordons withdrew into brigade reserve. On the 7th the battalion sent its pipes and drums to Istrane aerodrome for the entertainment of the Italian Crown Prince. On the 12th, being now at Cusignano, it gave a demonstration of tactics in the attack for the Italian officers. On the 14th it was inspected by Sir Herbert Plumer. Then on the 24th, when it was again in front line on the Montello front, word came that it was to return to France. The news must have been received with mixed feelings. France stood for heavy losses. Even those, the vast majority, who had little conception of what was to happen in March and April in Picardy and Flanders, knew that much. On the other hand, France was the decisive theatre of the war where the issue must be decided. The Gordons had been living a life as pleasant as could be expected in a great war. The people were friendly and kindly. Casualties for the month of February numbered ten.

After relief the Gordons marched to Vedelago, where the pipes and drums beat retreat, "which was much appreciated by the inhabitants". At Camposampiero half the battalion and transport went to the station to entrain on March 4th. The movement was stopped by the sudden receipt of an order to stand fast. The explanation was that a message from London had been received by G.H.Q. that the 5th Division was to go instead of the 7th. The latter remained in Italy for the rest of the war.

Hints of a change to very different surroundings came in the shape of a lecture on pack transport attended by the transport officer, Lieutenant P. H. Adshead, who was to win an outstanding reputation for reliability and animal management, and his sergeant ; of hill-climbing instruction ; then of exercises in mountain warfare. On March 17th the commanding officer, Lieutenant.-Colonel F. M. Crichton Maitland, visited the Asiago Plateau to study the probable divisional front of the future. The XIV Corps had just been relieved in the Montello sector and was to be transferred westward to the mountainous part of the battle-front. Four miles south of the most advanced trenches ran a mountain chain with summits nearer five than four thousand feet high, on the north slopes of which ran a rear line of defence. Thence the ground dropped to a shallow basin, rocky, rugged, and largely pine-clad. Along the bottom of this slope was the front line. The Austrians held the plateau itself, named after the bashed little town of Asiago.[1]

Things moved rather slowly in Italy. It was some time before the Gordons were called on to take over part of the front. Meanwhile they played a great deal of football, nearly always with success, but were beaten by the 1st South Staffordshire of the 91st Brigade in the final of the divisional competition. In late March they went up to the high ground, but still in divisional reserve. It was not very interesting because nothing of the country could be seen through a cushion of thick cloud. Nor can one particular exercise with which authority varied the monotony, that of "climbing hills in gas masks", have been regarded as a pleasant diversion. Monte Pau, near which the camp of huts lay, was itself upwards of fifteen hundred feet in height—and there had been heavy snow-falls. Though three to four miles from the front line, it was not a pleasant location.

At last the day came when the Gordons were "warned for the line". On April 20th they moved up in daylight, with platoons at fifty yards interval, and relieved the 2nd Queens of the 91st

---

[1] The name "Asiago Plateau" was used in two senses. More strictly, it stood for the area behind the Austrian front, but it often included the British area between the mountain chain and the front line. The Gordons speak of being stationed "on the Asiago Plateau".

Brigade. The sector, near the centre of the British front, was known as that of Monte Lemerle, after the feature across which the support position ran. The trenches and shelters had been blasted out of the rock, but the former were shallow and inadequate. North of the front line the ground dropped sharply to the Ghelpac, at this time a nearly dry torrent-bed. The Austrian position ran along a crest beyond.

On April 22nd more snow fell. Despite the special winter clothing which had been provided for the troops in the mountains, the men felt the severe weather acutely. The front was quiet, with occasional interchange of artillery fire. By the beginning of May the worst was over, though there was still a fair amount of rain. The battalion then found itself in the left sector, next to Italian Bersaglieri. It took the brigadier two hours to visit two companies.

The British divisions carried out a number of raids, with a good proportion of successes. The turn of the 2nd Gordons came on May 15th. The battalion was then resting at the camp of Monte Pau. Three officers and 52 other ranks were taken up as far as possible by lorry and then made their way afoot to the front-line village of Cesuma. The enemy was found on the alert and the fire encountered was so hot that the operation was broken off with a loss of 16, including 2 officers wounded. The party withdrew to caves north of the Ghelpac. The 2nd Border Regiment was more successful and brought back 5 prisoners.

After two months on the Asiago Plateau the Gordons returned to the plains on May 26th. It has been mentioned that the battalions in France have not recorded much information about the influenza epidemic. This is not the case with the battalion in Italy. On June 1st a large number of men were affected by what was described as " fever ". Next day about 200 were stricken. A move had to be postponed, and the Gordons were left behind by their brigade. This type of influenza was still so obscure that a toxicologist came from France to investigate it in the ranks of the battalion. It did not last long. On June 14th the Gordons record triumphantly that their tug-of-war team easily beat that of the 22nd Brigade, despite " the late fever ". It had earlier beaten French and Italian teams and made something of a name for itself.

The whole of the 7th Division was then back in reserve in the plains. On the day after the tug-of-war, June 15th, the Austrians launched their big offensive (Battles of the Asiago and of the Piave). In the mountain it looked dangerous at one moment. However, the maximum penetration of the British front did not exceed a thousand yards and all ground lost was recovered either the same day or early on the morning of the 16th. Against the French on the British right the Austrians had not even an initial success. Against the Italians further east, between the Brenta and the French sector, the enemy penetrated to a depth varying from one to two miles. With the rest of the 7th Division the 2nd Gordons were put at two hours' notice to move on the morning of June 15th but in the evening news came through that the situation was well in hand. After that the Gordons had an hour's physical training and games.

On the Piave the business was far graver, though in part the Austrian attack was repulsed by the Italians. The enemy had bad luck in the form of heavy rain on the 16th which swelled the river. He made further gains on the 17th, however, at one point to a depth of three miles. But the rise of the Piave and bombing of the bridges by the R.A.F. made his position untenable. He began his withdrawal on the night of June 22nd. The effect on the Austrians, who—as distinct from troops of other nationalities of the Empire—had attacked gallantly, was disastrous.

The Gordons then had another spell on the Asiago Plateau, where losses in July reached a total of 40, a higher figure than any yet experienced; but the continued quietude is shown by the fact that over half this loss was the result of a single day's exceptional activity on the part of the Austrian artillery. Back they went once more to the plains in mid-October, to do some strenuous training, as far as possible before 9 a.m. and after 6 p.m. owing to the oppressive heat.

On September 1st, Lieut.-Colonel Maitland gave up the command, to be succeeded by Lieut.-Colonel H. A. Ross. Training and sport are the topics of the diary in September. By early October the weather had changed and became very wet. The khaki drill clothing was withdrawn and replaced by woollen active service dress. The Gordons did not know this time that for some days they were due to return to France, the intention being to exchange the 7th Division for a tired and depleted division from that theatre. Lord Cavan, however, appealed to the C.I.G.S. to give the Italians more substantial support now that they were prepared, after long and insistent urging on his part, to undertake an offensive. The move of the 7th Division was then cancelled for the second time. General Diaz, the Italian Chief of the General Staff, created a new army, appointed Lord Cavan to command it, and placed an Italian corps of two divisions under his orders. Headquarters of the XIV Corps was re-formed, and Major-General Sir J. M. Babington was appointed to command it. It comprised the 7th and 23rd Divisions and was to take part in the main offensive, on the Piave. The remaining British division, the 48th, was to fight on the Asiago Plateau in an Italian corps. The intention of General Diaz was to make a decisive break-through on the Piave which would separate the Austrian armies on the river front from those in the Trentino.

The 7th Division marched to the Vicenza area between October 5th and 7th. The brigades now consisted, as in France, of three battalions only, the Gordons having lost old friends with whom they had been brigaded for over three years, the 8th Devonshire. Another wave of influenza swept the divisions, but it began to disappear when the troops left billets, though the weather was very wet and it was cold work bivouacking in fields and vineyards.

After the concentration round Treviso the Gordons were given some training in boats. The Piave was a very formidable obstacle because of the strength of the current, and the number of experts in navigating such a torrent whom the Italians could lend the British divisions was minute. On October 18th the corps commander, General Babington, watched five scows, each manned by two Italian *Pontieri*, carry the battalion across the Sile in an hour and twenty minutes. It was good going, and the boatmen were skilled and plucky, but the Sile was a much slower river than the Piave—and there was no fire to face on an exercise.

The original intention had been to open the offensive on October 16th, but rain caused a postponement, prolonged as the river continued to rise. The men of the Gordons were in high spirits and full of confidence, but for officers who understood all the factors there was cause for some anxiety. Numerically, the Austrians were practically as strong as the allies on the Piave, and it seemed a very powerful position. The river, rather than the Italian troops, had defeated the Austrians in June. If the Austrians fought reasonably well now, the passage of the Piave was going to be difficult and risky. We now know that the Austrians believed they could smash any bridge and defeat any attack.

Lord Cavan's Tenth Army was to be the spearhead of the attack. It faced the long, low island known as the Grave di Papadopoli, which was to be used as a stepping-stone. After its capture it would have to be linked by a pontoon bridge to the south bank, and the crossing of the channels between it and the north bank would have to be undertaken.

On the night of October 23rd the 22nd Brigade crossed to the island and on the 25th cleared it completely. The fighting does not concern us, but it is interesting to note in passing that the Lieut.-Colonel O'Connor of the 2/1st H.A.C. who was in charge of the landing operations became in another war General Sir Richard O'Connor.

The main part of the operation, the establishment of the XIV Corps on the north bank, was postponed until October 27th owing to delay in throwing a bridge. That which was eventually established was made up of both British and Italian pontoons, but, as there was no time to finish it, about half of it was completed as a footbridge of duckboards on trestles. The troops were issued with one day's hard ration in addition to the iron ration, an extra bandolier of s.a.a., and wire-cutters.

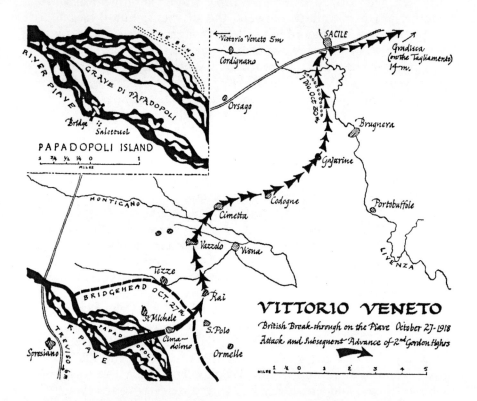

The 2nd Gordons led the march, leaving their bivouacs at 6.30 p.m., and crossed by the bridge from the village of Salettuol. The 22nd Brigade, which had secured the Grave di Papadopoli, was of course on the island already. The 23rd Division, attacking on the left of the 7th, crossed simultaneously. An Italian division also crossed to the south-east end, using two smaller islands as stepping-stones. In the small hours of October 27th a drenching shower fell, not improving the prospects of supply should the fighting on the left bank of the Piave prove tough.

All over the island Austrian shells, high explosive and shrapnel, were now bursting. Shelling always seems even more unpleasant by night than by day, but, if this made a great noise, its effects were small. The island was four miles long and where the Gordons stood over a mile in breadth, and in the dark the gunners had no particular targets except the former Austrian trenches, which the British troops avoided. Still the bombardment and the rain combined were trying to the waiting men. The time must have passed slowly.

At last the signal came. At 5.30 a.m. the Gordons, who were to lead the attack of the 20th Brigade, began crawling forward over the wet shingle on hands and knees. Zero had been fixed at 6.45 a.m., so that it should be just light when the troops advanced ; to have put it earlier would have been dangerous in view of the water obstacles to be crossed. The number of channels varied according to the position of small islands north-east of Papadopoli. On the front of the 20th Brigade there were four, the furthermost known to be three feet deep.

The first objective was a grim one. It was known by the Anglo-Indian name of the " Bund ", and was a stone-and-gravel embankment or flood-wall, reinforced with concrete at the curves, roughly ten feet high and six feet wide at the top. In front of it were two belts of wire, deliberately left uncut by the allied artillery. It was a horrifying obstacle on which to advance across four streams completely exposed to fire from it. No man who waded and scrambled towards it that morning knew its weakness, that machine guns emplaced on it could not be depressed enough to cover the last eighty yards in front of it. The Austro-Hungarian Army was rather careless. Germans would have put that matter right.

The Gordons plodded through channel after channel, linking arms by sections and dragging feet in the deeper places because if one foot were lifted from the bottom the other might be knocked away by the current. Machine-gun bullets whipped up tiny spurts of water, but again there was practically no loss.

Then men began to fall. It looked for a moment as though the advance would be bogged, but the support company was moved up and companies of the 8th Devons filled a gap which had opened between the 20th Brigade and the 91st on its left. This gave the extra impetus needed. The troops surged forward, cut the wire where thick, trampled it down where thin, or found the paths through it left for patrols. Then they swarmed up on to the Bund. The fight was short. The Hungarian troops in this sector had not fixed their bayonets, and had no stomach for fighting Highlanders at close quarters. Many prisoners were taken.

Some disorganization followed, due chiefly to the eagerness of the men to get forward, but the leading companies pressed on into Cimadolmo. The little place was strongly held and some 200 prisoners were taken in or near the church. Open country lay ahead. Resistance now came chiefly from barricaded houses. It was overcome by playing Lewis guns on them while parties worked round to their rear. Against better troops than the Hungarians were at this stage of the war the tactics would doubtless have succeeded, but at very high cost, since there was practically no cover and not a sign of the Italians who were supposed to be advancing on the right. It is probable that it was a burst of fire from this flank which caught battalion headquarters during a short halt before the advance to the second objective. The commanding officer, Lieut.-Colonel H. A. Ross, killed, and the adjutant, Captain R. D. Cameron, severely wounded, were among the casualties. The troops became still more disordered, but the n.c.o.s were by this time well trained and they carried the men in small parties on to the objective, where the advance ceased. The penetration was not deep, only about a mile and a half from the north shore of the Piave on the front of the Gordons, but, as may be imagined, an arduous engineering and administrative task lay behind. Though a few batteries were established on Papadopoli with commendable speed, it was not until the 29th that a bridge for wheeled traffic could be built to the mainland.

It was a fine feat of arms. The men of the two British divisions had shown themselves high-mettled, ever eager to close with the enemy. The Austrian official account remarks that the very sight of them *löste einen Massenschreck* (let loose a mass panic) and that the Hungarian and Yugoslav troops were quite unable to cope with them. It also reveals something which the British already suspected, that the hostile artillery pulled out much too early and left the infantry in the lurch. But for this factor the losses would certainly have been heavier. Those of the 2nd Gordons were the biggest in the 20th Brigade, but lighter than in any major action fought by the battalion in this war.[1]

Besides the British bridgehead over the Piave, two others had been established further west, by the Italians in the Montello Sector and by the French upstream of them at ‐ clerobba. They were all expanded on October 28th. Behind Lord Cavan's Tenth Army the roads were dangerously congested. Italian troops moving up were bombed by the Austrians with heavy loss during the night of the 27th, and next morning the Salettuol bridge, by which the Gordons had crossed to the Grave de Papadopoli, was broken by the current and could not be repaired. The invaluable *Pontiere* rebuilt it a little downstream, but meanwhile rations and ammunition had to be carried by pack mules.

During the night the 2nd Border Regiment had taken over half the brigade front from the 2nd Gordons. On the morning of the

[1]	Killed	Wounded	Missing
Officers	3	3	—
Other ranks	11	54	4

28th the whole front was taken over by the Borders, who led the advance. It was scarcely contested, though the only artillery support was an 18-pdr. battery which had forded the Piave to Papadopoli island. In the afternoon, therefore, the corps commander, General Babington, ordered the advance to be continued to the river Montecano, which crossed the front about five miles north of Papadopoli. This was not reached, but was closely approached. Efforts to secure an intact bridge led to an accident, typical of pursuits. A strong patrol of two platoons of the Borders went ahead to cover the bridge north of Visna, but did not discover that it was charged. In the night the enemy blew it up. Some hundreds of Austrians still south of the river then attacked and captured the patrol. The ironical feature of the incident was that the Austrians would probably not have dreamt of attacking had not the patrol stood across their road home.

So the 20th Brigade, which must have hoped that its wading was over, had one more river to ford. It was not, however, called on to undertake a forced crossing north of Visna, as was the first intention. As it was on the British flank and the Italians were far in rear it was naturally later than the 91st Brigade and the 23rd Division on the left. After they had forced the passage of the Montecano in really heavy fighting against fresh troops, the divisional commander, Major-General T. H. Shoubridge, decided not to lose any more men, as he was sure the enemy would be unable to remain on the river at any point. The Gordons found shelter in the hangars of an abandoned Austrian airfield.

That day the Royal Air Force had brought in reports suggesting a general retreat of the enemy. The XIV Corps was ordered to advance to the Livenza, which involved a slight wheel to the eastward. The 22nd Brigade had by great exertions been brought up from Papadopoli island and led the advance of the 7th Division. The 20th Brigade was in reserve. Though the opposition was trifling, the advance was slow. The men were footsore as well as weary. Boots, soaked in the crossing of the Piave and in some cases the Montecano, had dried hard, and it was impossible to bring forward even clean socks. The XIV Corps halted for the night along the Livenza and scarcely moved on the 31st. Ammunition was very short and it had not been possible to bring bridging material to the scene. The river was up to one hundred yards wide and swift flowing.

Major W. Gordon had now assumed command of the battalion. He was the third man of his name to command the 2nd Gordon Highlanders and the sixth to command a battalion of the regiment on active service. The name was well represented throughout. Major Gordon was given time for inspection and reorganization.

16

He found the troops in bounding spirits. Despite continuous exposure and indifferent rations, the sick list was remarkably low. No man wanted to miss the dramatic scene now unfolding.

On November 1st a series of bridges over the Livenza were constructed. On the 2nd the Gordons crossed at Sacile. There was fantastic congestion at the bridge owing to the Italian lack of road discipline, but the Gordons' diary does not complain and they probably crossed before the Italian double-banking began. No opposition was met with. The road was strewn with the refuse of a defeated, bombed, and demoralized army : dead horses, abandoned guns, rifles and equipment thrown down to lighten backs. Shops by the roadside had been looted. A halt was called about half way to the Tagliamento, which ran eighteen miles east of the Livenza. The Gordons were received with " great enthusiasm " in Torre, where they spent a cold night. Packs and officers' rolls had been left behind, and there were no blankets.

On November 3rd the advanced guard of the 20th Brigade, commanded by Major Gordon, consisted of the battalion, a battery of the 22nd. Brigade R.F.A., cyclists, and machine gunners. On approaching the Tagliamento the advanced guard ran into what it describes as " a peace conference " on the bank. Brig.-General H. C. R. Green, commanding the 20th Brigade, halted the column to find out what was happening. He was informed by an Italian cavalry commander that an armistice was in force, a fact of which neither he nor his divisional commander was as yet aware. Major-General Shoubridge, on arrival at the Gradisca bridge—cut in three places but partially restored—met Austrian *parlementaires* who showed him a telegram stating that an armistice had in fact been signed and that the river had been fixed as a line of demarcation. He replied that, being without official intimation of this news, he meant to cross, and in the hearing of the Austrians ordered forward his artillery, little if any of which could in fact have been brought up.

He decided, however, to do no more that day than secure the bridge, which was just passable to men on foot. Two companies of the Gordons were therefore sent across the mile-wide river to form a bridgehead. They were the first infantry to cross the Tagliamento, an occasion perhaps of sentimental satisfaction only, but one which no man who took part in it would forget.

Next day, November 4th, the rest of the battalion crossed to the east bank and was employed in guarding the prisoners'-of-war compound or finding escorts for prisoners sent back across the Tagliamento. The scene was fantastic. In three big fields beside the road about 7,000 prisoners had been collected. Some units were complete with transport. There were hundreds of horses and vehicles and an ordnance workshop with all its equipment. Huge fires made by breaking up vehicles were blazing. The officers had been escorted back separately, but the under-officers took charge and kept the camp orderly. Officially the armistice came into force at 3 p.m., but in fact all fighting was long over.

It is unnecessary here to describe the Austrian break-down in the mountains, where the British 48th Division was engaged, or to go into the complex details of the armistice. To put it shortly, the Emperor Karl was, perhaps unavoidably, the agent of his own empire's destruction. It was inclined to totter even before the allied attack on the Piave, though its military situation, unlike that of Germany, was good enough on paper. The Emperor's action came as the final blow which brought about the collapse. The other influences were the defeat of the June offensive on the Piave ; the disasters suffered by the senior partner, Germany ; the allied victory in the Balkans and the capitulation of the Bulgarian Army, which laid open the road to the Danube ; unrest and dissatisfaction in the non-German States of the Empire ; and economic distress amounting in fact to widespread hunger.

On October 16th the Emperor had issued a proclamation creating a "federal state". He had hoped by this to close the ranks but actually forced them open. States and nationalities—Hunggarians, Czechs, Slovaks, Serbs, Slovenes, Italians, Poles, Rumanians, and others—broke away or reached the point of so doing. Their troops got out of control and refused to obey orders. With an army that would not fight there was no alternative to the course of seeking an armistice. So ended the famous Austrian Empire and with it the famous *Kaiserliche und Königliche Armee.*

On October 6th Major-General Shoubridge congratulated the battalion on its "splendid behaviour". Next day it started a leisurely but uncomfortable move to the Trissino area. On November 27th it formed part of a brigade made up of one battalion from each of the brigades of the 7th Division reviewed by the King of Italy on the airfield of Castelgomberto. It had only four days' preparation, but Lord Cavan, a Guardsman, said in a special order of the day that he did not believe a better review had ever been held in time of war. Unhappily, for want of time, the King made his review from his car, a perfunctory performance.

In December, educational classes—and also dancing classes— were organized. On the 23rd the first party to be demobilized, 2nd Lieutenant J. Walker and 20 other ranks, left for home. Thereafter the battalion shrank rapidly to the cadre which was the role of all battalions : for the regular to be followed by reconstruction, for the Territorial by demobilization, and for the New Army by dissolution.

All that need be said of the achievement in which the 2nd Gordon Highlanders had shared may be put into the words of the best of the Italian army commanders, the Duke of Aosta, when he came to say farewell to Lord Cavan in January 1919 : " Goodbye, General, I am indeed sorry that you are leaving Italy. Without the presence of you and your troops there would have been no Vittorio Veneto."

CHAPTER XXII

VICTORY AND ARMISTICE

AS the month of September drew to its end Marshal Foch decided that the time had come to employ " all the allied resources " in convergent action against the vast German salient from Verdun to the coast. On four successive days four big offensives were to be launched : on September 26th by the French and Americans between the Meuse and Reims ; on September 27th (the left centre) by the British Third and First Armies, roughly between Péronne on the Somme, and Lens ; on September 28th by the British Second Army, the Belgians, and the French, from Armentières to the sea ; and on September 29th (the right centre) the British Fourth Army and the French First, from north of Saint-Quentin to the Somme.

The 3rd Division took part in the second of these mighty operations, each deadly to the enemy in itself and in combination disastrous. It formed part of the VI Corps, so that yet again Gordon Highlanders were to fight under the orders of the most distinguished Gordon Highlander then holding a senior command in the field, Lieut.-General Sir Aylmer Haldane. The 3rd Division was called on to break the Hindenburg Line south of Flesquières, that ruined village on a hill-top where battalions of the regiment had been held up in the Battle of Cambrai.

The 3rd Division was to take the first and second objectives. It attacked with the 9th Brigade on the right and the 8th on the left. After these brigades had secured the first objective, the 76th was to pass through the 8th and in company with the 9th—which had a shorter distance to cover than the 8th—to advance to the second objective. This was the tough nut. It included the rear Hindenburg trench, which ran across the Flesquières ridge and past the southern outskirts of the village. The division's task was made harder by the fact that the first objective ran aslant across the front and the division on the right was not moving forward until three hours later.

On September 26th the 1st Gordons rested from 2 to 5 p.m., those who could sleep on the eve of an offensive doing so. In the evening they marched to their assembly trenches. The night was quiet, and the enemy appeared to suspect nothing. The quietude was rudely broken at 5.20 a.m. on the 27th by the first tremendous crash of the British artillery, heralding a day of din.

Twenty-five minutes later the leading battalions of the 76th Brigade, 8th King's Own and 1st Gordon Highlanders, went forward. The Gordons were at this stage of the war an eager but young battalion, with inexperienced platoon commanders. It is therefore not surprising that some delay and confusion occurred in getting through a gap in a line of barbed wire. However, all were determined to go forward. Some further disorganization followed when they got involved in the fight for part of the first objective, where the leading companies suffered considerable loss. The commanders of the leading and support companies on the left, where most of the trouble occurred, had no time to reorganize. They simply collected every man they could and pressed forward to follow the new barrage to the second objective.

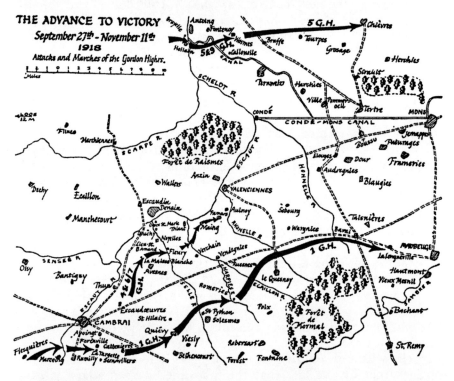

THE ADVANCE TO VICTORY
September 27th – November 11th
1918
Attacks and Marches of the Gordon Highrs.

The enemy's resistance was stout at this stage. Apart from the Hindenburg system, the ground was covered with a maze of old trenches and fortified shell craters. Some German machine-gun detachments kept up their fire till rushed from close quarters under the cover of Lewis guns and showers of rifle grenades. The Hindenburg trench skirting Flesquières did not prove a particularly difficult obstacle, but in the southern part of the village confusion became greater than ever. Realizing this, Captain C. H. Lee scraped together some sixty men, burst into the north part, cleared it, and came out on the eastern side in touch with the Irish Guards of the Guards Division on the left. This is what is meant by the saying that it is junior officers who win battles. Captain Lee received the D.S.O. as an immediate award.

There the advance was halted in face of fire from a sugar factory north-east of Flesquières and from field artillery firing over open sights. Then the 62nd Division passed through and completed the capture of the second objective, but after heavy fighting was unable to advance more than about a thousand yards beyond it.

Commenting on the attack the battalion diarist points out that it went into action short of n.c.o.s and lost a high proportion ; section commanders were lance-corporals or privates ; platoon commanders were mostly inexperienced, though some of them did very well ; a fair proportion of the privates were lads aged between eighteen and a half and nineteen. Casualties were naturally increased by lack of experience. Then he fails to give figures for these casualties. It is, however, known that those of the 76th Brigade were 614, of whom over 500 were wounded. The Gordons can, therefore, be expected to have lost a little under one-third of this figure.

What had been accomplished represented a great feat of arms for young troops. It was indeed a wonderful proof of the fortitude and endurance of British stock that after over four years of war and a death roll for the British Isles only and the Army alone now approaching 700,000, it was still capable of winning so great a victory. The foe, indeed, was not what he had been, but the British Army had taken a great part in wearing the shine off him.

The 1st Gordons spent the next couple of days in trenches or the ruins of Havrincourt Château. Meanwhile the advance was carried forward on this part of the front by the 62nd Division, which secured a bridgehead over the Escaut (or Scheldt, to give it it's Belgian name) and its canal at Marcoing, but was held up in front of Rumilly, three and a half miles south of Cambrai. It was in consequence of this check that the 76th Brigade was suddenly and unexpectedly called into action once more.

Between 1 and 1.30 a.m. on October 1st the 2nd Suffolk and 1st Gordon Highlanders moved to assembly positions beyond the canal. The Suffolks were to take the village itself. The Gordons were given two distinct roles : two companies to the left of the Suffolks were to move west of Rumilly if the attack on it should be checked. The other two were to advance in rear of the 8th King's Own on the right and to fill a gap which seemed certain to develop between the 76th Brigade and the New Zealand Division on that flank. These right companies had to hurry but otherwise fulfilled their task without much difficulty.

It was otherwise with the left half of the battalion, under command of the doughty and reliable Captain Lee. In the first place, troops of the 62nd Division, which was pulling out, left unoccupied some ground in front into which the enemy promptly pushed forward a number of machine guns. These, of course, escaped the British barrage, with the consequence that the Suffolks were held up and became engaged in close fighting. Their right company did get on to Rumilly, but it was never secured.

Meanwhile the left wing of the Gordons had pushed on west of the village till brought to a halt by fire from the railway sidings north of it. These two companies had done a very fine job, but could not complete it. A renewed attack was then organized, to take place at 6.30 p.m. under a fresh barrage, after a bombardment of Rumilly by heavy artillery. The two right companies (A and C) were brought into position to carry it out. As they were very weak the commanding officer, Lieut.-Colonel the Hon. W. Fraser, organized them as five bombing squads, allotting one section of the village to each.

The barrage, arranged in haste, was ragged. Nevertheless, the attack was successful. Lieut.-Colonel Fraser, on his way back to his headquarters, laid hands on about a hundred men of the Suffolks and sent them forward to help his men in mopping up. About eighty prisoners, including a battalion commander, and a number of machine guns were captured. The losses were light and mostly due to " shorts " in the British barrage. Once again the 1st Gordons, weak in numbers and weary as they were, had given proof of their grit and determination. Once again, too, junior officers, quickly learning their work, had shown skill as well as bold leadership. A couple of days of this open fighting and manoeuvre taught them more than a series of trench-to-trench attacks—and left more survivors to profit by the lessons.

For the next six days, October 2nd to 7th, the only change on this part of the front was that the outpost line was pushed forward about a quarter of a mile. Just to the north the enemy still held the large and sprawling town of Cambrai, out of which he would have to be squeezed by pressure to north and south.

The advance of the VI Corps was resumed at 4.30 a.m. on October 8th, with the 3rd Division on the right and the 2nd on the left, represented by the 9th and 99th Brigades respectively. The 1st Gordon Highlanders stood by till the afternoon. At 4 p.m. Lieut.-Colonel Fraser was ordered to report to Brig.-General H. C. Potter, 9th Brigade, under whose command he had been placed two hours earlier. The attack had run into trouble. The Germans had counter-attacked with a division supported by five tanks. Both British brigades, which had taken most of their second objective on the line Seranvillers-La Targette-Forenville, had been driven back to the first. The German tanks had been engaged by two British tanks and by Stokes mortars, with the result that three had been knocked out, one had been captured, and the fifth had made itself scarce. The British advance had, however, been stopped and some of the troops were a bit shaken. It was in itself a trifling incident, but it was enough to make British observers thankful that the Germans had not led the way in producing tanks and could not afterwards make the industrial effort needed to build them on more than a very small scale. In fact, they found their few captured British tanks more effective than their own.

Brig.-General Potter told Lieut.-Colonel Fraser that if the 2nd Division succeeded in retaking Forenville he would have to attack La Targette. The battalion had already started to move on earlier orders, but was caught by messengers and concentrated at a crucifix a mile east of Rumilly. The new attack was to be launched at 6 p.m.

Lieut.-Colonel Fraser had to make his way to the headquarters of the 8th King's Own, which was to attack on his left, to concert plans. As Seranvillers was reported in British hands and the situation further north was obscure, it was decided to attack from the south. The commanding officer reached his own battalion at 5.30 p.m. and gave his orders verbally. Those of the brigade arrived five minutes after the advance had begun. Seranvillers was found to be still held by the enemy and had later to be mopped up by the 2nd Suffolk. Yet the Gordons took La Targette in the dark. On the road running north to Cambrai a machine gun prevented a junction being made with the King's Own for another hour, but then the whole objective was secured. Next morning the Guards Division passed through to continue the advance. Once more the Gordons had done all that had been asked of them.

On the morning of October 9th the enemy began to retire. He covered the movement by a multitude of machine guns, skilfully handled though rarely fought to the last, and contrived to impose on his pursuers a certain respect for a series of slender rear guards. His next real stand was on the Selle, which in the zone allotted to the VI Corps ran through the large village, or small town, of Solesmes. This retreat was one of twelve miles. To defend the Selle line he brought up fresh divisions and heavy artillery, so that another set battle to break his defence became necessary.

The 1st Gordons spent ten days resting, " cleaning up ", and reorganizing after their success on October 8th. They received three drafts amounting in all to 7 officers and 299 other ranks and at Marcoing drew from the quartermaster's stores new clothing for the whole battalion. On the 19th and 20th they marched through Cattenières to Quiévy, behind the new front. They had the welcome experience of seeing and sleeping in undamaged houses.

In fact, when the 62nd Division of the VI Corps attacked Solesmes on the 20th the full barrage crept past the town on either side of it and only shrapnel was fired over it so that the civilians, warned to descend to their cellars, should be in no danger.

On October 20th the 62nd and Guards Divisions broke the enemy's front on the Selle and established themselves on the high ground beyond. This victory did not at once loosen up the fighting because the enemy stood again in strength on the next river, the Harpies, two miles to the north-east. Lieut.-General Haldane now decided to pass his reserve divisions through again to take over the advance.

There was a good deal of German shelling as the 3rd and 2nd Divisions marched up and deployed, but all was ready up to time. The Gordons, moving up to their assembly position four hundred yards west of Romeries in the small hours of October 23rd, suffered a number of casualties and became disorganized. Matters were quickly put right with the aid of the moon. The objective was the village of Romeries and a light railway a quarter of a mile beyond.

The attack was launched at 3.20 a.m. Some machine guns in the orchards on the near side of the village remained in action after the barrage had passed over them. The Gordons, with the 2nd Royal Scots of the 8th Brigade, waded—it is said in a few cases actually swam—across the Harpies. A ferocious and costly fight took place in Romeries but ended with the death or surrender of every defender. The objective was reached, and after a halt upon it the 2nd Suffolk and 8th King's Own passed through to pursue a badly shaken and demoralized enemy.

Lieut.-Colonel Fraser's comments on the success are worth recording. He pointed out that field-gun fire had virtually no effect on machine-gun detachments installed in well-built houses. He was certain that his tactics of immediately establishing posts at previously selected points in Romeries were correct in village fighting. It was from these posts that the mopping up had been effected. He attributed much of his loss to an s.o.s. signal sent up—apparently not in his own battalion—during the assembly and explained how much harm this might cause. Finally, he considered that the recruits of eighteen and a half now coming out should not be taken into action. Ten per cent. of them, he said, did excellently, but the rest were nearly useless where stamina was called for. He thought that even a very weak battalion was better off without them. It must be added that this last view was by no means universal. It seems more correct to say that the value of these young recruits depended to a large extent on the battalions they came from and the length of time they had been in the theatre of war.

The 3rd Division continued the pursuit in face of rear guards for another six miles, the Gordons following in reserve as far as Ruesnes, west of Le Quesnoy, where they came in for some heavy gas shelling on October 28th. Then, after a move rearwards, they followed the leading divisions of the VI Corps eastward in the direction of Maubeuge. They were at La Longueville, three miles east of Bavai, and preparing to move on when a message from brigade headquarters announced that an armistice would come into force at 11 a.m.

So for the 1st Battalion active operations came to an end on November 11th, 1918, eleven miles from the position on the outskirts of Mons on which, on August 23rd, 1914, it had first been engaged.

The 4th and 6/7th Gordons in the 51st Division took part in an advance not very far north of the 1st and of a similar type. On October 11th the 152nd and 154th Brigades moved forward by congested roads to the neighbourhood of Escadoeuvres, two miles east of Cambrai. On the front of the 154th the 4th Gordons were in reserve and were not engaged. On that of the 152nd the 5th Seaforths were on the right and the 6/7th Gordons on the left. The first objective of the latter battalion was a mile and three quarters from the starting line and ran from the north western outskirts of Avesnes-le-Sec to a farm called La Maison Blanche. The attack was fixed for noon on October 12th. In the early morning, however, patrols of the neighbouring division reported that the enemy had disappeared and its commander thereupon decided to cancel the rolling barrage and begin the advance at 10.15 a.m. The 51st Division's patrols did not at first confirm the enemy's retreat, so Major-General Carter-Campbell, decided to attack at the hour originally fixed and to keep the barrage. This was a reasonable view, and the information it was founded on may have been correct, but the late start may have enabled the Germans to prepare a better resistance.

The 6/7th Gordons reached their objective without difficulty. When, however, they tried to advance to the second, they were sharply checked by fire from Lieu-Saint-Amand. The Germans were making a fresh stand.

Though they were now often showing signs of demoralization their better divisions were not to be trifled with. Those who argue that they should have been more boldly hustled should note what happened next day, October 13th. The 51st Division was ordered to push advanced parties over the Selle, three miles ahead, to cover the throwing of bridges. They advanced after bombardment of Lieu-Saint-Amand and other localities but without a rolling barrage. The result was calamitous. Again the 4th Gordons did not attack in first line, but the 6/7th were very badly shot up. Altogether they had upwards of 300 casualties, though a high proportion of these were suffering only from whiffs of mustard gas, from which recovery was normally quick. Among the wounded was Lieut.-Colonel Thom, a fine commanding officer.

A brief halt followed, to prepare for the passage of the Selle. On October 19th the 51st Division was ready to renew the attack. Up to noon Lieu-Saint-Amand was occupied by the enemy, but when the 153rd Brigade advanced at 3 p.m. after a bombardment of the village it was found empty. The brigade reached the railway on the west bank of the river without opposition. The 154th Brigade also moved forward and met no resistance in crossing the Selle. The 4th Gordons occupied the hamlet of Fleury on the east bank. The division's right was in the air, since the 4th Division's front further south was still half a mile west of the river. In view of the fact that the latter division was attacking in the small hours of the 20th, this situation represented little danger. Indeed, a pontoon bridge from Fleury was established on that day. Meanwhile the 4th Gordons formed a defensive flank facing south.

On October 20th the 154th Brigade again advanced but was held up by fire on the road from Fleury to Croix-Sainte-Marie. Further north the 153rd Brigade also crossed by extemporized bridges. Next day these two brigades moved forward in face of very slight resistance. However, though they reached the road from Verchain to Thiant and took the latter, they did not persist when they found the left bank of the Ecaillon, the next tributary of the Scheldt and here running two and a quarter miles east of the Selle, held in strength. Their orders at this stage were to gain ground only when opposition was not strong " and he continues to withdraw ". On October 22nd the 51st Division stood fast, as did the 4th Division on its right, waiting to renew the offensive in conjunction with the left of the Third Army further south. The 4th Gordons remained in Fleury until the 23rd, when they were relieved and moved back to rest in Douchy. Civilians who had cleared out to avoid the fighting were already returning to the villages in British hands. The 152nd Brigade, in reserve, had moved up to the Selle on October 21st, the 6/7th Gordons billeting in Noyelles. A new commanding officer, Lieut.-Colonel C. J. E. Cranstoun, had taken over in succession to Lieut.-Colonel Thom on the 17th.

On October 24th another " full-dress " attack was launched. The 153rd Brigade, covering the whole front of the 51st Division, forced a passage of the Ecaillon and after hard fighting took the village of Maing, a mile and a half east of Thiant. The bridging

work was brilliant at this stage. Two bridges to take field artillery
were finished at 10.30 and 11.45 a.m. on October 25th and a heavy
bridge for lorries and tanks by 7.50 a.m. on the 26th.

The enemy was being allowed the shortest possible respite.
That he was not being pressed even harder was mostly due to the
state of the roads. The delays were caused in part by the craters
blown in them, especially at junctions, but sheer wear and tear
was responsible for a great proportion of them. Once again it
must be stressed that those conversant only with the conditions of
the Second World War can have little conception of the effect of
heavy vehicles with solid rubber tyres on roads not treated with
tar macadam.[1] And the Germans, whose transport had passed
over all the main and most of the secondary roads in their retreat
were so short of rubber that their heavy vehicles were shod with
iron and acted almost like ploughs on muddy surfaces. Local
quarries were altogether inadequate to supply the road metal
needed and the expedient employed on the Somme of tipping into
craters and spreading over roads the stone and brick of ruined
villages wholesale could not here be employed. It said much for
administrative skill and energy that the advance was as steady as
was the case, that the troops were always on full rations, that
ammunition was generally adequate, that bridging was effected so
quickly, and that the wounded were carried back with so little
delay.

The 152nd Brigade now took over the right half of the front of
the 153rd and the two attacked at 7 a.m. on October 25th. The
6/7th Gordons was on the right of the 152nd. The 4th Gordons
who had had a relatively easy time, were detached from their
brigade and placed under command of the 152nd Brigade, but were
held in reserve. The first objective, a line of German rifle pits
seven hundred yards ahead, was captured without much difficulty.
There the support companies went through and closed up with the
barrage, which had halted beyond the rifle pits. The next objective, the Le Quesnoy-Valenciennes railway, was reached despite
hot machine-gun fire from the village of Famars and a wooded
knoll, Rouge Mont, south of it. The final objective, a road running into Famars from the south, was then captured with about
100 prisoners. No exploitation was possible in face of strong resistance a few hundred yards ahead.

At 5 p.m. the enemy launched a counter-attack behind a heavy
barrage. The 6/7th Gordons and 6th Seaforths were driven back
to the railway, but made a stand behind it. The 4th Gordons
relieved the Seaforths after dark and orders were issued for the
renewal of the offensive at 10 a.m. on the 26th under a creeping

[1] See p. 70.

barrage, fired on the whole divisional front by six field artillery brigades and one heavy. The 152nd Brigade was to gain first a line through the middle of Famars and then one east and north of the village.

The two battalions of the Gordons, 6/7th on the right, 4th on the left, attacked side by side. The 6/7th worked round the south side of Rouge Mont and killed or captured all its defenders. The 4th Gordons came in for stiff opposition. First of all their right met heavy fire from Rouge Mont before it had been taken by their sister battalion. Then the left company had a hard fight in Famars, but by 11.30 a.m. the objective had been secured. The position was uncomfortable because the 6/7th were somewhat in rear and the right flank of the 153rd Brigade was considerably more so.

At 2 p.m. the 4th Gordons reported to the brigade that the 6th Black Watch on their left was giving ground and that they had formed a defensive flank. To do so they had used platoons standing by to secure a bridgehead over the next river, the Rhonelle. The Germans evidently set store by Famars and they had plenty of artillery to support efforts to regain their hold upon it. On they came again at 5.30 p.m. after a smashing bombardment. The 6/7th Gordons held their ground and the extreme right of the 4th appears to have remained with them. The right company in general, however, being now without an officer, fell back. The left, which thus had both flanks exposed, followed suit. The brigade commander, Brig.-General W. H. E. Seagrave, issued an order that Famars must be recovered that night, but that the establishment of the projected bridgehead beyond the Rhonelle could be postponed. The 4th Gordons were rallied, reorganized, and led forward again. The men were as willing as ever to advance. Once more they cleared the village, and by 11 p.m. the front was established as before.

The 152nd Brigade was not, however, yet done with Famars. Most of the brigade was to have been relieved that night, but the forward move of the relieving brigade, the 154th, was checked by gas shelling. It suffered a number of casualties and was unable to take over from its detached battalion, the 4th Gordons, in the village where they were living cheek by jowl with some hundreds of civilians in the cellars. On the 27th, at 11.30 a.m., the enemy launched yet another counter-attack, with two battalions. He reached the northern fringe of Famars, slipped a number of machine-gun squads into it, and by noon had pressed the Gordons back to the western edge. Once more they attacked, overran all opposition after close street fighting, and before 3 p.m. regained their former position. In the two days they had taken 122 prisoners at a cost of 210 officers and men, of whom 36 were missing.[1]   That night the battalion was relieved and withdrew to Maing, the 6/7th being close at hand.

The struggle for Famars had been as hot and hard and as prolonged as any such fighting in the course of October.   It will be gathered from the narrative that the infantry on both sides was readier and more willing to attack a position than to hold its gains when won.   The opposing forces were equally fatigued ; there was a certain weariness—and small wonder !—among the older soldiers, many of whom had been wounded and a good few more than once, and still a certain rawness among the young recruits, though they had quickly improved in minor tactics.   The British were the fitter, because they were better fed.   They were also the more numerous counting by battalions, and the fighting strength of their battalions was rather higher.   On the other hand, the German battalion had more and better light machine guns than the British and these were invaluable weapons in rear-guard actions. And though, as has been stated, the British had a certain superiority in numbers, they had nothing like the three to one majority which was the stock recipe for success on the offensive, and which the Germans had achieved against the Fifth Army in March.

The essential difference was that British morale was the higher. The British surrendered less easily.   They responded better to prolonged calls on their determination and endurance.   Thus virtually all the most prolonged struggles ended as did that for Famars, in a British victory.

The two battalions of the Gordon Highlanders in the 51st Division could be well satisfied with what they had accomplished. The 6/7th in particular had had a gruelling time of it and had been highly successful.   The 4th had not been so heavily engaged, but had made a triumphant ending at Famars.

It was indeed practically the end for both battalions.   The 51st had a little more fighting but was relieved on the night of October 29th.   When the armistice came into force the 4th Gordons were in Cambrai and the 6/7th four miles north at Thun-l'Evêque.   The men of the 4th, we learn, showed no signs of rejoicing, and the diary comments that " such a day is difficult to realize ".   At least equal interest appears to have been excited by the divisional order that in future column of route formation, except on ceremonial parades, should be threes instead of fours. " Much discussion " was aroused by this innovation.   The 6/7th was sufficiently enthusiastic to light a huge bonfire.

[1]	Killed	Wounded	Missing
Officers	1	7	1
Other ranks	7	159	35

The 15th Division had been transferred to a part of the front south of the La Bassée Canal and with its right on Loos, which lay between the two big salients created by the Germans in their March offensive on the Somme and their April offensive on the Lys. It was therefore unaffected by the enemy's withdrawal from these salients under pressure. Loos still lay within the British lines ; Mazingarbe, which must have housed as many British battalions throughout the war as any French village of its size, was still a regular billeting place for troops coming out of the front-line trenches. Not only was this sector outside the earlier withdrawals of the enemy ; it was also outside the fronts of the offensives projected by Marshal Foch and Field-Marshal Sir Douglas Haig. The troops were, therefore, thinly spread, only two divisions, 15th on right and 16th on left, holding the front from Loos to the canal, a distance of over six miles. The enemy might be given a prod or two, but otherwise it would be a case of waiting till he withdrew, as he must sooner or later if the offensives to north and south continued to go well. General Sir William Birdwood, commanding the reconstituted Fifth Army from Loos to Armentières, was, however, most anxious that when this occurred every effort should be made to ensure that contact was not lost as in previous German retreats and that the enemy should be given no respite.

It was on the night of October 1st that the Germans pulled out, their withdrawal of front-line garrisons beginning at 4 a.m. on the 2nd. To start with, despite long expectation that the enemy would go, the old story was repeated. Contact was lost, and the troops met practically no resistance as they moved eastward over the flat coalfield. The first stage of the withdrawal could hardly, in fact, have been simpler than it was from the German point of view. The enemy had only to get back over the Haute Deule Canal, here three miles east of his abandoned front and parallel with it. By October 3rd he was to all intents and purposes back upon it. It was a strong position, which he had partly flooded by cutting the canal bank.

The 5th Gordon Highlanders began to advance as reserve to the 44th Brigade. It saw no Germans next day, but it did see many lorries ditched by mines. On October 4th the battalion took over the advance, its zone being from Wingles towards Meurchin, on the far bank of the canal. On the 5th its right company was checked with considerable loss in a wood on the Meurchin road. Little further change took place for the next week. The Germans were holding fast and shelling heavily, having unlimited ammunition which they could not move. It was clear, however, from the fires and explosions east of the canal that they did not mean to remain upon it for long. On October 12th the 9th Royal Scots attacked successfully at Vendin-le-Viel, taking 29 prisoners.

On October 15th, having heard explosions in Meurchin during the early hours, 2nd-Lieutenant Barrow and two men scrambled over the broken road bridge and found that the Germans had gone. They were indeed in retreat on the whole army front. The 5th Gordons took pride in the fact that before a field company R. E. could reach the scene their A Company had roughly reconstructed the bridge. That day the battalion advanced a mile and a half beyond the Haute Deule Canal. On the 16th, after a brief hold-up at a " Fosse ", it reached Carvin, two miles on. The village was heavily shelled, but the Gordons pushed on. Owing, however, to some confusion or delay in the orders, they covered only another thousand yards. On October 17th a company of the 13th Royal Scots passed through, and was shortly reported to be going ahead " like a prairie fire ".

The 44th Brigade now passed into divisional reserve, but continued to march eastward. On October 20th the 5th Gordons billeted in Capelle, twelve and a half miles east of the canal but seven miles behind the line reached that day by the leading troops. Though the roads were so bad, the houses were in good condition. The region was agricultural, showing few outward signs of the long German occupation. The troops were warmly welcomed and found the inhabitants kindly. They themselves were in high spirits.

The role of the pioneer battalion, the 9th Gordons, had now become important in the extreme, and very strenuous. Day after day the battalion made an early start to repair the roads sufficiently for the first-line transport to use them. The war diary claims that the advance was never held up by the state of the roads and that the mine craters proved insurmountable until the pioneers came along. The roads also had to be cleared of trees and telegraph poles. During the last ten days they found the work getting easier. The enemy seemed to have had less time to exercise his " devilish ingenuity ".

The 44th Brigade went into the lead again on October 29th, but with the 5th Gordons in reserve. The Germans had halted anew on the Scheldt, and as the advance closed upon it their artillery once more became active, firing large quantities of gas shell. Despite this fire, the 44th Brigade established posts in the village of Bruyelle, south of Antoing, on November 3rd. Meanwhile, since there was a halt in front, Lieut.-Colonel Lord Dudley Gordon organized a football competition in the 5th Gordons. At 10.30 a.m. on the 8th the divisions on either flank reported " enemy gone ", but the 8th Seaforths were held up by machine-gun fire. At dusk, however, patrols crossed the Scheldt both at

17

Bruyelles and Hollain. The 5th Gordons crossed next day and, since the rest of the brigade had gone into the blue, had a long march to rejoin. No man fell out. Did the troops realize that they were skirting the battlefield of Fontenoy ? A Company of the 9th Gordons worked non-stop for thirty-six hours with the 17th Field Company R.E. on bridging the Antoing-Pommeroeil Canal, which leaves the Scheldt just south of the former town. The divisional commander, Major-General Reed, afterwards gave the company high praise for its devotion to duty.

On the night of November 10th the 5th Gordons, then in billets at Tourpes, were ordered to pass through the 8th Seaforths next day and make good the high ground beyond the village of Chièvres, which lay five miles ahead. The battalion set off in open order across country. Then, after some rumours, came definite news that an armistice would come into force at 11 a.m. It is extraordinary that the news should have come so late, since it was widely known that there was to be an armistice and in a number of cases wireless messages picked up by signallers had revealed the date. This, however, is the evidence available as regards the 5th Gordons. Brigade headquarters states that it got the news at 10.45.

The 5th Gordons formed column of fours and marched eastward, singing and whistling. All previous welcomes were put into the shade by that met at Chièvres. The inhabitants lined the streets ; gifts were distributed ; Major Wood, the senior officer with the leading companies, was formally received by the mayor and acclaimed " hero of the town " ; and a minute of the proceedings was entered in the official records and signed by the officers present. The battalion put out a company on outpost duty, but the remainder was free to enjoy the amenities of Chièvres. As for the 9th Gordons, the nearest they come to referring to the armistice is found in the words, " work as usual ".

An effort has been made in this narrative to keep up a running commentary on the background, though in a regimental history it is not possible to devote much space to this. For the same reason the final comments must be few and brief. Where the victorious allied offensive of " the hundred days " (August 8th to November 11th) is concerned all that need be said is that there was never a break-through and, though vast numbers of prisoners were taken, large sections of the enemy's array were not cut off. As the German front in September formed a huge salient from the coast to Verdun, the most deadly strategy would have been, in theory, to break-through on both flanks. The tangled and wooded nature of the Argonne, west of Verdun, and the relative inexperience of the American troops attacking there—magnificently as they fought— were the chief obstacles to a breach of the front in that region, where it would have counted most. Even as it was, the approach to the last main railway south of the Ardennes had a crippling effect on the enemy.

ALLIED OFFENSIVE : 1918

Starting Line ━ ╼ ╾ Line before German ╲•╱•╲
Armistice Line ▪▪▪▪▪▪ Offensive

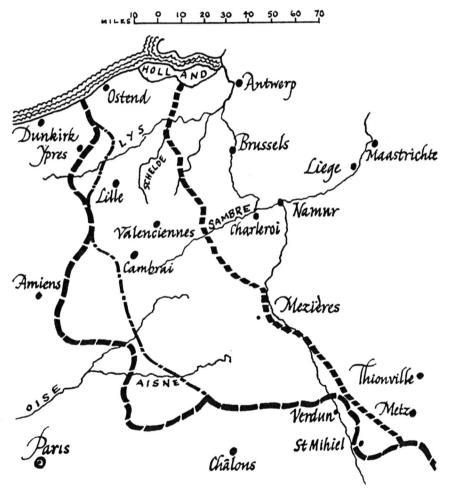

Once the worst devastated area of the Somme battlefield had been left behind, the greatest speed was attained by the best troops, at this stage the British, and over the best ground, a great part of it rolling downs. Marshal Foch did not plan that the British should advance the fastest, but that is what happened, with the result that they became the spearhead and dictated the course of the offensive.

Looking at the war on the Western Front, in which the Gordon Highlanders were almost exclusively engaged, as a whole, it was undoubtedly in the main a war of attrition. It is not for a moment suggested that clumsiness and slow reaction to circumstances were absent from the allied leadership. On the other hand, the suggestions so often made that with more imagination and better tactics circumstances would have been entirely changed, the war would have been greatly shortened, and losses halved, have little warrant in the evidence. With troops as thick on the ground as they were and so closely approximating in military value, manoeuvre would always have been limited. Mechanical transport was developing, but it was not yet sufficiently advanced to provide full mobility.

Means of communication were another bar. They were splendid, even brilliant—up to the final stage where they most mattered from the battalion's point of view, that is, from brigade headquarters forward. (They might hold in battle up to battalion headquarters, but only at the expense of keeping the battalion commander far back.) The system of reeling out telephone cable with the advancing troops had to be abandoned because it was almost inevitably cut by fire, and later by tanks. There was no portable wireless. So chief reliance had to be placed on runners, a slow method.

Far from the grind of trench warfare being avoidable, it would have been to the advantage of the allies to practise the old methods of fortress warfare to a greater extent than they did. In particular, though constant mining was carried out, they might have made greater use of their tunnelling companies, which were superior to those of the enemy.

Despite the formation of an expeditionary force of excellent quality by Haldane, Britain was wholly unprepared for a war of masses, and yet forced to undertake one or see France utterly defeated and occupied. Something has been said of the state of the New Army and Territorial Force divisions in the early stages. The latter, with slightly the better start, were still far behind the German reserve divisions as regards readiness. One respect in which the Army did better in the Second World War than in the First was training at home. It was much more realistic, but it was given more time, in the later war. This applies also to production of heavy and medium artillery and to shell for both. The British Army undertook the Somme offensive inadequately provided with either, and it was not until 1917 that it could be said to be properly equipped.

The result was losses which may indeed be described as needless, but only on the assumption that the issue of the war could have been decided in some other theatre, which is most unlikely. The Germans, with far-reaching preparations and many more trained officers and n.c.o.s than the British, suffered on the British front, from the Battle of the Somme onwards, casualties at least as high as ours. The most remarkable feature of the war from our point of view is the manner in which our men defied and shook off their shoulders the burden of its slaughter and miseries, and maintained their fighting spirit.

In this respect the Gordon Highlanders take an honourable place. All battalions had their share of bad luck and most went through periods when losses reduced them to a level below their best. But their best was high, and they recovered lost ground. One sign of good morale common to all was their smartness and the pride they took in their turn-out, even in unfavourable circumstances. This is constantly illustrated in their records. Five days after the armistice Sir Douglas Haig told Captain MacDuff, commander of the guard of honour of the 6/7th Battalion mounted for Marshal Foch, when the British Commander-in-Chief brought the Commander-in-Chief of the Allied Armies on a visit, that the guard was the equal of any he had seen in pre-war days. He was not the man to say this merely for the sake of politeness to a unit which had made a creditable effort. The battalions served in good divisions and lived up to their top standard. The regiment of later generations can rest assured that its children of the First World War carried on its traditions worthily, that their record is high, and that, whether they fell in battle or survived, they deserve to be looked back upon as examples of brave and steadfast soldiers.

CHAPTER XXIII

THE RHINE—DEMOBILIZATION

THE rest of the story is for the most part that of the demobilization of the greatest army Britain had ever put into the field. The Gordon Highlanders played a prominent part in the forces of occupation in Germany. That country was, however, occupied only up to the Rhine, with three deep bridgeheads beyond the river. The northern of these was British.

The 3rd Division was one of those destined for Sir Herbert Plumer's Second Army in Germany, renamed Army of the Rhine (never " British Army of the Rhine " except in international usage). The start of the long march was delayed because the bridges near the final battle front had been cut before the armistice came into force. The troops did not mind ; they enjoyed the Belgian *cabarets*. Some halts occurred later, mainly owing to delayed-action mines on the railways. On the whole, however, progress was remarkably steady. The 1st Gordons, moving through the Ardennes, marched on five days of the week from November 24th to 30th, on which day they reached Ciney. From December 4th to 19th they marched on every day but one. They received an enthusiastic welcome from the Belgians.

The battalion crossed the frontier on December 11th. A ceremony befitting the occasion was observed. The divisional commander, Major-General C. J. Deverell, and his Staff rode at the head of the column, which marched past the corps commander. Unhappily, rain fell all day. On December 19th the 1st Gordons reached their destination, the villages of Kierdorf and Bruggen, west of the Rhine. The billets were very good, and within a few days a sergeants' mess was opened and dining halls were secured for the men.

Germany was a comfortable station. Though the people had been reduced to hunger by the blockade, the country was hardly damaged by war. Fraternization with Germans was forbidden in the early stages, but no such gulf yawned between occupying troops and people as when the B.A.O.R. began its occupation after the Second World War. The opera was enjoyed by music lovers at Cologne. There was an abundance of sports and games. Educational classes, both academic and for a large number of trades, were well attended at first. The work was, however, unsatisfactory from the teachers' point of view because of the speed of demobilization.

Since the policy was to reduce many battalions, including all the regular, to cadres, it was necessary to create temporary divisions for the first phase of the occupation. The ten formed had no numbers and were named Northern, Southern, Eastern, Western, Midland, London, Lancashire, Highland, Lowland, and Light. So far as this measure affected the Gordon Highlanders it was as follows. A new division was built up on the 62nd (2nd West Riding) Division, then widely dispersed in the thinly-populated hilly Eifel country, west of the Rhine. Highland infantry was gradually drafted into it as battalions, as companies or contingents withdrawn from battalions which were being reduced to cadres and sent home, or as units of young soldiers from home still liable for service. In every case all ranks were either regulars—these, except for officers, only for a short time—or came late in priority for demobilization. The latter were known as " retainable ". These troops passed to the command of the 62nd Division, with which, by a coincidence, the Gordon Highlanders had had frequent association during the war, with respect on both sides. Meanwhile that division's own battalions were disappearing by a similar process. The incessant and highly complex movements were well carried out, in great part owing to the efficiency of the German railways.[1]

When the process was more or less complete the 62nd Division ceased to exist and the Highland Division came into being, on March 15th, 1919. Especially in the senior ranks, many officers dropped a grade. All the brigadiers of the Highland Division had commanded divisions and some battalion commanders had commanded brigades.

A large number of officers and men were transferred from the 1st Battalion to the 62nd Division in the course of its transformation in March 1919. By this time the battalion had moved into barracks in Cologne. It had sent home various demobilization parties, but was still fairly strong until it parted with these drafts. Ten officers and 60 other ranks joined the 5th Gordon Highlanders, and 11 officers and 197 other ranks the 4th, which had recently joined the 62nd Division. On March 10th the 1st Battalion handed over its horses, harness, and vehicles to the 51st Northumberland Fusiliers, a " Young Soldiers " battalion.

The cadre left Cologne on April 6th and arrived at Dover on the 9th. On the following evening it reached Invergordon and was ferried across to Cromarty. There the reconstruction of the battalion began shortly afterwards.

The 4th and 6/7th Gordons had a quiet time in Belgium, where they moved to the area east of Mons in December 1918. In a

---

[1] The writer is compelled to declare an interest in paying this tribute. As a young G.S.O.3 of the 62nd Division and afterwards for a short time of the Highland Division, it sometimes fell to him to draft movement orders, put in demands for special trains, meet battalions on arrival, and always to keep the list of locations up to date.

Highland dancing festival held on January 21st, 1919, every event was won by the dancers of the 6/7th, which must at this time have been the most genuinely Highland battalion of the regiment. On February 18th orders were received by the 152nd Brigade that drafts of " retainable " men from the 6/7th would join the 4th Battalion, and that the latter would then move to Germany, which it did on February 23rd, arriving next day. These transfers completed the reduction of the 6/7th. On April 6th and 7th the cadre entrained at Manage for Dunkirk.

The 5th Gordons remained for some time at Nivelles. They were represented by their pipes and drums at King Albert's review in Brussels on January 26th. The battalion as a whole had not the good fortune to take part in this splendid and memorable ceremonial event. One infantry brigade only was called for. The 44th Brigade, in which the Gordons served, being all Highland, and the 46th all Lowland, Major-General Reed selected the 45th, which was composed of two Highland battalions and one Lowland.

On February 6th Lieut.-Colonel Lord Dudley Gordon relinquished command and was succeeded by Lieut.-Colonel A. Greenhill Gardyne. On the 21st the battalion, having picked up a draft of 6 officers and 237 other ranks from the 9th Gordons (P.) for the Army of the Rhine, reached Mechernich, passing under command of the 62nd Division. It took all its vehicles with it but only nine animals, to draw the vehicles from the detraining station to a park and for other immediate needs until it had been issued with other animals.

The 9th Battalion was the only remaining one of the New Armies of Lord Kitchener. On December 6th it provided a guard of honour for a visit by King George V. It then moved to Tubize, where training was carried out all through February 1919. On the 24th Lieut.-Colonel R. A. Wolfe-Murray, who had been wounded when in command of the 1st Battalion in August 1918, took over command.[1]

The battalion was reduced to cadre strength, 4 officers and 44 other ranks, on March 28th, but the cadre party was kept kicking its heels until June 12th, when it left Tubize for the United Kingdom.

Not all the battalions of the Army of the Rhine had war service. Large numbers of youths liable to military service being available, the Army Council decided to form " Young Soldiers "

---

[1] In the Rev. P. D. Thomson's *The Gordon Highlanders*, it is stated that Lieut.-Colonel T. G. Taylor, who commanded the battalion for two and a quarter years but for a break of three months in 1918 due to a wound, remained in command up to the disembodiment. This is not quite correct, though Lieut.-Colonel Wolfe-Murray commanded only a skeleton battalion for the last five weeks prior to reduction to cadre strength.

battalions for occupation service, either to be retained as such or if necessary to be broken up on arrival to provide drafts for others. Three of these battalions were the 51st, 52nd and 53rd Gordon Highlanders.

The 51st arrived in March, the 52nd and 53rd in April, 1919. The divisional commander of the Highland Division, Major-General Sir David Campbell, was successful in his plea that they should not be broken up. The 51st joined the 4th and 5th Battalions to form a Gordon Highlanders brigade, numbered the 2nd Highland. The 52nd formed part of the 1st Highland Brigade. The 53rd became the divisional pioneer battalion and was reorganized as such. Thus five of the ten battalions in the Highland Division were Gordon Highlanders.

The records of these Young Soldiers battalions are scanty—for the 51st non-existent, except for references to it in divisional orders. There is only a single event of interest in their brief careers and in those of the two Territorial battalions before their demobilization. This, however, must have caused no little excitement in the minds of the young soldiers who had come out in the belief that their job was merely to help fill the ranks of a temporary and placid garrison, with no prospect of any more active duty than that of tiding over the period of demobilization and of the re-establishment of a peace-time army.

The German delegates to the peace conference at Versailles refused to sign the terms presented to them, though these were on the whole moderate, and the urgent demand of Marshal Foch for a frontier on the Rhine had been refused by the political chiefs. The allies determined to stand no nonsense. They prepared to advance from their bridgeheads into unoccupied Germany. Their plans were thorough and stern. For example, the possibility of the use of gas shell, long-range bombardment, and air bombing was provided for. Such measures were, however, subject to considerations of humanity. Their employment was precluded except against places known to be occupied by hostile forces who were resisting actively, insurgent populations, or those in rebellion against their own Government, and it was to depend upon the sanction of G.H.Q. Even high-explosive shell for field artillery was not to be fired without the permission of the corps commander.

The experiences of two Young Soldiers battalions may be given. The first warning received by the 52nd Gordon Highlanders came on May 22nd, 1919. It was preparing to move to a training area next day when the move was cancelled and it was ordered to be ready to cross the Rhine on or after the 25th. However, this action was postponed. A month passed before the battalion entrained at Düren on June 19th, and travelled to Opladen, marching that evening to a nearby billeting area. On the 22nd it received instructions for action on the day of the renewal of " hostilities ".

On June 17th the 53rd Battalion moved by train to Solingen, one of the lesser Ruhr towns, but highly industrialized and with a thriving cutlery trade. The young troops were comfortably billeted and were interested in their surroundings. The people seemed friendly. On June 28th news came that the peace terms had been signed. The battalion stood by in case of trouble, but the inhabitants of Solingen took the news quietly and there was not the slightest disorder. The troops from the west of the Rhine returned almost immediately to their former stations.

In August 1919 the Highland Division was suddenly ordered to return to the United Kingdom and to be stationed in Northern Command at Clipstone, Catterick and Cannock Chase. The five battalions of the Gordon Highlanders entrained between August 8th and 13th. The reason why they were not reduced to cadres was presumably that the Territorial battalions were mostly, and the Young Soldiers battalions were wholly, made up of retainable personnel. Demobilization for the former and disembodiment for the latter were not, however, long delayed.

The 2nd Gordons had a pleasant enough time of it in Italy. The people were most friendly, and the Highland dress appeared to confer a special privilege on the wearer. Football, hockey, boxing, cross-country running, and wrestling on horseback were quickly improvised. There must have been plenty of dancing also, since dancing classes for the men were numerous. Yet the one desire was to get home again, and there were few volunteers for the four battalions of the mixed brigade destined to remain for an indefinite time in the country.

On January 19th, 1919, Lord Cavan, who was returning to England, made a farewell speech, in the course of which he said : " No commander ever had his task made so easy for him owing to the loyalty, steadfastness, and enthusiasm of you all. . . . With all my heart I thank you." Certainly no force serving in the difficult circumstances of his could have had a finer commander.

By early February the battalion had been reduced almost to cadre strength. The cadre, with the colour party, arrived at Aberdeen on March 24th.

It will thus be seen that, with the exception of the 2nd Battalion in Italy, every one of the six battalions which survived until the armistices and also the three Young Soldiers battalions either formed part of the Army of the Rhine or sent drafts to join it. On the whole, Belgium would seem to have been considered the pleasantest post-armistice station, as was to be the case after the Second World War. Yet few save the regulars and a certain number who re-enlisted on short engagements found much pleasure in any station. What they looked forward to was the railway station nearest their home. Some unrest occurred, though it was never so serious in formed units as in troops held at the bases. It never became at all serious in units with good commanding officers, but not all those who had learnt their trade in war and proved successful in it could be regarded as good in the very different atmosphere of peace.

Part of the trouble lay in the structure of the demobilization scheme, which had been drawn up with the best of intentions, the rapid reconstruction of the country's industry and, where possible, the immediate provision of jobs for the demobilized. Coal miners came first in this programme. The Gordon Highlanders had in their ranks a considerable number from this trade. The diary of the 1st Battalion records that its first demobilization party, 40 strong, which left for home on December 28th, 1918, was mainly made up of miners; the first draft of the 5th Battalion, which entrained on December 11th, consisted of 34 men, all miners. Next came "pivotal" men belonging to the most essential trades and professions. There was also a category released on the basis of "Employers' Letters", formal notification by employers that positions held by individual men before they had been called up as reservists, had volunteered, or had been conscribed, were open and that the former holders were urgently required.

About the priority of the miners the troops probably did not worry much. They did, however, find it unfair that large numbers of men of other categories should be released before men with longer service. This was the chief grievance. First in, first out, seemed to them the fairest principle, though if it had been put into force from the start of demobilization it would have resulted in even more unemployment than actually occurred. The programme was subsequently modified.

No mention of trouble appears in the records of the Gordon Highlanders during this unsettling period. Discipline seems to have pulled them through. It would be unjust to many other good regiments to say that the Gordons' discipline was outstanding. Let us put it that it need not fear comparison with the best. Conceptions of discipline and the means of establishing and preserving it have changed in the period of nearly forty years between the arrival of the battalions on the banks of the Rhine and the completion of this record of the regiment's history in the First World War. Yet discipline must survive in its essence if a regiment is to maintain a high standard. The traditions of the past—and few are so rich as those of the Gordon Highlanders—and the discipline of today are the foundation on which all else must be built, including the good name of the regiment.

APPENDIX I

‡ HONOURS WON BY GORDON HIGHLANDERS IN THE GREAT WAR

Honour	1st Btn.	2nd Btn.	*3rd Btn.	4th Btn.	5th Btn.	6th Btn.	7th Btn.	•6/7th Btn.	8th Btn.	9th Btn.	10th Btn.	8/10th Btn.	§ Total
V.C. . . .	—	2	1	—	—	1	—	—	—	—	—	—	4
C.B. . . .	2	2	—	1	—	—	—	—	—	—	—	—	5
C.M.G. . .	4	4	—	1	—	1	—	—	1	—	—	—	11
D.S.O. . .	13	9	3	5	3	6	3 1 Bar	—	3	4	—	2	51
M.C. . . .	21 and 2 Bars	20 and 1 Bar	3	‡21	15 and 3 bars	39 and 6 Bars	33 and 3 Bars	—	1	9	2	11	175
D.C.M. . .	30 ‡	27 ‡	4	20	16	46 and 1 Bar	15	—	4	5 ‡	4	22 and 1 Bar	193
M.M. . .	47 and 3 Bars ‡	81 and 6 Bars	—	‡84	73 and 4 Bars	148 and 12 Bars	157 14 Bars 1 dble.	—	‡	42 and 1 Bar	†1	‡40	1054
M.S.M. . .	‡ ‡	‡3	—	‡	3	4	9	—	—	6	—	4	71
Foreign Decorations .		17	—	‡1	‡	16	16	—	—	15	—	‡	65

‡ The list is incomplete, the records of Honours in some battalions being defective.
* Honours distributed among other battalions.
Totals correct as regards rank and file.

THE VICTORIA CROSS

DRUMMER WILLIAM KENNY

" For conspicuous bravery on 23rd October, 1914, near Ypres, in rescuing wounded men on five occasions under very heavy fire in the most fearless manner, and for twice previously saving machine guns by carrying them out of action. On numerous occasions Drummer Kenny conveyed urgent messages under very dangerous circumstances over fire-swept ground."

CAPTAIN JAMES ANSON OTHO BROOKE

" For most conspicuous bravery and great ability near Gheluvelt, on the 29th October, in leading two attacks on the German trenches under heavy rifle and machine-gun fire, regaining a lost trench at a very critical moment. He was killed on that day. By his marked coolness and promptitude on this occasion, Lieut. Brooke prevented the enemy from breaking through our line at a time when a general counter-attack could not have been organized."

PRIVATE GORDON MCINTOSH

" For most conspicuous bravery when, during the consolidation of a position, his company came under machine-gun fire at close range. Private McIntosh immediately rushed forward under heavy fire, and reaching this emplacement, he threw a Mills grenade into it, killing two of the enemy and wounding a third. Subsequently, entering the dug-out, he found two light machine guns, which he carried back with him. His quick grasp of the situation and the utter fearlessness and rapidity with which he acted undoubtedly saved many of his comrades, and enabled the consolidation to proceed unhindered by machine-gun fire. Throughout the day the cheerfulness and courage of Private McIntosh was indomitable, and to his fine example in a great measure was due the success which attended his company."

LIEUTENANT ALLAN EBENEZER KER

" For conspicuous bravery and devotion to duty. On the 21st March, 1918, near St. Quentin, after a heavy bombardment, the enemy penetrated our line, and the flank of the 61st Division became exposed. Lieut. Ker, with one Vickers gun, succeeded in engaging the enemy's infantry, approaching under cover of dead ground, and held up the attack, inflicting many casualties. He then sent back word to his Battalion Headquarters that he had determined to stop with his Sergeant and several men who had been badly wounded, and fight until a counter-attack could be launched to relieve him. Just as ammunition failed his party was attacked from behind with bombs, machine guns and the bayonet. Several bayonet attacks were delivered, but each time they were repulsed by Lieut. Ker and his companions with their revolvers, the Vickers gun having by this time been destroyed. The wounded were collected into a small shelter, and it was decided to defend them to the last and to hold the enemy as long as possible. In one of the many hand-to-hand encounters a German rifle and bayonet and a small supply of ammunition was secured, and subsequently used with good effect against the enemy. Although Lieut. Ker was very exhausted from want of food and gas poisoning, and from the supreme exertions he had made during ten hours of the most severe bombardment, fighting and attending to the wounded, he refused to surrender until all his ammunition was exhausted and his position was rushed by a large number of the enemy. His behaviour throughout the day was absolutely cool and fearless, and by his determination he was materially instrumental in engaging and holding up for three hours more than 500 of the enemy."

APPENDIX II

REGIMENTAL ROLL OF THE FALLEN IN THE GREAT WAR

	1st	2nd	4th	5th	6th	7th	8th	9th	10th
Ori- ginal Units {Officers	68	65	81	45	51	40	29	12	10
{Other ranks	1970	1379	1065	817	899	777	213	342	186

	6/7th	8/10th	1st Garrison India	51st	52nd	53rd	3rd	11th	Depot
Later Units and Depots {Officers	1	8					3	9	1
{Other ranks	90	531	40	4	8	6	40	5	8

	2/4th	2/5th	2/6th	2/7th	1st London Scottish	2nd London Scottish	King's African Rifles	W. African Frontier Force	Attached Gallipoli
2nd Line and Attached . . .	24	13	17	8	32	26	6	2	1

	Staff	R.F.C.	M.G.C.	T.M.B.	Attached various units				
Officers Seconded	4	7	2	1	16[1]				

THE TOTAL CASUALTIES were over 1,000 Officers, and over 28,000 Rank and File.

[1] Some of these Officers may have been serving with battalions of the regiment. Owing to the many cross postings it was extremely difficult to trace casualties by battalions. The *totals* given above agree with the official lists.

APPENDIX III

BATTLE HONOURS

THE GREAT WAR—21 BATTALIONS

MONS
LE CATEAU
Retreat from Mons
MARNE, 1914, '18
Aisne 1914
La Bassée, 1914
Messines, 1914
Armentières, 1914
Ypres, 1914, '15, '17
Langemarck, 1914
Gheluvelt
Nonne Bosschen
Neuve Chapelle
Frezenberg
Bellewaarde
Aubers
Festubert, 1915
Hooge, 1915
LOOS

SOMME, 1916, '18
Albert, 1916, '18
Bazentin
Delville Wood
Pozières
Guillemont
Flers-Courcelette
Le Transloy
ANCRE, 1916
ARRAS, 1917, '18
Vimy, 1917
Scarpe, 1917, '18
Arleux
Bullecourt
Pilckem
Menin Road
Polygon Wood
Broodseinde
Poelcappelle

Passchendaele
CAMBRAI, 1917, '18
St. Quentin
Bapaume, 1918
Rosières
Lys
Estaires
Hazebrouck
Béthune
Soissonnais-Ourcq
Tardenois
Hindenburg Line
Canal du Nord
Selle
Sambre
France and Flanders, 1914-18
Piave
VITTORIO VENETO
Italy, 1917, '18

INDEX

(Only officers and other ranks of the Regiment or attached, and senior officers who had formerly served in it, are indexed. The senior rank in the war, when known, is given in the index.)

CPSIA information can be obtained at www.ICGtesting.com
Printed in the USA
LVOW08s1217060814

397816LV00002B/104/P

9 781783 311057